By-Way Biking
in
The Chilterns

Henry Tindell

Published by Sigma Leisure – an imprint of
Sigma Press, 1 South Oak Lane, Wilmslow, Cheshire SK9 6AR, England.

British Library Cataloguing in Publication Data
A CIP record for this book is available from the British Library.

ISBN: 1-85058-381-1

Typesetting and Design by: Sigma Press, Wilmslow, Cheshire.

Cover picture: Bridleway, Christmas Common to Stonor.

Printed by: MFP Design & Print

PREFACE

"The turning onto the bridleway was easily found; to the right lay the grand club house of the golf course – on a bright and breezy early May afternoon, it is easy to imagine Lord Nuffield (of Austin-Morris fame) feeling at home here. At 700 feet, the route is bound to descend and, past Elderberry Cottage, it does so gently – allowing a highish gear (middle chain wheel) to be used comfortably.

Entering the mixed woodland again, the sun-dappled light on the track picked out its changing texture – generally quite firm, with silver birch, beech and oaks twisting the track and exposing occasional roots. Sporadic dips provide a dried-up muddy patch with its inevitable mass of horseshoe imprints, but neatly circumvented by way of the adjacent bank.

Then, unexpectedly, a fox appeared ambling along the route, surely upwind from me, because I was almost upon it before its startled reaction caused it to leap right-wards, almost becoming enmeshed in the plain-wire strands of the fence at the edge of the wood. A frantic lurch and it was away like a shot, leaving me smiling aloud."

Such are the simple pleasures of biking in the Chilterns – for, a little earlier, a few roe deer crossed my path, I passed extensive carpets of bluebells, patches of primrose, banks of rhododendron bushes preparing to bloom, rode around the Maharajah's Well in Stoke Row, the last remaining old brick kiln in the area and saw the magnificence of Joyce Grove that was once Ian Fleming's home, in Nettlebed.

All this provided a delightful culture shock, as I had spent the morning in West Bromwich, on business, sampling the delights of a Black Country iron foundry, finishing with the 'fettling' bay where workers operate pneumatic chisels and grinders and the air is thick with grit and the noise incredible. So, I'm reluctant to castigate the M40 planners, in spite of bisecting the Aston Rowant Nature Reserve, as the effect vanishes in minutes on a bike. And such ready access to the small world of the Chilterns shows that in many important respects it has changed remarkably little over the last few centuries, and this is the joy that I hope I can share in this book.

The routes presented are by no means exhaustive, but do provide over 250 miles of tracks and by-ways that lead through some of the most interesting areas of the country – for what the Chilterns area lacks in sheer height, steepness, crags and vast open-spaces of the National Parks and Highlands, it makes up for in beauty on a scale that is ideal for riding and walking.

As perception is aided by preparation, a little background to the environment (from places of interest, to natural history and geology) is provided. I hope that you, like me, might become so enthralled as to pursue the subject through first-hand experience, and to read about its literature and many literary connections.

Henry Tindell

Dedication

'To all my family'

CONTENTS

The Rides

Grades are for guidance; distances are approximate

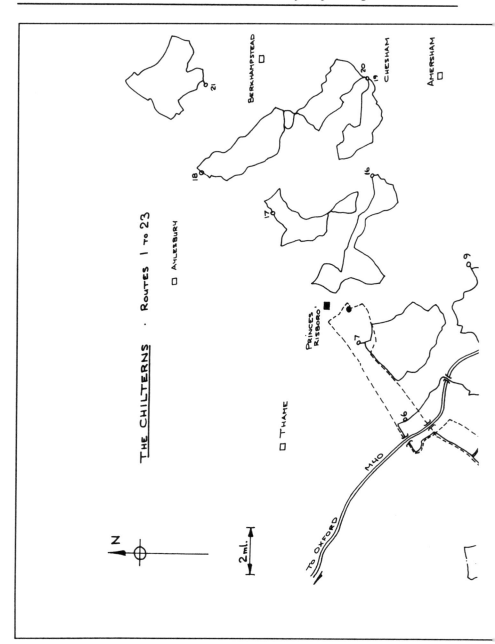

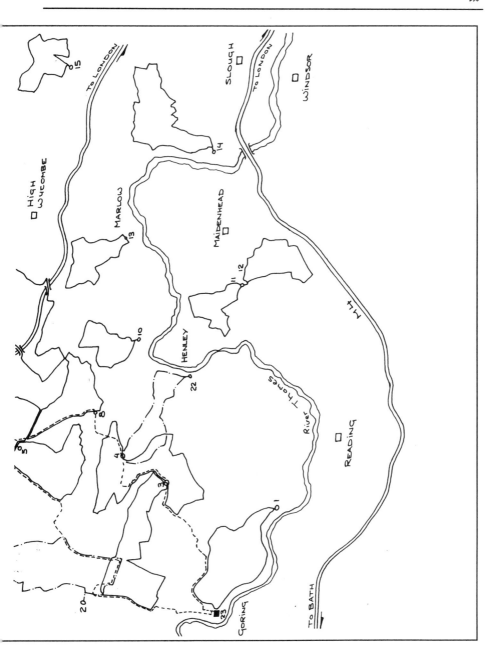

INTRODUCTION

The Chilterns were designated an 'Area of Outstanding Natural Beauty' (AONB) in 1965, and exploring by bike can provide one of the most invigorating means to glimpse the treasures within.

Getting There

Although the boundaries of the region are nowhere precisely defined, it matters not – in general terms it runs in a broad arc some twenty miles deep, on a radius of some thirty-odd miles from Central London; beginning around the Thames at Goring and running forty odd miles north-east towards Dunstable and Luton.

Access from the capital is quite ridiculously easy; by train the westbound line from Paddington provides a connection for Goring and the Southern Chilterns. Other lines radiate out through the region en-route for Banbury, Aylesbury and Milton Keynes, each line conveniently providing terminals in the Chilterns. By road, the M40 ploughs through in the Wycombe area, cutting a swathe through the Aston Rowant Nature Reserve, but creating only a local dislocation and disturbance, whilst providing excellent access from the Midlands and North West. The M4 serves to delineate its southern aspect, and the M1 lies beyond its north-eastern limit.

It has been identified as between 300 and 800 square miles in area; I would suggest (as do the Chiltern Society) around 650 square miles, or about the area of Oxfordshire. It takes in parts of Oxfordshire, Buckinghamshire, Hertfordshire and Bedfordshire, and I have strayed a little further south into Berkshire, and the lowlands of Buckinghamshire; indeed, even to the outskirts of John Betjeman Metro Land!

There are twenty-two circular routes described in detail. These range from about seven to twenty miles, often with a surprising Height Gain of over 1000 feet. The final route takes part of the ancient 'Ridgeway' from station to station (Goring to Princes Risborough) for approximately twenty-five miles – and it is possible to return through places passed on earlier routes on the 'Lower Icknield Way' and the 'Oxfordshire Cycleway', albeit partly on surfaced roads, making a circuit of well over fifty miles. The Ridgeway/Ickneild Way embodies much that is typical of the area, from the lowlands of the Thames, through Medieval Ewelme, skirting along the base of the chalk hills and through the ubiquitous Beech Woods – providing a link with drover and traveller since pre-neolithic times, along a line that can be extended from Dorset to the Wash.

A little background is prescient, with features of the area such as its 'clay with flints' surfaces, woods, brickyards that provided housing from the Middle Ages, Windmills, Manors, Farms and Gardens (although Chequers was bequeathed to the nation, lamentably it is reserved for the Prime Minister).

And most of all, the wonderful network of Bridleways that provide the key to this treasure of an area, the surprise being that apparently it is such a well-kept secret. So, please don't tell anyone that would look but not search for the magic beyond the handlebars!

Discovering the Chilterns

Although a background of the Chilterns – from its geology, geography and history – is by no means essential to its enjoyment, some such understanding can only enhance a journey in this delightful area.

For the Chilterns are, indeed unique, and contain a rich variety of landscape that has been formed not only by natural forces, but also by the people, past and present, inhabiting this area.

When the Chilterns were designated an 'Area of Outstanding Natural Beauty' (AONB), this excluded the major towns like High Wycombe and Marlow. It is important to recognise the pressure on the AONB in the late twentieth century, for although only 10,000 people actually live within its boundaries, some half million live within 2 miles, and over 10 million within 25 miles! Indeed, the Dunstable Downs have received significantly more visitors in a year than even the most popular National Parks. However, responsible bikers need not strain this fragile balance between the needs for recreation and the needs of the area; for one thing as a biker one tends to occupy little space and need inflict no disturbance – hopefully following the precept of this guide and travelling in small groups (two or three is ideal), will serve this balance.

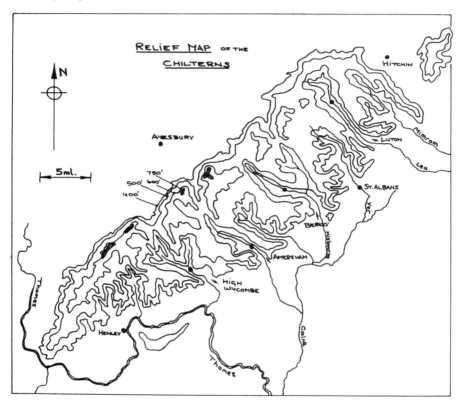

Although by no means a student of Geology, I find its interest inescapable, in this area particularly. The origins of the landscape have determined, to a large extent, its subsequent shape and 'colour'. We begin with the most obvious elements – chalk and flint.

GEOLOGY MAP
CHALK

ICKNIELD WAY
AYLESBURY
OXFORD
LONDON
Thames
READING
CHALK

Chalk and Flint

In the late 17th century the historian Camden wrote in his 'Britannia' that, "Chiltern hath its name from the soil, cyle or chilt, a Saxon term signifying chalk, for it riseth in the most part in chalky hills, covered with woods and groves of Beech". This provides not only the origin of the name, but also an accurate description of the region at the time (although not necessarily before), and even so today. The tree cover (predominantly Beech) is certainly extensive. One quarter of the region is tree covered, making it one of the most densely forested areas in the country.

Although chalk-land covers a large swathe of south-eastern England, it has produced in the Chilterns a landscape quite different from that to the west (such as the Berkshire Downs); south (North and South Downs); or north-east (East Anglia). Another of the Chilterns distinct features is the 'clay-with-flints' upper layer, often found at the crest of the scarp.

The origins of chalk lie in the sediment, deposited in seas of the Jurassic period (65 million years ago). This 'calcareous mud' comprised enormous numbers of tiny shells and plants (coccoliths and coccolithophorids). These were compressed, over time, to its present state; a pure-white, soft rock, possessing a permeability to water.

Some 50 million years later, the colossal earth surface upheaval that produced the Alps, was also responsible for setting the initial shape of the Chilterns, throwing up this layer of chalk and clay-with-flints, atop the hills and along the dipslope south eastwards. Subsequently Ice Ages, and a later warming towards our present climate, also had a profound effect on the shape of the Chilterns. The exposed layer of permeable chalk remained initially frozen and impenetrable to water, causing vast runnels to gouge out the familiar valley and ridge pattern that runs at right angles from the scarp, down towards London and the Thames Valley basin.

As the population of Britain grew, the porous nature of the chalk had a distinctly retarding effect on the colonisation of the Chilterns, for water shortage was always a problem. It remains a severe problem today, although it can now be overwhelmed by technology – at a price, including the near extinction of rivers like the Misbourne. In chalky areas without a clay-with-flints soil, pits were once dug and lined with clay, to catch the rainfall and so provide some water for the local inhabitants. An interesting example of this water deprivation is met on the routes that pass Stoke Row, where the famous 'Maharajah's Well' was dug (by hand!) to a depth of 346 feet (twice the height of Nelson's Column) before water was reached.

Surfaces of chalk, well drained but slippery in the wet, and flints with their hard surface and often sharp edges, are highly significant to the biker – as will soon be seen! The flints provide interest in a number of ways, as with their silica composition they are extremely hard. They were of prime importance during the late Stone Age (Neolithic period), for use as tools. This in turn significantly impacted on the landscape. It was at this period that the 'Icknield Way' was formed – of which more later.

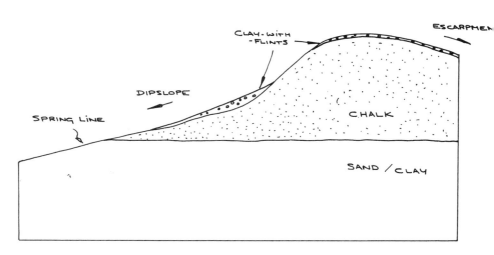

Section through THE CHILTERNS
(schematic)

Beech

Neolithic man was the first human to have a dramatic effect on the Chilterns, by clearing areas of the dense (mainly oak) indigenous forest, with his flint tools. In fact, it was not until the late medieval period that the oak and elm were supplanted by the present predominance of beech, as remarked by Camden earlier. For it was from the 17th century that Beechwood had a commercial value, and was grown to supply the ever-rising demand for charcoal, and for London's fuel needs. Also during this time began the growth of the furniture industry, particularly around High Wycombe. This area is still recognised as an important wood working centre; having the High Wycombe Chair Museum to record the craftsmanship of the past, and the Timber Research and Development Association (TRADA) to, hopefully, create the future. The woods around this area supported many craftsmen, pre-eminent among whom was the 'Bodger'. (Route 9 – West Wycombe passed the 'Bodgers Arms'). Recent misuse of the word as an 'inelegant' DIY-er probably derives from 'botcher'; for the bodger was (sadly, now almost extinct) a fine craftsman who took the green product from the beeches and shaped them, using early tools such as 'pole' lathes. They provided the elements from which fine furniture was rapidly produced in the towns, such as the 'Windsor' chairs that are now of great value.

The beech has a shallow and broad root system that enables it to grow not only on the rich loam soil and clay-with-flints, but also on the chalk. Growing up to 100 feet in height and with a dense cover, it can often lead to almost complete exclusion of light, so denuding the ground of the variety of fauna seen on other deciduous woods. It can, however, lead to the most glorious bed of leaf mold and deep, dry leaves, in the autumn.

All of these aspects affect the biker – for the roots provide interest on the ground (and can promote unexpectedly intimate contact if they are not spotted in time!). These fallen leaves provide a fine texture, but rapidly become wheel clogging if too wet.

In spite of the above features, there is still a great variety of flora and fauna in the Chilterns; for example, its orchids are a singular feature, with the Purple White-Helliborine, Birdsnest, and Ghost Orchid – the latter being unique to the area. Fortunately, the Berks, Bucks and Oxon

Naturalists Trust (BBONT) are extremely active in the area. Its work is seen, for instance, along the bridleway from Nettlebed to Nuffield (Route 4). The BBONT's first reserve (Hurley Chalk pit) is seen from the path back to Knowl Hill (Route 11).

Settlement in the Chilterns

Another feature of the areas unique character is man's contribution, often linked to the land, as well as his dwellings. The fact that the AONB is much as it was in the late Medieval period is due to factors such as the water shortages mentioned earlier; its impenetrable woodland; and the demand of wood, for sale in London, which promoted the spread of the Beech Woods. By the time that this trade began to wane, it had deterred the expansion of the open farming methods adopted in areas such as the Aylesbury Vale. When its proximity to the capital, and the industrial centres of Reading and Slough, had been appreciated it was, thankfully, saved the worst of the ravages of dormitory town status. The 'New Towns' of the post war era went to Welwyn Garden City, Luton, Milton Keynes, and Bracknell; and nearly to Princes Risborough!

The Ridgeway (Icknield Way)

The earliest local traces of human occupation came from discoveries by a Victorian amateur archaeologist, who found at Caddeston what was later dated as remains of around 125,000 years ago, amongst the earliest found in Britain but not as early as finds in Southern France of 400,000 BC. The early occupations are of only academic interest to us, although relatively soon after the English Channel had formed, separating England from Continental Europe around 6000 BC, the Stone Ages began. As mentioned earlier, the Neolithic Age brought about the use of flint tools, and the Icknield Way is generally dated from this period. It was used as a route for travel from the chalk-lands of East Anglia, along the Chiltern scarp, and down to the coast in Dorset. This make the Icknield Way, dating from 4000 years ago, the earliest of its ilk in Europe.

The track split in the Chilterns, with the 'Upper Icknield way' probably the winter line, being part-way up the scarp (now, basically, the route of the Ridgeway). The summer route – having dried from the winter rains –

runs along the bottom of the scarp or into the vale, and is still known as the 'Lower Icknield way'. Although the former route is primarily bridleway (hooray!), the latter was adopted in Roman times. From the early part of the twentieth century it became metalled, still being marked as the old road at many points (Route 20 – Aston Clinton – starts here). An excellent book on the Icknield Way, re-published in 1980, is by the Poet Edward Thomas, killed at Amas in 1917. He wrote in 1913 about his travels on the Icknield Way(s), at a time just prior to the metalling of the roads. Fortunately, the Ridgeway is preserved for use by bikers much as it was, not only in Edward Thomas's time, but even hundreds, if not thousands, of years ago.

The nature of the landscape in the Chilterns is also important as its development contrasts with the adjacent Vale of Aylesbury, which was more easily worked, and so radically changed by agricultural progress. This produced what the geographers call 'planned' landscape, whereas the Chilterns often provide basically unchanged areas of 'ancient' landscape. This results in examples of 1000 years old hedges (as 'Black hedge' from Princes Risborough to Winter Hill). However, not all such features are ancient – as in the chalk crosses ('Whitelead Cross' – passed on Princes Risborough – Route 16, or 'Bledlow Cross' – Route 7) which date only from the 17th century; or the 'Whipsnade Lion' (seen on Route 21 – Aldbury) created in the 1930's.

Chilterns Ages

One of the features attributable to the people who inhabited the Chilterns between the New Stone and the Romans, is that of 'Grim's Ditch'. A Saxon name for the Nordic God Odin, Grim's Ditch is thought to date from the Iron Age, around 100 BC. Its purpose and use remain a mystery, but the geometric patterns it makes in the Chilterns seems to indicate a boundary. Although smoothed by the ages, it is often clearly visible, and traces straight lines and right angles on the map, such as when we follow it on Route 16 (Gt. Missenden), over both easy and difficult terrain. A different area, around Wallingford, also contains a Grim's Ditch. Route 3 Stoke Row follows if from Nuffield, a fine stretch of riding on its bank, which also forms part of the Ridgeway.

The Roman period left less obvious traces than might have been imagined, although the ways through the Chilterns were established as

'Akeman Street' (via Berkhamstead), 'Watling Street' (via Dunsable) and 'Ermine Street'. All of these roads have been incorporated in modern highways, as the A41, A5 and A1 respectively. It is also probable that they further developed the Lower Icknield Way; but although there were a number of Roman Villas in the Chilterns, the main centre was Verulamium (St Albans). St Albans was attacked and destroyed in AD69 by Queen Boudica (Bodacia), long before the Roman departure around AD400. Her tribe, the Iceni, are thought to have provided the name for the Icknield Way.

There must be plenty of Roman history buried beneath the surface, and we pass by the find of a hoard of Roman coins, discovered in 1953 near Ewelme park, (on Route 4: Christmas Common).

Between the end of the Roman occupation and the arrival of William the Conquerer, the Anglo-Saxon period was generally reckoned to be the 'Dark Age'. But its legacy in the Chilterns is significant, for a great many place-names were established. The Saxon language was rich in descriptive power for the location of settlements, and the shape of the countryside can often be discovered in these names. No just 'end' as in Cadmore End and Lane End – the furthest reaches for access; 'hill' and 'ridge' as in Coleshill and Bledlow Ridge; but also 'den' – a long winding valley as in Hambleden, and 'coombe' as in Swyncombe. In fact, the descriptive nature of the language extended considerably, and adds an interesting facet to the region.

Before the arrival of the Normans, the layout of the Chilterns had been established much as it is today, providing long strip parishes that began at the foot of the scarp, ran up and over the hill, and down the dipslope. Thus providing a spring line at the start, steep ground to the crest, clay-with-flints and chalk, then fields and woods, running down to a further spring line in the lower ground.

Certain of these areas were designated hundreds', as in the 'Aylesbury Hundreds' and the 'Chiltern Hundreds'. The latter comprised of Stoke, Desborough and Burnham (visited on Route 14 – Burnham Beeches), which are known today as the method by which Members of Parliament resign their seats. Since 1760, MPs applying for stewardship of the Chiltern Hundreds took an office that was dedicated to the eradication of the lawless characters who frequented this densely wooded and sparsely populated area, where travelling was a risky business!

After the fall of King Harold at Hastings in 1066, William the First marched through the South-East and across the Thames at Wallingford (see Route 2 of that ilk). It was not until he reached Berkhamstead that the Saxon noblemen finally capitulated. The Normans built their first 'motte and bailey' castle here, but only ruins remain at Berkhampstead and Wallingford.

Perhaps the most obvious feature of the Norman period, seen today, is in their churches. In fact, few Saxon examples remain, although for example, Stoke-Poges has some Saxon origins within predominantly Norman surroundings. This provided Thomas Gray with the setting for his 'Elegy written in a country churchyard', (near to Route 14 – Burnham Beeches).

The Civil War inflicted remarkably little damage to the Chilterns, although the famous Church at Ewelme was only just saved from desecration. Today we can marvel at the 15th century tomb of Alice, Duchess of Suffolk. This has a graceful effigy above, and a horrific one below a plinth. Alice, granddaughter of Geoffrey Chaucer ('Canterbury Tales') was instrumental in founding the Ewelme Almshouses in 1437, and the school – the oldest of its kind in the country. An endowment by the Suffolks at that time has supported the Almshouses throughout the centuries, and they remain a beautifully preserved example of Medieval England. Also in the church-yard is the grave of Jerome K (for Klapka) Jerome, author of the immortal 'Three men in a boat'. Ewelme is visited on (Route 2 – Wallingford).

John Hampden (of Gt. Hampden – visited on Route 16 – Gt. Missenden) will be forever linked with the Civil War. Killed in a skirmish in 1643 at Chalgrove Field, near his old Grammar school in Thame, he lies buried in the Gt. Hampden church-yard. A great Chiltern landowner, he played a part in sparking off the Civil War by refusing to pay his 'Ship Tax' to King Charles I, whilst member of Parliament for Wendover.

We visit Wendover in Route 17, an old established town, which later had the important political figure of Edmund Burke (from 1765) as its MP. By all accounts Burke lived an exciting life, rising from obscurity to fame under the wing of the local landowner, the Marquis of Rockingham, who effectively secured his seat in Parliament. In spite of his limited resources, Burke purchased the mansion of 'Gregories' in Beaconsfield for some £22,000 in 1768, equivalent to several millions today. It formed the centre for great literary and political gatherings for the next thirty years, until Burke died with much of the enormous mortgage still unpaid.

Beaconsfield is another place with many historical connections, being on the old coaching route (now the A40) from London to Oxford. Happily the M40 has relieved much of the traffic pressure, and Beaconsfield church once more provides a, relatively, quiet church-yard for Burke, Waller and G.K. Chesterton, who wrote the 'Father Brown' stories here during his 25 year stay. Surprisingly, Enid Blyton receives inadequate recognition, living here until he death, and adding to her prodigious output of children's books. The Jordans Route (no. 15) passes near here, and the model village of 'Beckonscot' is well worth a visit, supporting local charities as it has since its inception in the 1930's.

Another local association is Benjamin Disraeli, Earl of Beaconsfield, for his house 'Hughenden Manor' will be found just north of High Wycombe, not far from his father, Issac's house in Bradenham. Bradenham also has an excellent Youth Hostel, and lies within a couple of miles of Bledlow Ridge (encountered on the 'Bledlow' Route 7).

The Jordans route visits several features dating from the early Quakers, with the 'Friends Meeting House', the 'Mayflower Barn' and the Youth Hostel all from the era of William Penn. Extraordinary characters; Penn visiting America twice, and founding Pennsylvania, returning to face suppression of his faith at home. His simple grave by the meeting House is passed en-route for the village of Jordans, still managed by the trust, and a fine place to linger.

Further around the 'Jordans' route is the delightful village of Chalfont St. Giles. Before stopping there, however, 'Milton's Cottage' (just before the village centre) is well worth a visit. Although Milton only spent a year here, coming from London to escape the ravages of the plague in 1665, the cottage provides a marvellous insight into his world. His fame rests with *Paradise Lost*, completed at Chalfont, but it led to *Paradise Regain'd*, late in a remarkably turbulent life. In early life a gifted academic, from a well-off background, he travelled to Europe after a long stay at Cambridge, meeting giants such as Galileo. An outspoken republican, he became what today would be called a top PR man for Cromwell, being paid £1,000 to write a counter-work to the Royalists – making him immensely rich at the time. Later times, following the Restoration, saw him entombed in the tower and fortunate not to lose his head, before starting his famous works. 'Paradise Lost', although somewhat inaccessible today, as a best seller netted him some £20. Paid in £5 instalments, he died before getting the last payment and his heirs sold the copyright for a few pounds (sounds like a 1960's rock star!).

Continuing this literary vein, notable is Marlow (Route 13), like Henley another bustling Thames town. It features a fine suspension bridge, which provided its Victorian architect with a commission for the bridge which links Buda with Pest, gateway to the East. It was in Marlow that Percy Shelley made his only home of much duration, living a short and dramatic life that ended in an Italian lake. His house was a centre for young Radicalism in the early 19th century, but is marked merely with a plaque now. Perhaps reaching a wider audience was the creation of his wife, Mary Godwin, whose book Frankenstein, was written here, in this town betwixt the Thames and Chiltern Hills. This was the time soon after the Battle of Waterloo.

And so on as we travel round many places in the Chilterns with important historical and literary links. There are also the great houses dating from the Elizabethan age onwards, such as the Blount family at Mapledurham (Route 1, Mapledurham), the Camoys at Stonor Park (Stonor, Route 8), the deGreys at Rotherfield (Greys Court, Route 22 – Henley on Thames), the Astors at Cliveden (Route 14, Burnham Beeches).

All these fine houses can be visited at certain times. Later arrivals include the Rosthchilds, who settled around Tring. Although some of the original manor houses have gone, there is a fine legacy in the Zoological Museum in Akeman Street, Tring, now a part of the British Museum. West Wycombe (at the start of Route 9 of that name) provides the grand West Wycombe House. Nearby stands the Mausoleum, and church with its 'Golden Ball' (able to seat several people inside!) above the tower. These were long connected with the Dashwood family. Sir Francis Dashwood was a notorious character, and founder of the 'Hell Fire Club' that used the house and some fascinating tunnelling under the hillside, in the hill above the village. Other places, such as the mansions of Wormsley Park, owned by Paul Getty II, we can only view from a distance, but the park through which we travel (Route 6, Aston Rowant) is more than adequate compensation. Nearby Nettlebed (Route 4) was the home of Ian Fleming (of the 'James Bond'), with the magnificent 'Joyce Grove' now serving as a fine Sue Ryder home.

And so the Chilterns background provides many such associations, but their true richness is to be found in the country and on the by-ways leading on until:

I know each lane, and every alley green,
Dingle or bushy dell of this wild wood,
And every bosky bourn from side to side,
My daily walks and ancient neighbourhood..."

John Milton, 1634.

Further Reading

The Bridleways of Britain, by A. Whittet, publishers – Whittet Books, 1986.

The Ridgeway by N. Curtis, publishers – Arum Press, 1989.

The Ridgeway Path, by S. Jennet, publishers HMSO, 1976.

A Visitor's Guide to the Chilterns, by N. Lands, publishers – Moorland, 1982.

The Chilterns, by L. Hepple and A. Doggett, publishers – Philimore, 1992.

Equipment and other Basics

Bikes

Perhaps the only essential pre-requisite – as in the reply of possibly the 20th century's greatest explorer, H.W. Tillman (who just happened to be educated in the Chilterns, at Berkhampstead), when asked what was needed in preparation for an expedition, was – "put on your boots and go!" One could almost adopt a similar approach to these routes in the Chilterns – for they don't pose the same threat of exposure, or the like, as the truly mountainous regions of Britain. However, a few preparations can smooth our journey, which may be made surprisingly arduous if tackled 'out of sympathy' with the terrain.

Although the virtue of a bike lies in its versatility, and no matter how unsuitable a type it can be dragged, pushed, carried or thrown over most obstacles, it is nevertheless obvious that the preferred type is the well known genus of Mountain Bike. On the 'Easy' and parts of 'Moderate' graded routes a road bike would be ok, but for the 'Meat' of the routes the Mountain bike is absolutely ideal.

I prefer the aesthetes' approach to bike preparation (also consistent with a distant Scots ancestry!) in that all items not regarded as essential shall be jettisoned. Off, therefore, go mudguards, drinking bottles, stands, reflectors, speedos and sundry gizmos; and on goes closed-foam padding for lifting. I prefer a rucksack, but the essential pump and spare tube can find their way back onto the bike. The object of the exercise is simply to reduce bike weight – mountain bikes have a tendency to being overweight and this has to be strenuously fought before setting out – or even more painfully tackled up the hill or through the mud!

As usual, the beginner should be guided by a recommended enthusiastic local bike shop, who can also advise on, and do if necessary, the minor repairs and upkeep of a machine suitable for these routes. Don't worry – I've done them all for an outlay of under £100, although I must admit to some prior experience!

I prefer as big a tyre section as possible, with a ribbed type rather than aggressively-studded tread pattern – these features both inflict the minimum damage on the ground and prove the most suitable for the variety of going – including some road-work. As a high level of skill in off-road riding is developed it should be used to preserve the environment – always aim to leave virtually no trace of ones passage – call it enlighted self-interest if you like.

Before starting, all bearings (wheels, bottom-bracket, gears, sprocket and chain) should be checked for 'play', adjusted (not too tight!), and capaciously lubricated. I prefer the modern 10-50 engine oil, which is cheap in bulk and has a fair compromise between low viscosity (being able to run into the bearings) and retention for the time of a route. I therefore *always* carry an oil can, particularly to lubricate the chain after every circuit – one only has a small 'engine' with which to drive the machine!

A note on riding – the enemy of the Chilterns off-road biker, as far as I am concerned, is mud which gets into the chain and gears. I therefore do my best to avoid getting these parts any more muddy than is absolutely necessary, for its effects can transform a well-oiled and efficient machine into a creaking and groaning thing that may soon demand replacement of chain and, possibly, rear sprocket. Usually such patches of mud can be skirted around, but if all else fails I prefer to carry the bike through, as it's usually easier and faster to clean footwear than gears!

The other main item of importance is, obviously, brakes. Their importance in aiding safe descents of some 'interesting' ground is self-evident. Riding skill is just as important and obviously such areas should be treated with care (e.g. dismount!), until sufficiently experienced. Given the above, I have found virtually none of the downhill unridable, in good conditions at least.

Spares, Tools and Information

Before setting out, I always prefer to have at least a minimal tool kit; consisting of an adjustable spanner (large enough for wheel nuts), Allen keys/small spanners/adjustable for cables etc., large and small screwdrivers (also useful as emergency tyre levers), puncture outfit, chain-link extractor and a few links, pump and spare tube, small pair of pliers and roll of plastic tape. Such a selection is only a reflection of personal preferences and perhaps an excessive 'insurance' for, providing a route can be completed on foot in good time, it could be argued that a tool kit could be dispensed with entirely – I prefer not to tempt fate!

Similarly a small first-aid kit should be packed to cover the sort of emergencies that could occur.

Regarding 'information', I would find it unthinkable to sally forth without an OS map, for all of these routes are encompassed by two of the 'Landranger' series 1:50 000 (1cm to 1km or $1^1/_4$ inch to 1 mile). These maps provide a good scale for biking and a tremendous amount of information (such as contour detail and alternative routes) to complement this guide. The more detailed 1:20 000 'Pathfinder' series requires too many maps to cover the Chilterns and is, perhaps, more useful for those on foot. Maps of lesser detail than the Landranger series I find totally useless.

The only problem with maps and, to a lesser extent guides, is handling them on the bike and keeping dry in inclement weather. I don't find the walker's/runner's map-cases too convenient, and usually manage perfectly well by inserting it into an A4 sized clear plastic wallet, folding and keeping it inside my shirt/jacket. This can also be craftily deployed as a wind-cheat for a downhill road section!

Clothing

As remarked earlier, the probability of exposure by falling foul of severe conditions is not a major hazard in the Chilterns. However, one could become uncomfortable to a significant extent if unprepared for the normal English weather, if exposed to it for a few hours! A hazard in summer that shouldn't be overlooked is vegetation along the routes, particularly nettles which often invade the smaller tracks. My thoroughly old-fashioned loose tracksuit top and bottoms serve very well to balance heat loss against hedgerow attacks, and can be removed easily, as conditions demand. For occasions of serious nettle-grappling, I also whip out the every-ready pair of woolly gloves to see me through the worst.

Footwear, again, is almost entirely dictated by personal preference, mine being for walking boots (of the 'bendy' variety) and thick socks – ideal unless the weather is warm. In the latter case I use old trainers – for although fell running shoes are ideal I prefer to keep them for their primary use! A studded pattern is to be preferred, but I find familiarity and comfort the best criteria!

I am most impressed by the high proportion of road cyclists sporting helmets, and this would seem the logical and sensible headgear here, so I will refrain from disclosing my own preferences.

Finally, outer-wear. Undoubtedly the ideal is a modern breathable fabric over-jacket, light and reasonably waterproof. Even if such is not available (being rather pricey) some sort of waterproof should always be carried, even if only to provide cover against the wind, or an enforced halt. Leggings I find less important, for providing one has sufficient leg cover to prevent too much chilling by rain, then staying dry is not particularly necessary on these routes.

A By-Ways Biking Code

❏ DO NOT ride on Footpaths.

❏ Bridleways are OK, but careless use could lose this right of way to bikers. Always give way to walkers and horse riders – they have a legal priority.

❏ Avoid upsetting other users of by-ways, landowners and farmers, and disturbance of the environment.

❏ Be especially careful approaching others from behind, if in doubt wait behind.

❏ Observe the normal common-sense rules of the countryside (obviously attending to gates and the like).

❏ Prepare bike and self appropriately (see text).

❏ Survive to enjoy the next route!

Have fun – I did!

Footnote

I have retained the use of good old 'Imperial' units throughout the book (miles, yards, feet, not to say pints in the pubs!), partly because I find it infuriating to have every unit in both 'metric' and 'imperial', but mainly because it is very much 'in-character' with the region. I have, so far, come across only imperial distances on signs on the routes, so it is quite practical to use them exclusively. For those poor souls who have never been familiar with them, perhaps the following rough conversions will assist...

1 yard	3 feet
1 foot	12 inches
1 metre	3ft 3in (1.1 yards)
1 km	$5/8$ mile

1. Mapledurham

Route: Mapledurham – Goring Heath – Woodcote – Goring – Whitchurch – Mapledurham

Brief Description:
Grading – Moderate
Terrain – 60% off-road
– Tracks in good condition where unsurfaced, generally straightforward. Fine ride, with superb settings. Quite possible to reach from Reading Station – to experience some remarkable contrasts, between city, hamlet and unspoilt countryside.

Distance: Total – 15 miles; Off-road – 9 miles

Time: 2 hours

Height Gain: 625 feet

Start/Finish: Mapledurham

Map: OS Landranger 175; start – GR 671770

---

a – b: Mapledurham to Woodcote

Begin from the Mapledurham House car park, as it is unlikely that parking for private transport can be found within a mile of the house, as restrictions abound. However, payment for parking here rewards one with an opportunity to stroll around the hamlet. Alternatively, a start can be made from Goring Station – pleasant enough – but it cannot compare to the former setting.

A further possibility exists for the keen who could ride from Reading station across the Thames to Caversham, then onto the bridleway that leads directly to Mapledurham, proving dramatic contrasts from city-centre to mediaeval hamlet, of a few centuries in as many miles...

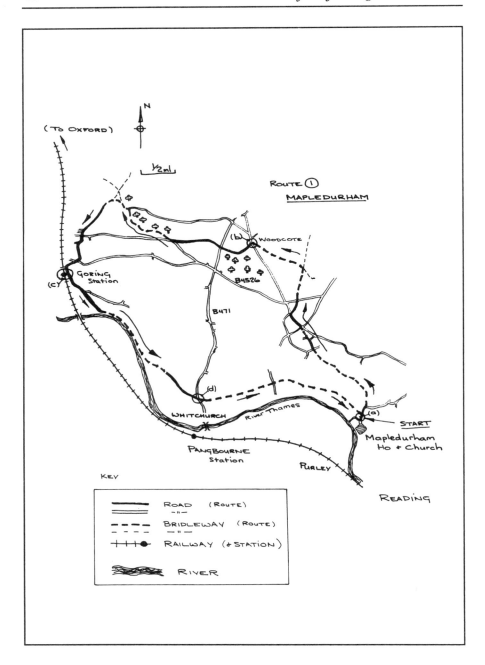

(TO OXFORD)

N

½ml.

ROUTE ① MAPLEDURHAM

(b) WOODCOTE

(c) GORING Station

B4526

B471

GORING Station

(d)

WHITCHURCH

River Thames

(a) START

Mapledurham Ho + Church

PANGBOURNE Station

PURLEY

READING

KEY

―	ROAD (ROUTE)
– ii –	
– – – –	BRIDLEWAY (ROUTE)
– ii –	
– – –	
+++●	RAILWAY (+ STATION)
〜〜	RIVER

From the Mapledurham car park field turn left onto the lane for $1/4$ mile and then left, clearly signed bridleway 'Goring Heath $1^1/_2$ miles'. Continue pleasantly and without great effort along this good path to reach the metalled track at the thatched and timbered house, then take the left fork (no signpost) passing 'Elm Cottage' and so into the bridleway.

This comes out to the cross-roads at Goring Heath where we go across to follow the Goring road, shortly passing the Alms houses (now with 'Latimer Contracting') on the right. On reaching Hillbottom Road (on the left) take a right turn into the track and continue straight over the next road, following the signpost 'Exlade Street, $1^1/_2$, bridleway.' Continue for less than a mile in Common Wood and turn left at the tree marked 'CH70' (not terribly obvious, but in the clearing). Through the wood, and straight on over another bridleway crossing, steadily uphill, but rideable all the way! Finally emerge from the wood onto a good track, to 'Green Lane' at Woodcote.

b – c: Woodcote to Goring

From Green Lane turn left then next right down 'Potkiln Lane'. This leads across the B471 (care!) and a rush downhill, turning right at the bridleway signpost, (which is found shortly after passing the road coming in from the left).

Follow the bridleway, a well drained, if rather steeply cambered, chalk path gaining height painlessly until the wood is left and the track suddenly leads out to a metalled junction. Fine views are revealed from this high point, out across the Oxfordshire plain, with the cooling towers of Didcot Power Station in the distance. Bear left and downhill all the way, along 'Iknield Road' to a T-junction (through Cleeve) and turn right for Goring. Still downwards to the station, and the 'Queens Arms' (Morrels pub on the left).

c – d: Goring to Whitchurch

Leaving the station on the right continue along the minor road, with the railway line on our right, until after $1/2$ mile we take the right fork, a signposted bridleway to 'Whitchurch $2^1/_2$ miles, Gatehampton Farm and

Manor'. This is a metalled track initially. Continue straight on past the next signpost (also marked 'Whitchurch $2^1/_2$ miles'). The track now takes us within 50 yards of the Thames, providing delightful riding between the river and the rolling foothills of the Chiltern on the left. This peerless track leads on along a nice surface, occasional rise and fall with ever-changing scenery.

Mapledurham: manor house and church

When the fork is reached, follow the blue bridleway arrow left, leading to a steepening, and a sharp series of boarded steps that can invoke a short carry to reach the road.

Continue straight on, past 'Elm Cottage', then right (a signpost points back 'Bridleway, Goring 3 miles').

d – a: Whitchurch to Mapledurham

After 150 yards turn left along a track that leads straight on through tall wrought-iron gates and an old (cast-iron) sign 'Bridle-road to Caversham', on the right-hand side of the track. Splendid views around. On past the impressive 'Hardwick Stud' on the left, with plenty of evidence of its equine occupants. We can see down across the slope on the right to the river, and over to Purley on its opposite side. A cub scout camp often adds further to the ambience, if not the quietness! Soon through the exit gates, matching those passed earlier, and the clearing provides a glimpse of Mapledurham House a mile ahead.

Along the track to meet the lane, with a signpost pointing back 'Bridleway, Whitchurch $2^1/_2$ miles', and a right turn returns us in a few yards to the start.

2. Wallingford

Route: Wallingford – Carmel College – Ewelme – Berrick Salome – Wallingford.

Brief Description:
Grading – Moderate/Dificult (if wet).
Terrain – 67% off-road.
– Good tracks, but can be very heavy if wet. Ewelme and Wallingford worthy of attention. Interesting.

Distance: Total – 17 miles; Off-road – 11.4 miles

Time: $2^1/_2$ hours

Height Gain: 425 feet

Start/Finish: Wallingford (station)

Map: OS Landranger 175; start – GR 607894

---

a – b: Wallingford to Ewelme

From Wallingford centre, cross the Thames on the Henley (A423) road and after 150 yards turn right into the track, although there is, remarkably, no signpost. It is immediately before the 'Bridge Villa International Camping Site'. Then bear left at the fork, keeping hard by the camping site and through a pleasant covered glade, then right at the junction and straight on past 'Newnam Farm'. Nice riding leads to a paved surface and an underpass (the Ridgeway footpath turns left here) where we keep straight on towards 'Carmel College'. Follow the College signs around to the left, ignoring the Bridleway straight ahead (this is taken by Route 3 – 'Stoke Row'). A steep rise is soon encountered, leading in $1/_3$ mile to the junction with the A4074 (Wallingford to Reading).

Across the A4074 (care!) and enter the small road that runs behind it, enabling the next left turn to be made in 100 yards into the bridleway (well signed), without recourse to the A4074, by keeping to the wide

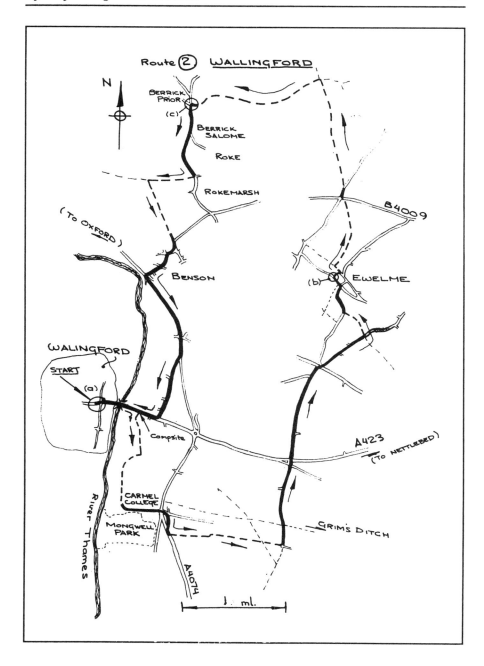

grass verge. Across the open field, with pig farm on left. At the end of the field turn left and through the farm (waymarked, just about), and across the next field (surface a bit rougher). Across another field (bridleway sign), which could be designed for bikes with suspension – flat but lightly rutted, transverse to travel direction! Straight over the tarmac road and now the surface is much improved (gravel) to the road, in $1/4$ mile. Turn left here, joining the 'Swan's Way' and heading north along this pleasant lane, past the Ridgeway crossing. Straight on at the minor crossroads, and the next which in 200 yards crosses the A423 (care!), signed Ewelme 2 miles. After a mile the next junction requires a right and immediate left turn, following signs 'Swinton' and 'Swincombe'.

Ewelme – water-cress pond

Pass the gravel pit workings and go left at the bridleway ('Love Lane') signpost. Between the fenced-off gravel pit and landfill site to the road crossing. Ignore the bridleway straight on and turn right at the road to Ewelme. As the road begins to descend, a bend suddenly reveals a glimpse of Ewelme – across the small valley – a magnificent view! Down the road past the old farm buildings and the route turns left at the T-junction, then first right at the thatched cottage and water-cress ponds (from which its name derives), and up the hill; shortly turning left into 'Chaucer Court'.

b – c: Ewelme to Berrick Prior

From Chaucer Court turn left, following the bridleway signs, then right at the gravelled track (ignoring a bridleway sign straight on) past the timbered buildings (now private houses, 'North Barn' and 'South Barn'). The good track leads across fields via an interesting high-handled gate, presumably designed for non-dismounting horse riders, steadily uphill to reach the crossing of the B4009 in good order.

At this point the route has bridleways that can provide a wheel-clogging mud in wet conditions. An alternative route is to turn left at the B4009, then second right to Roke, forking left at Roke, and coming out to the next bridleway, by way of lanes.

For the more determined(!), turn left at the B4009, then right after 20 yards and along a road for 150 yards to a left onto the bridleway (signposted), with posts to deter the motorist. The track gets increasingly bumpy with plenty of undergrowth, but rideable as flat or slight decline. At the first track crossing, turn left (straight ahead up a small incline is Whitehouse Farm). Straight on over the road crossing and we finally emerge from the increasingly muddy track onto the road to Berrick Prior. Ignoring the first left, keep straight on to the crossroads where we turn left, past 'The Chequers' (Breakspears Inn).

c – a: Berrick Prior to Wallingford

From Berrick Prior take the right fork at Berrick Salome (signposted Benson), past a couple of thatched cottages and, at the outskirts of the village, turn right into the bridleway. There is no sign, except for one pointing left to Roke, but the turning is 300 yards from Rokemarsh. This track is a definite improvement from the previous one, level and a bit bumpy, breaking out across the field. Shortly after leaving the small, almost hidden stream, we need to take a sharp left turn, towards Benson. Although there is no signpost, after making the turn the track becomes more obvious as it runs back through a clearing in the hedgerow, across the streams. Very soon, the track becomes surfaced, and we pass 'Hale

Farm' and 'Walnut Cottage'. This is Hale Road. The road widens and we bear right towards Benson. Pass the 'Sun' (Ushers Pub) and turn left at the War Memorial, following the signs to Wallingford past the fine parish church of St. Helen.

50 yards brings us to the A4074 Wallingford-Oxford road, where we turn left towards Wallingford, past Benson airfield on the left, until after a mile a fork appears on the right. This is Benson Lane, but is 'No-Entry' to traffic from this direction, so we can push across the A4074 (care!), and along the 200 yards of path, until re-mounting at the 'Hydraulic Research Station' where the road becomes two-way, and quiet. At the end of Benson lane turn right at the T-junction, with the 'Queens Head' opposite, past the Penny Farthing mounted outside the antique shop, then the parish church of St Mary Magdalin. Shortly we retrace our steps to the bridge over the Thames and back into Wallingford, where refreshments abound!

3. Stoke Row

Route: Stoke Row – Mongewell Woods – Grim's Ditch – Carmel College – Drunken Bottom – Hailey – Well Place – Stoke Row.

Brief Description:
Grading – Difficult
Terrain – 65% off-road
– Contrasting bridleways – Ridgeway to Carmel College very fine, later tracks can be difficult if wet. Several points of interest and some pubs. Varied, if muddy.

Distance: Total – 14.6 miles; Off-road – 9.5 miles

Time: 2$^1/_2$ hours

Height Gain: 975 feet

Start/Finish: Stoke Row

Map: OS Landranger 175; start – GR 684842

---

a – b: Stoke Row to Carmel College

From the main road through Stoke Row and the 'Crooked Billet' turn northwards along Newlands Lane. This shortly runs downhill until at the apex of a left bend the bridleway leads off to the right, into the woods. This is signposted with a small blue arrow, although the path has a log across part of it, no doubt to deter motors. Follow the track down through the wood, taking a left and then right fork, to arrive after a few hundred yards at the road in the bottom, where we turn left.

After $^1/_2$ mile turn left (there is a small signpost on the right). Follow the track around to the right (a footpath goes straight on here) and uphill on the surfaced track, which gradually changes into being unsurfaced and in places muddy, but rideable throughout. Continue over the top of the rise, having emerged from the wood, past the mansion on the left, and then gently downhill. Straight across the (Nuffield-Stoke Row) road,

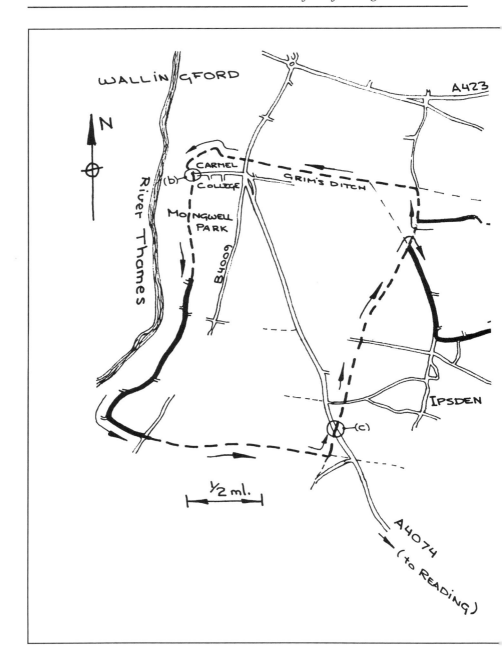

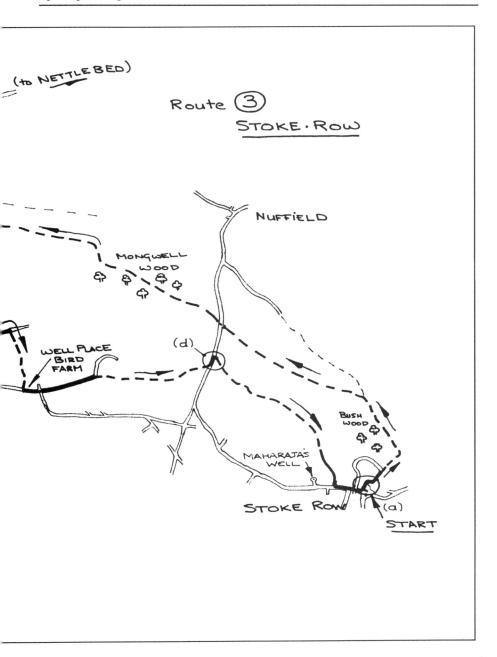

continuing along the surfaced bridleway past Copperhouse Farm at the high point, providing good views. Downhill easily on the good track, following small green waymarking arrows as the track changes texture, but any mud presents few problems. Bear left at the fork with signpost, down through Mongewell Woods; a superb ride! Suddenly breaking out to open ground and a small road at which we turn right (the 'Swan's Way' joins here).

After $1/4$ mile turn left on to the Ridgeway (bridleway), well signposted as the Ridgeway crosses the Swan's Way. Continue for $1/2$ mile straight on over the metalled road and into the covered grove forming the path – most useful in bad weather! The path runs almost imperceptibly over the rise marked by the trig point (height of 98m) and then gently down to a delightful track, although the occasional gullies and roots can catch the unwary! On arrival at the road crossing, continue straight across and through the gates of Carmel College. Keep left, following the college signs past the Preparatory School until reaching a junction where we leave the road (which turns left), instead continuing straight on at the bridleway sign.

b – c: Carmel College to Icknield Way/A4074

Continue straight on following a green arrow, then sidestep a few yards left onto the well-surfaced flat track along the edge of the wood as we leave the college grounds. Another Ridgeway signpost points this way, now encountering a couple of muddy patches, that can be eased around, reaching a substantial stake with the marking "Oxfordshire CC Judges circular ride, opened by the Duchess of Kent 17 June 1992".

A further 100 yards takes us onto a metalled road, and over the river which also runs beneath the first house of the picturesque and well-kept hamlet of North Stoke. This is 'The Street' which soon bends to the left. At this point we carry straight on, signpost 'Longride'. Behind this sign, as for many others on this route, is the Judges circular route blue arrow showing a clockwise circuit. Out across open fields until meeting the surfaced road where we go straight on, towards Littlestoke Manor, until the B4009 crosses our route. Continue straight on along a good track across open ground, slightly undulating, with traces of chalk again.

A long drag uphill (rideable for the keen) is rewarded by a complementary ride downhill but, $1/4$ mile before reaching the road at the bottom, turn left at the crossing of the (Iknield Way) bridleway. To the right is 'Icknield Farm', and there is a signpost 'Bridleway' and 'Swan's Way'. In summer this leads right through tall crops, although the path can just about be discerned through the foliage – during wet weather I found it an experience akin to riding through a car-wash! After $1/2$ mile we reach the A4074 which we cross diagonally, to re-enter the field through the obvious gap in the bank, at the bridleway signpost.

c – d: Icknield Way/A4074 to Ipsden Heath

Follow the path across the field, through a small copse (marking on tree), with a road crossing immediately after the exit from the copse.

At this point the route follows straight on along the Icknield Way, crossing the next road, then turning right at the following road (Drunken Bottom) for Hailey; each junction being well signed. However, unless under dry conditions this part of the Icknield Way can provide 'clinging' mud that is less than ideal for biking. For those with an aversion to such conditions a right turn after leaving the copse followed by a left at Ipsden brings one to the turning at the top of the hill to Hailey, from the opposite direction.

From Drunken Bottom pass 'Poors Farm' and turn left at the top of the hill towards Hailey. This road leads past the 'King William IV', 20 yards after the old barn (on the right), turn right onto the bridleway (signpost pointing out the route across the hill). Fine views from here. A fine ride downhill, then a short uphill leads to the road where we turn left, and so pass 'Bird Place Zoo' after 200 yards on the left. Straight on along Urquart Lane following signs to 'Bird Place'. At the end of the surfaced track, the bridleway carries straight on and up the hill stiffly on a good surface, past 'Harwood Lodge'. The track improves as it reaches the road crossing at Ipsden Heath.

d – a: Ipsden Heath to Stoke Row

Again, this point marks alternative routes, for those wishing to avoid the last muddy track by simply turning right on this road (away from Nuffield) then bearing left and back directly to Stoke Row.

For those not deterred by a little mud, turn left at the end of 'Urquart Lane', and after 200 yards turn right into a bridleway (no signpost)

making an acute angle with the road. Opposite, is a road marked
'Homer only'. There is a slight decline, but this is more than compensa-
ted for by some decidedly heavy going before reaching a better track,
and the road. This soon leads to a left turn at the junction of the main
road through Stoke Row, passing the 'Maharajah's Well' on the left, then
the 'Cherry Tree', with Newlands Road on the left for the next lap!

Maharajah's Well, Stoke Row

4. Nettlebed

Route: Nettlebed – Park Corner – Nuffield – Stoke Row – Checkendon – Satwell – Nettlebed Woods – Nettlebed.

Brief Description:
Grading – Moderate – Difficult
Terrain – 68% off-road.
– Generally, excellent bridleways and several points of interest, but of deceptive length and Height Gain. In good conditions take it easy and savour the surroundings!

Distance: Total – 17.5 miles; Off-road – 12.2 miles

Time: 2³/₄ hours

Height Gain: 1020 feet

Start/Finish: Wallingford (Brick Kiln Common)

Map: OS Landranger 175; start – GR 702868

---

a – b: Nettlebed to Nuffield

The route starts from the small common, near the impressive brick kiln (more of which elsewhere), on the side road that lies just off the main Henley to Wallingford road (A423), and the junction with the B481 (Watlington) road. Some 200 yards away is the roundabout where the A423 meets the B481 to Sonning Common. These roads, whilst useful for access by car, inevitably detract from the adjacent parts of Nettlebed, but we make scant use of them by bike, fortunately.

From the former junction (B481/A423) we take the lane towards Crocker End, past the kiln on our left, and along for ¹/₃ mile to the fork. Take the left fork, signposted 'Magpies' (ignoring the right turn to Crockers End). Continue straight on past the sign 'Soundess House' and 'Unsuitable for Motors'.

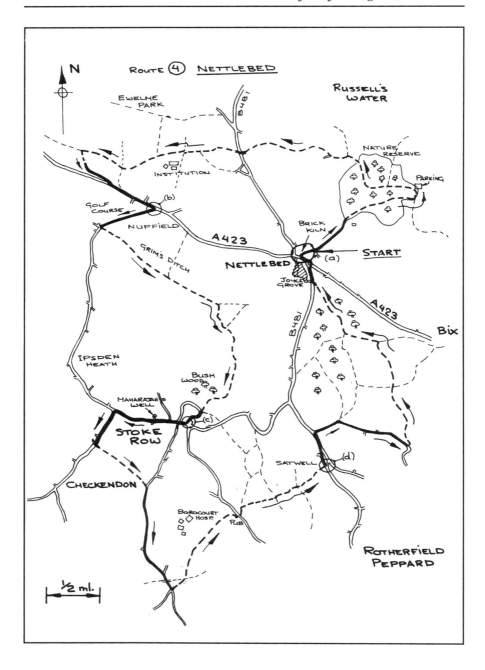

Bridleway approaching Park Corner

Passing Soundess House, we enter the BBONT (Buckinghamshire, Berk-shire, Oxfordshire Naturalists Trust) Nature Reserve, where we run down pleasantly, on a good bridleway, through the wood to the junction at the bottom. Turn left here, shortly passing a car park with BBONT information – rather surprising on a bridleway – but it is discreetly managed and the Trust has done, and continues to, a lot of good work in the area. In Spring there are banks of bluebells in an area dominated by silver birches rather than beeches. Go past 'Pages Farm' and straight on, ignoring the bridleway off to the right. Gently up the incline, keeping left at the next bridleway junction, and on past 'Westwood Manor Farm'. Continue all the way along the good track, steadily rising, until the metalled lane is reached. Bear left, then right, and out to the crossing of the B481 on its way from Nettlebed to Waltington.

The signpost pointing back is toward 'Bix Bottom', and we turn right onto the B481, then left after 40 yards into the bridleway, with its sign partly obscured by vegetation. This track is delightful, a slight decline and narrow twisty track through (Springtime) bluebell and primrose filled banks. A popular but unspoilt path. Care is required with route finding now, as we reach the crossing of tracks, where we turn right at the beech with 'NU14' marking. Down the rutted track for 150 yards, then turn left into the wood at the 'NU7' sign on the tree, by the muddy stretch. These turnings are easily missed, and going straight on at the former brings one to the 'Young Offenders' centre, (not bridleway status). From the 'NU7' sign the route becomes rutted but manageable through the wood, and crosses over the Ridgeway (footpath) at a clearing, continuing steadily down, rather overgrown and ill defined, until suddenly out from the wood and to the crossing of the lane, where we turn left, This soon becomes surfaced and the gradient rises as we pedal up to the junction of the A423.

Turn left onto this rather busy road, running parallel to the track (hidden in the wood across the fields on our left), and steadily uphill to the high point some $1/2$ mile away, where we turn right, shortly after 'The Crown' (Breakspears pub) and the bus stop, at the sign to Nuffield.

b – c: Nuffield to Stoke Row

The road runs through the grand 'Nuffield golf course', and over on the right stands the clubhouse. We turn left at the bridleway sign (an upright post with blue arrow), immediately after 'Timbers', the large house on the left, at the end of the green. Along the good track to turn left at 'Elderberry Cottage', nicely downhill at a gentle rate. The bridleway route now extends all the way to Stoke Row, by initially following the track then turning right to go through the woods. Easy going in dry weather but can become muddy in wet conditions, being well frequented by horses, and rather soft in places. Still slightly downhill, to the farmhouse with the timbered barn mounted on stone plinths. Onwards and down until suddenly out to a small fork, keeping right, over a metalled road, following the blue bridleway sign. Continue straight on across the metalled road after 100 yards, then left at the fork following the blue bridleway sign (ignoring the yellow footpath sign to the right). Straight on past the fallen tree and up the sort rise that should be rideable (I pushed again!), with its good, flinty, base. Emerging from the wood, where the bridleway exit contains a large log to detract non-approved users, we turn left at the lane. This leads directly to the main road through Stoke Row, by way of Newlands Lane, with ample opportunities for refreshment.

c – d: Stoke Row to Satwell

At the end of Newlands Lane, turn right (signpost 'Nuffield 3 miles'), along the main road past the 'Cherry Tree', then the 'Farmer Inn', the famous 'Maharajah's Well' (seen easily from the road), and the church. A left turn is made at the signpost 'Checkendon 1 mile, Woodcote $2^1/_2$ miles', and also 'Oxfordshire Cycleway'. Downhill on Uxmore Road, and at the bottom of the dip turn left into the bridleway (opposite the road on right). The wooden sign on the bank is now virtually indecipherable, but points to a good track, tarmac initially, that leads down through Ipsden Wood, (Chiltern Forestry Commission land).

Out to the metalled road junction where we turn right, and on for a mile to cross over the first small junction, then in 200 yards turn left at the bridleway which crosses the road (good sign – green with blue arrow). Soon out to the road and turn right, then left after 20 yards into the bridleway marked 'Kingswood Common $1^1/_2$ miles'. Downhill all the way, past the big house on the left, along the delightful narrow track, down and up a little, across the metalled road to Borocourt Hospital, straight on over another track. Through lovely beech woods, glorious on a sunny day with butterflies fluttering around. Across another tarmac road, where 100 yards on the right is the inviting 'Grouse and Claret'. Another green bridleway sign with a blue arrow points us straight on and across a road and down a narrow track before finally arriving at a track crossing with sign 'Satwell $1/2$ mile', plus bridleway sign showing the way straight on. Down a steeper run to the bottom then up through the lovely bluebell-filled wood (a few fallen beeches about) and to the road, where we turn left following the sign for the 'Lamb Inn' (Bears-pears).

d – a: Satwell to Nettlebed

Pass the Lamb Inn (on the right) and a minor road on the left, and continue on to turn right at the road marked 'Oxfordshire Cycleway'. Straight on past various footpath crossings and 'Roses Farm' then gently downhill, to turn left into the well signposted bridleway, as the road bends to the right. Along the bridleway, to the muddy area where the paths cross, and we turn left here. An exciting downhill stretch is followed by a mixed path, flint base, rather overgrown in places, but a fine wood. Steadily uphill, on and off the bike for me, until the house comes into view. Follow the track around to the left, and through 'Bromsden Farm and Stud'. Straight on over the tarmac road, heading towards 'Westleaze Cottage'. Open field to the left, popular with phea-sants, down to the bottom and left, and up to keep right at the fork and a long, steady, pull up the good track containing an ample supply of small flints that makes it not too easy a task.

Although still within the wood, the road to Nettlebed (B481) is reached, and we turn right here, towards the roundabout in Nettlebed $1/4$ mile away. Directly across the road from the bridleway exit lies the fabulous mansion and grounds of 'Joyce Grove'. Now a Sue Ryder home, it was previously the home of Ian Fleming, an appropriate origin for the creator of James Bond. Along the B481 to the roundabout and left, past the other entrance to Joyce Grove, to the start in Nettlebed, just before the B481 to Watlington, and the brick kiln.

Brick kiln at Nettlebed

5. *Christmas Common*

Route: Christmas Common – Icknield Way – Ewelme Downs – Park Corner – Russell's Water – Pishill – Christmas Common.

Brief Description:
Grading – Moderate/Difficult
Terrain – 70% off-road
– When dry the paths are an absolute delight, with only short stretches of difficulty. Quite strenuous and entertaining!

Distance: Total – 14 miles; Off-road – 9.8 miles

Time: 2 hours

Height Gain: 1000 feet

Start/Finish: Christmas Common (N.T. car park)

Map: OS Landranger 175; start – GR 709936

---

a – b: Christmas Common to Ewelme Park

The National Trust car park is situated in an unrivalled place for footpaths and sorties around Watlington Hill, making an interesting contrast to the bike routes. At the top of the hill from Watlington, a few hundred yards from Christmas Common, it is discretely shielded from the road, although well signed.

From the car park turn right to the crossroads at Christmas Common where we go left for 200 yards to the bridleway, marked 'PY4'. Left into the bridleway, with some insignificant mud at first, through the copse, and then out to fine views across the plain towards Oxford and Thame. Continue down the hill, quite exciting, good dry going, past the wood-yard on the left. This forms part of the 'Oxfordshire Way', a fine long-distance path which contains footpaths as well as bridleways. At the bottom, the Ridgeway crosses the Oxfordshire Way and we turn left here at the appropriately marked signpost.

Follow the Ridgeway, across the first road, then gently down, some (avoidable) muddy bits, to the second road crossing. Continue straight on along the metalled road. At the road off to the right, keep left and onto the unsurfaced track, signposted 'Leys Farm'. Along past the next road crossing, surfaced with gravel. Then a little muddy and interesting riding, gently down, and out to the metalled road which we follow straight on for 50 yards before turning left at the bridleway sign. This is now part of the 'Swan's Way', a 65 mile, predominantly bridleway, route from Goring to Salcey Forest (sounds good!). Pass the pig farm and go gently uphill on the rutted track, over a crossing, having negotiated a sharp little ditch to catch the unwary. Across open ground to turn left at the post with blue arrows denoting the bridleway. Ahead is a small copse running in a line across the field. After the mainly flat going before, this presents a steady rise on a pitted track that had me pushing up to meet the road to Ewelme Downs.

b – c: Ewelme Downs to Russell's Water

The road leads to 'Ewelme Place', the large house and grounds, where the Ridgeway (footpath here) crosses our bridleway. Pass the house and go along an avenue of Cherry trees, alight with blossom in April, and turn right at a small road joining from the left. At the T-junction turn right onto the B481, then immediately left at Park Corner along the surfaced track. Ignoring the footpath on the left, to Priors Wood, continue on the unsurfaced track down to the first gate and straight on past the farm on the left, heading directly for the wood, fencing both sides of the track. Nicely down through the wood, a little rough but rideable. Into the bottom, rather prone to collect a muddy section, continuing up the short rise in similar vein, possibly benefiting from a short carry. Fine example of a restored brick/timber/flint/ thatch house to the left as we leave the wood to turn right at the sign to Maidens-grove, just before the tarmac track. Continue alongside the buildings, which leads down a narrow track with a dry, flint studded, base. Now quite steeply to the bridleway junction. Turn left here, a delightful enclosed track. In 150 yards it steepens, flints seem to increase in size, banks rise either side, and a short carry is appropriate. This gradually develops into a rideable track as the gradient eases off and the surfaced lane leads to the green in Russell's Water.

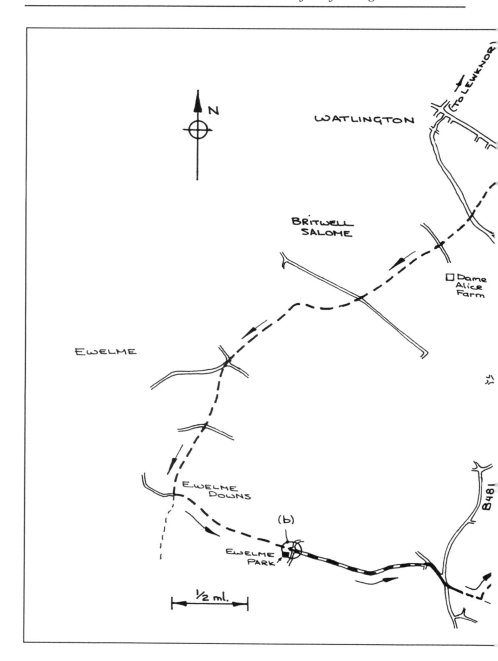

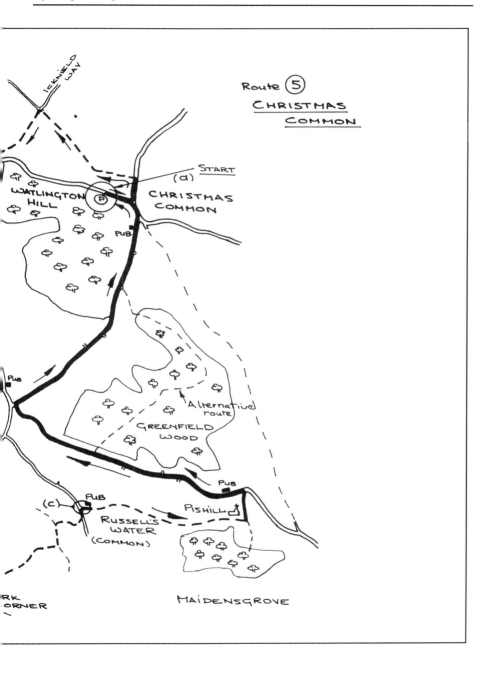

c – a: Russell's Water to Christmas Common

At the junction turn left, then right in 100 yards past the 'Old Chapel' and the duck pond. Along this track, with 'The Beehive' almost hidden on the left, and follow the bridleway sign 'Pishill with Stonor $1^1/_2$'. Altogether a fine place to linger. Across the fine open heathland common and then through the farmyard, the oak wood, and muddy narrow track. This part displays a generous array of broadleaf trees, not being overwhelmed by the ubiquitous beech. The slight decline aids rideability and is waymarked by white arrows on the trees, past the crossing of footpath 'PS20', and continuing along 'PS22'. The track steadily improves to the superb downhill run turning left onto the surfaced lane at Pishill hamlet.

Pass the old Vicarage, with fine views at Pishill parish church. Quickly down to the bottom to meet the B480, although the views from the church should not be missed. Turn left at 'The Old School House' onto the B480, past the magnificent 'Crown Inn', and up the steadily increasing incline to the plateau. Although we follow the road to the junction at the top of the hill, there is an alternative of the bridleway that runs by the houses on the right. This is part way up the hill starting from just after the postbox, and footpath 'PS21' marked on the left. This bridleway runs from Pishill Bottom across the steep field and through Greenfield Wood to fork left to Greenfield.

At the top of the road turn right (signpost 'Christmas Common $1^3/_4$') and along the almost flat and pleasant road, past the pig farm, and then the 'Fox and Hounds' as we reach Christmas Common. Straight on at the junction then left at the road to Watlington – this is a high-point with the transmission mast nearby. Along for $^1/_4$ mile and left into the car park from which we began.

6. Aston Rowant

Route: Aston Rowant – Lower Icknield Way – Lewknor – Icknield Way (Ridgeway) – Christmas Common – Stokenchurch – Aston Wood – Aston Rowant.

Brief Description:
Grading – Moderate/Difficult
Terrain – 58% off-road
– A muddy start to the first bridleway belies the true nature of the route, but it contains some steep uphill tracks (from Ridgeway to Christmas Common) and downhill (Aston Wood), between magnificent going. Well worth the effort!

Distance: Total – 13.5 miles; Off-road – 7.7 miles

Time: $2^1/_4$ hours

Height Gain: 900 feet

Start/Finish: Aston Rowant (village)

Map: OS Landranger 165 & 175; start – LR 175 GR 727990

---

a – b: Aston Rowant to Christmas Common

The village of Aston Rowant has retained its secluded aspect by being off the nearby B4009 Chinnor to Watlington Road. Just far enough away for the M40 not to intrude, it lies with its neighbour Kingston Blount (reached by a footpath) at the foot of the Chilterns, which makes it a convenient place to start.

In the centre stands the church, where we begin along Church Lane. In 200 yards the metalled surface changes into a muddy track. We continue along this for a short distance to encounter the bridleway joining from the right, and, after 50 yards, a not particularly pleasant muddy area. Turning left here takes one across the furrowed track and free from the mud at the junction. No signs around. This track leads in $1/_2$ mile to a better surfaced track, then the A40 crossing.

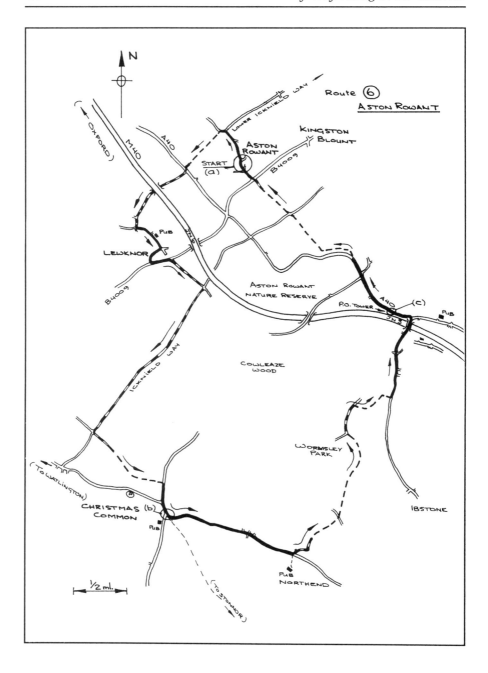

Left along the A40 for only 20 yards and right into the bridleway, with its sign rather hidden in the hedge, by the gate. A good track now leads easily to the tunnel under the M40. Continue to the junction at 'Moor Court', and left to Lewknor. Straight on through Lewknor to the T-junction and turn right past the 'Leathern Bottle' and to the B4009. Turn left along the B4009, then first right after 200 yards at the sign to 'Hill Farm'. Along this track for $1/3$ mile to the bridleway crossing, where we turn right, following the Ridgeway (it having recently emerged from under the M40, now behind).

This is archetypal Ridgeway travelling, often a broad track, sometimes with muddy patches, but always interesting as it follows a line at the base of the Chilterns, heading south west. Along for a couple of miles until we turn left at the well-marked 'Oxfordshire Way' bridleway. We soon begin the ascent of the hill to Christmas Common, past the wood-yard on the right, and up the track through the copse at the top, to the road. This is the reverse of the early stage of Route 5. At the road turn right, then bear left after 200 yards, and then left again on the road to Northend.

Bowley's Wood, on the way to the Telecom Tower

b – c: Christmas Common to Telecom Tower

Along this road for a little over a mile and turn left into the well signed bridleway, almost opposite the road in Northend that leads to the 'White Hart' (see Route 8). In 50 yards this bridleway leads through the gate into the Wormsley Estate (owned by Paul Getty II). The initially gentle decline gradually steepens, where in spring the hedgerows are full of primroses and bluebells amongst the beeches, a very fine track. Bear right down the hill, waymarked with arrows on the trees. Across a small road, continuing down and then through two gates close together. Straight on, heading for the woods and hills beyond, with a view of the Telecom Tower on the skyline ahead. An area often frequented by pheasants, the bridleway continues with white arrow markings on the trees – now a good, broad track, along the edge of the field burgeoning with hawthorne blossom in spring.

Eventually the path emerges to a metalled road, with the mansion of Wormsley Park on the far (left) side of the valley, perhaps $1/2$ mile distant. Along to the hamlet and then turn right just after the houses, following the bridleway sign. The path now pulls up through the wood, on a good track, regaining the height recently lost; still waymarked on the trees. The sting in the tail is a short stretch of muddy going as we near the crest, worth a push around. The track leads directly to the Ibstone-to-Stokenchurch road, where we turn left (towards Stoken-church). In $3/4$ mile the M40 is reached, and crossed over, followed by an immediate left turn onto the A40 in the direction of Oxford.

c – a: British Telecom Tower (Stokenchurch) to Aston Rowant

We soon pass the Telecom tower on our left, a useful landmark for several routes in this region, and from Buckinghamshire to Oxfordshire along on A40 that is often relatively denuded of traffic thanks to the adjacent motorway. Passing by the road off to Kingston Blount on the right, we begin the descent of the Chilterns, but as the A40 sweeps left, we turn off right at the apex, down a clearly defined bridleway. Down past the National Trust sign 'Aston Wood'. As we get to grips with the quite interesting descent, the bridleway forks right, marked on the tree and with a small white sign on a post. Steeply and impressively down into the bowels of the wood – surprisingly rideable with experience, passing some muddy areas, but nothing too problematical. Suddenly we emerge from the wood at the bottom of the hill and run out across the improving track at the start of the Oxfordshire Plain.

The track across the field leads over the Icknield Way (Ridgeway) and onto an excellent, flat track, past 'Woodhey Farm', across the road, and back to Aston Rowant. This way leads directly back to the beginning at Church Lane.

7. Bledlow

Route: Bledlow – Hampton Wainhill – Crowell Hill – Bennett End – The City – Bledlow Ridge – Bledlow.

Brief Description:
Grading – Difficult
Terrain – 84% off-road
– Most of the bridleways are fine, well drained, chalk based; but the high proportion off-road and some stiff uphill going make this an absolute gem for the fit, but equally as enjoyable (if not more so!) at a slow rate. 'The Lions' of Bledlow and adjacent tracks – epitome of Chilterns biking.

Distance: Total – 12 miles; Off-road – 10.1 miles

Time: 2$^1/_4$ hours

Height Gain: 925 feet

Start/Finish: Bledlow (village)

Map: OS Landranger 165; start – GR 777021

---

a – b: Bledlow to Crowell Hill

Bledlow is a delightful small village, one can normally find a place to park between the church and 'The Lions', and is only a couple of miles from Princes Risborough Railway Station. From the church, past the 'The Lions' and turn left directly onto the stony (chalk) bridleway, sign by the pub. Take the first right after 200 yards, gently down, then a steady grind up toward the house at the edge of the wood, good track all the way. Just to the right of the house and at the bridleway fork, take the lower (right) route, which skirts along the lower part of the escarpment. A most pleasant track, straight on over the next bridleway crossing ($^1/_4$ mile) out to a broader track on a smooth chalky base, past 'Stepping Hill' house and over the road, continuing along the Icknield Way/Ridgeway.

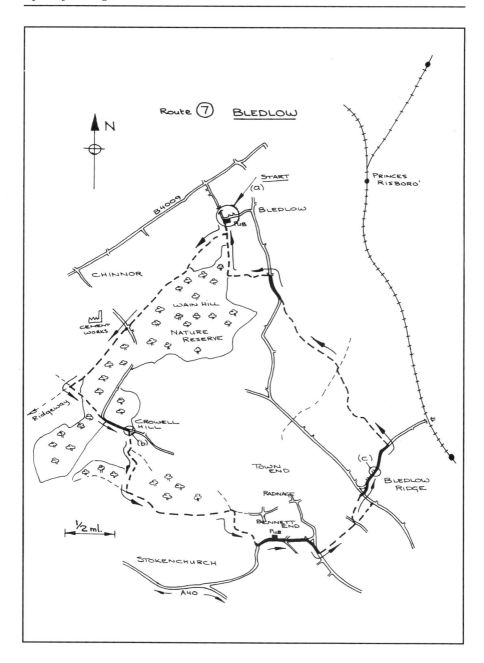

Route ⑦ BLEDLOW

Although the Chinnor Cement Works is nearby on the right, it is quite well shielded and doesn't intrude into the ambience of the track. At the next bridleway crossing, take the left turning up Crowell Hill. The sign pointing up there is missing, but the crossing is wide and obvious. A magnificent track all the way up (I soon resorted to pushing), and the road is suddenly reached at the top.

b – c: Crowell Hill to Bledlow Ridge

Turn right onto the metalled road, and from here the route follows some muddy going, so an easier alternative is to carry straight on, past Radnage, to pick up the last bridleway before Bledlow Ridge.

If undeterred, continue past the 'real' telephone box, almost hidden by the houses, and turn right at 'Crowell Hill Farm', following the small green bridleway arrow and 'CR12' marking. Then immediately after the house, drop down (almost literally!) into a narrow enclosed gully, that is truly muddy! A carry for me, trying to retain trainers on feet, but things improve soon and a white arrow provides the comfort of at least being on-route. Downwards to the fork and turn right, marked 'CR12'.

Continue through the wood, following white arrows, still muddy in places, but now often avoidable (one soon learns a technique for skirting around bad patches wherever possible, or alternatively how to cope with a mud filled chain – I prefer the former!). Then steeply down to the bottom, over a fallen beech, to the bridleway junction marked 'S87'. Turn left here, and soon to more mud, past another junction (follow S87), yet more mud and finally out, a certain relief, to an excellent dry track running through open country. This leads into another bridleway, and we bear left, running gently down all the time.

Directly behind, on the top of the hill, is the Post Office Tower. Straight on along good tracks to the tarmac road where we turn right, but only for 150 yards. Turn right again, at the bridleway sign pointing up the hill, along a good, dry track up towards Prophley's Wood. The track steadily steepens and is rideable (but not by me, at least on this occasion), to the surfaced road at the top, past the farm ('Prophleys'), a fine Chiltern brick building.

At the T-junction turn left towards The City (parallels with another city are not readily discernible), past the bridleway on the left, 'The Crown' (if closed!) and a thatched-flint cottage. Continue along City Road past Radnage School and then fork right along Green End Road, (signposted 'West Wycombe 3, High Wycombe 5'). After passing a road to the left, take a left turn at the bridleway sign, through the gate and adjacent stile.

Down steeply, quite bumpy, running out between two ploughed fields, with their sea of flints that can glisten white against the brown soil. Through a wooded patch and down to the bottom, leaving only 200 yards uphill to reach the road. A fine track. Turn left at the road, and then right at the next bridleway sign (rather hidden away) after only 100 yards. This is about as narrow a track as can be imagined, especially with summer foliage, but a dry firm base. It leads uphill, a definite push for $1/4$ mile to the surfaced track, and then the road crossing (Chinnor Road). Turn left here, and right after 20 yards, signposted 'Saunderton $1^1/2$, Princes Risborough $4^1/2$'.

c – a: Bledlow Ridge to Bledlow

Through Bledlow Ridge on How Lane, shortly dropping quite steeply down, under pylons, and then left 100 yards later, just before reaching the bottom of the hill, along the obvious bridleway crossing the road. Along in the direction of 'Lodge Hill Farm'. The good track leads under the pylons again, carrying straight on by following the blue arrows, ignoring the track to the farm on the left. At the next intersection keep left as a track joins on the right, then straight on at the next junction, following the 'Bledlow Circular Ride' sign, and so through the woody glade. A superb track, fully enclosed and quite dark as I travelled down in the evening. Through the gate ('Circular Ride' sign), then the next, and to the open field, straight on at the bridleway crossing and on to the road: a fine bridleway!

Right at the road (Wigan Lane), along for $1/4$ mile and downhill to the crossing (where the road to the right is signposted 'Princes Risboro' $2^1/2$, High Wycome 8'). We turn left into the clear bridleway, rising steadily to the crossing. Turn right here, down the hill, running out to the original track, and then 'The Lions'. I had the great good-fortune to arrive just before dark, and a more welcome opportunity for rehydration and relaxation is not easy to imagine...

Bridleway from The Lions toward Wainhill

8. Stonor

Route: Stonor – Turville – Turville Heath – Northend – Christmas Common – Stonor

Brief Description:
Grading – Moderate
Terrain – 55% off-road
– Relatively short and all bridleways in good condition, but some stiff little climbs and superb bridleway from Christmas Common to Stonor. Some peerless settings – altogether delightful.

Distance: Total – 7.5 miles; Off-road – 4.1 miles

Time: 1$^1/_2$ hours

Height Gain: 800 feet

Start/Finish: Stonor Village

Map: OS Landranger 175; start – GR 736886

a – b: Stonor to Turville

The route is described starting from Stonor, which is easily reached by road from, for instance, Henley. Alternatively, it could be started from the Christmas Common car park as described in Route 5.

The bridleway that starts the route runs directly off the road through Stonor (B480). From the Henley-on-Thames direction this is a right turn, 100 yards past the 'Stonor Arms'. The magnificent Stonor House is further up the road, although set back in a large estate. The bridleway soon rises up the hill, providing an early fitness test, or an excellent excuse to push and view Stonor Park, with its roaming deer herd. After $^1/_3$ mile turn left and then straight on to meet the metalled lane, continuing straight on (the sign 'Southend $^1/_2$ mile' points left). towards Henley. A further 100 yards and we turn left into the delightful 'Kimble

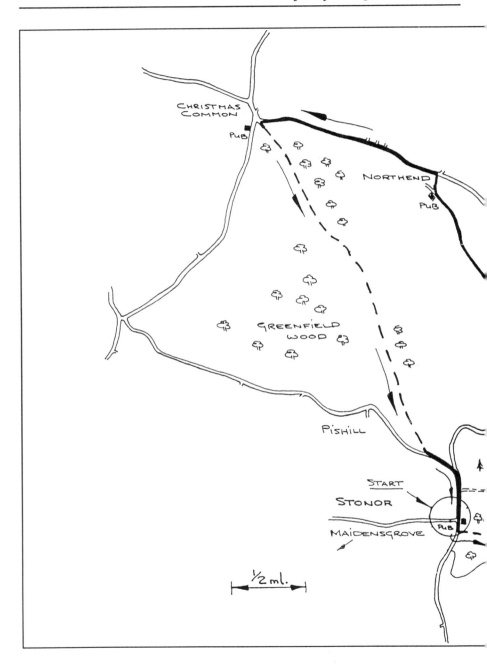

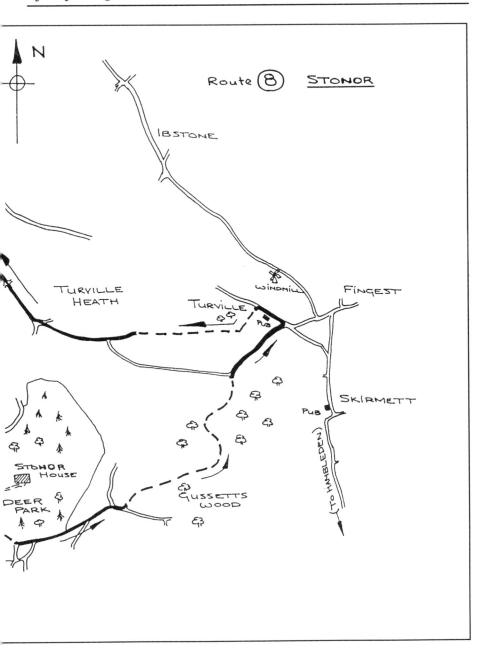

Farm', past the duck pond on a good track. Into a marvellous downhill run through 'Great Wood', often with pheasants to be seen. At the road turn right, with a distant view of the Windmill on the ridge above Turville, and then left into the village of Turville, as pretty as any in the Chilterns.

Turville

b – c: Turville to Northend

Ride into Turville past the 'Bull and Butcher' and left at the small green, between the pub and the church, up the little lane beside 'Sleepy Cottage', with its old-fashioned school sign almost buried by the abundant flora of the house. Pass the old school house to a particularly well looked-after bridleway going straight ahead. Its sign, requesting users to take care with the surface, should be respected. After 200 yards turn right on the bridleway to follow the edge of the wood and perimeter of the ploughed field. This path then leads directly across the middle of the field as the crest of the ridge is attained, the crown of the path depicting its line, amongst the densely flint-populated field. Looking behind, one can see across the valley to the opposite ridge and Turville windmill, giving an indication of the height gained and lost!

At the end of the ploughed field go straight on through the gate and up to the metalled lane, ignoring the bridleway on the right (a useful alternative back into the valley). Pass Turville Court, straight on past a road on the left to Turville Heath, and turn right at the junction, signposted 'Northend'.

c – a: Northend to Stonor

Pass the 'White Hart' (a more pleasant stopping place being hard to imagine), and head right at the village green towards the T-junction, passing the 'Beware of Toads Crossing' sign! Left at the junction, following the lane to reach Christmas Common in a mile, with no significant change in height. Turn first left at Christmas Common, immediately onto the bridleway, well marked as part (initially) of the 'Oxfordshire Cycleway'. Ignoring (for the purposes of this route) bridleway departures to the left, continue straight on down the good bridleway through the woods. Quite a long track, it gradually steepens to prove an exciting route to retain control, as control one must as it finally emerges directly onto the Watlington to Stonor (B480) road. A fine run! Left at the road, and a pleasant cruise down returns one to the start at Stonor in $1/2$ mile.

9. West Wycombe

Route: West Wycombe – Lane End – Bolter End – Cadmore End – Fingest – Horsleys Green – Bottom Wood – West Wycombe

Brief Description:
Grading – Difficult
Terrain – 39% off-road
– Although much of the Height Gain is on the road, the off-road can be tricky – initially with wild undergrowth in the middle with nice paths; and latterly (Bottom Wood) muddy but not quite desperate. A worthwhile challenge with rewarding stretches between the awkward bits.

Distance: Total – 16 miles; Off-road 6.2 miles

Time: 2^1/$_2$ hours

Height Gain: 1200 feet

Start/Finish: West Wycombe (car park near the Golden Ball atop the hill)

Map: OS Landranger 175 & 165; start –   Landranger 175 GR 827947

---

a – b: West Wycombe to Fingest

There is an excellent (free at time of writing) car park, adjacent to the Garden Centre, handy for the Dashwood Estate (Hell Fire caves, etc), that is found just off the A40 at the northern end of West Wycombe, a few yards along the Bledlow Ridge road.

From the car park return to the A40 and turn right, in the direction of Stokenchurch (signposted 5 miles), and then after 200 yards turn left into Tower Ridge Lane, marked by a 'No through road' sign. Steeply up the lane, which affords a fortuitous view and pause halfway up, through a gate to the striking West Wycombe House.

West Wycombe manor house

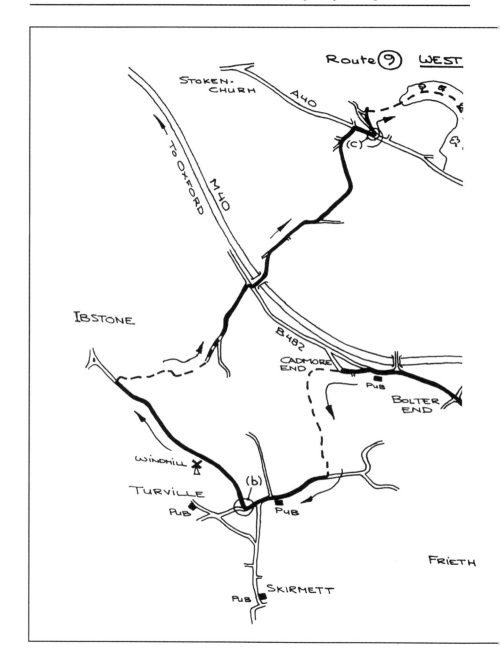

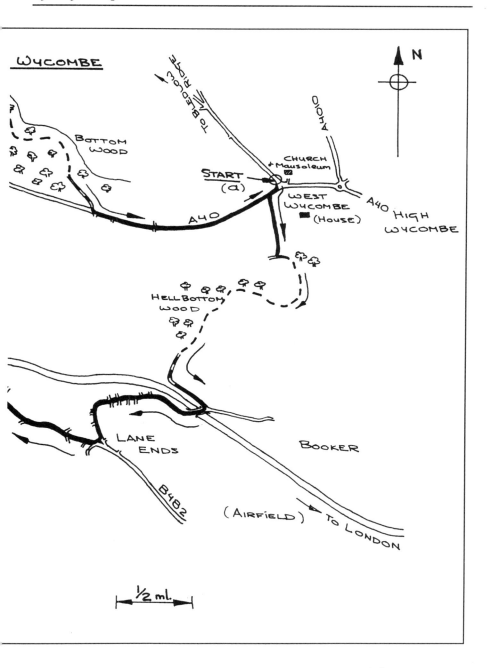

At the top of the hill the bridleway goes left or right. Taking the left route runs onto an unsurfaced (gravel) track, past the imposing statue of horse and rider, with the house directly below, on the left. Continue past the thatched cottage and at the last house ignore the footpath to the left and carry straight on, just to the right of a gate with a 'Private, Conservation area' sign. In Summer this bridleway starts off terribly over grown with nettles, and demands covering for exposed parts! Follow the track (impossible to do otherwise!) under the pylons, and the undergrowth relents as the open field is reached. A footpath runs straight on and into the wood on the other side of the valley, but we keep right, around the edge of 'Hellbottom Wood', rising up the other side of the valley until the wood is left behind and the rough track develops into a lane. A flinty incline leads to the high point (good views) and a track joins from the right. Continue straight on until the junction, where we turn left (farm on the right). Pass a copse of firs, with a camp, and down to the road.

Turn right at the road which leads over the M40 in $1/4$ mile, and through Lane End, by way of 'The Row' and the flint-faced 'The Chairmakers Arms' (Morelands pub), to the T-junction of the B482. Right here, along High Street, past 'The Old Sun'. The road now becomes Finings Lane and leads straight through Bolter End, past 'The Peacock' (ABC). Into Cadmore End and at the Primary School (on the right) turn sharply left, leading in 200 yards to the pleasantly secluded Cadmore End Church and small green.

Take the bridleway opposite the church, well signposted. Along a good track across the field, alongside a hedge, cinder surfaced initially, keep around to the left, heading for 'Hanger Wood', running gently downhill with fine views. Follow the blue bridleway signs through the wood, excellent track, with some exciting and bumpy riding to the gate, and metalled track that leads past Hanger Farm and Estate to the road. Turn right and into Fingest in $1/4$ mile.

b – c: Fingest to Studley Green

Go past the picturesque church with its unusual twinned tower, and 'The Chequers' on the left. Immediately after the church follow the signpost 'Turville $1/2$, Ibstone 2,' to the road on the right leading up the steep hill, signed 'Ibstone $1^1/2$, Stokenchurch 5'. A lovely road with enough gradient to exercise the fittest, and hedgerows to soothe the suffering ... Pass the windmill, near the road but remote as a private residence, and the footpath, recommended for the bike-less as an approach to Turville village from here.

Continue along the top of the ridge for $^3/_4$ mile to turn right at the bridleway sign, by the large gates, and through the adjacent wooden gate. Pleasantly down through the small wooded area, another gate after 200 yards, across the field, through a clump of trees and down through the path depicted with a regular row of posts either side, to the next gate. Turn right here, short muddy patch (avoidable), and left after 50 yards across open ground to the track which leads onto a steep concrete path past the house ('The Granery') and out to the road, which continues straight on past 'Chequers House'. It is only here that the M40 can be heard, and at the end of Chequers Lane turn right onto the B482 and left after 20 yards (signed 'Horsleys Green $1^1/_2$') and sometimes 'Cream Teas' ... Having crossed the M40, a rush down the hill is followed by an equally steep rise, past the 'Wycliffe Centre' (Bible translations) and onto the A40, where we turn right, in the direction of Studley Green and Wycombe (care).

c – a: Studley Green to West Wycombe

The last part of the route takes a rather muddy bridleway through Bottom Wood, which can be avoided by simply following the A40 back to the start; but if one has got this far then why not follow me ... Along the A40 to the first left at the 'Studley Arms'. Fork right after 100 yards (no marking) down the good, unsurfaced, track. At the bottom the bridleway sign points the way, right, and up to the gate. Through the gate, following the yellow arrow 'Lower Bottom Farm' marked on the barn, good track which continues across the well-marked field. Gently down, then up and straight on through the gate marked 'Bottom Wood, Chiltern Society, Nature Reserve'.

Follow the white arrows on the trees straight on and so into the muddy area. I find it preferable to carry through this going, in total under $^1/_4$ mile, and possibly avoidable just into the wood. Eventually one comes to a better track, occasionally a bit cut up (horses, as previously), going straight on and through a gate. Finally out to a wide gate and across an open field to the next gate in 150 yards. Through the next gate and turn left at the obvious track leading along to the houses in the distance. Ride past the farm after 200 yards and to the A40.

Turn left at the A40, and immediately past the 'Dashwood Arms' in Piddington, going gently downhill. In spite of its potential for traffic, in season the breeze downhill past the magnificent Copper Beeches, and the view leftwards to the West Wycombe church and its 'Golden Ball', above the Hell Fire caves, provides a fitting end to the route. Turn left at the signpost 'Bledlow' and around to the car park. And the Garden Centre even has a café!

10. Hambledon

Route: Hambledon – Pheasants Hill – Colstrope – Pheasants – Parmoor – Skirmett – Gussets Wood – Great Wood – Hambledon

Brief Description:
Grading – Moderate
Terrain – 37% off-road
– All of the uphill is on the road, pleasant lanes through glorious villages, churches and pubs. Off-road is lovely, good, narrow tracks, but demanding respect. Hambledon – an excellent centre for walking also.

Distance: Total – 7.5 miles; Off-road – 2.8 miles

Time: 1¹/₄ hours

Height Gains: 875 feet

Start/Finish: Hambledon (car park outside village)

Map: OS Landranger 175; start – GR 785855

---

a – b: Hambleton to Skirmett

The start point is the car park 1/4 mile north of the A4155 (Marlow to Henley road), along the Hambledon road. Although most easily reached by road it is only 3 miles from Henley-on-Thames Railway Station, along the aforementioned road. From the parking place the 'Hambledon' place-name shortly appears and we also finish the route by descending from the wood on the left, near here. In under a mile we can take the right turn that leads directly into the village of Hambledon, turning left immediately after the church, in the direction of 'Pheasants Hill'. As we leave the village by the Manor House, there is little difficulty in seeing this as the home of W H Smith (founder of the bookshops) the First Lord of the Admiralty parodied by Gilbert and Sulivan as the "head of the navee who never went to sea...". For this is a truly delightful place and a superb place for walking the footpaths as a complement to the rides.

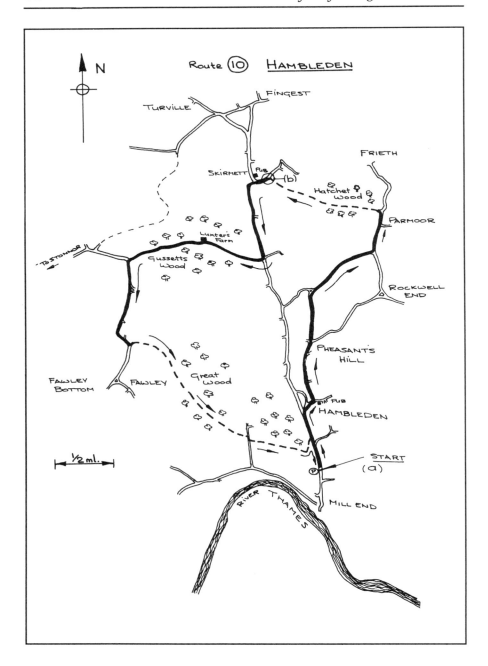

Although the route takes us along surfaced roads, they are secluded, and in such a fine setting that this is compensation for the relative scarcity of bridleways. But the going is no pushover, for the lane soon begins to rise out of Hambledon, and at the small crossing in the hamlet of Pheasant's Hill we turn right, and upwards all the way to Rockwell End before the gradient relents. Left at the fork, and then left again at the junction takes us in the direction of Parmoor, and Frieth.

Shortly after the road off to the right (which we pass by) we turn left into the bridleway (good sign), at the small triangular piece of grass with its three slender beeches. This leads past the house on the right and down a track that could have been designed for a mountain bike – narrow, steep, continuously interesting and demanding respect; but repaying with a superb ride (but watch out for horses). This brings us out to the lane where we turn left, and along to Skirmett in 200 yards.

b-a: Skirmett to Hambledon

As we run down to Skirmett we could turn right and sample 'The Old Crown', or, to remain on route, carry straight on and follow the road round a sharp bend toward Hambledon. A cruise down this road for less than a mile leads to the first turning on the right, with its signs to 'Luxters Farm and Vinery". A steep rise takes us up past the farm, and through 'Gussetts Wood'. This provides a pleasant run along flat ground, to the T-junction at the extremity of the wood. Turn left here, swooping down the road, past the footpath sign to 'Orchards', and along to a sharp right turn in the road, with the 'Round House' on the corner. Its unusual shape with an interesting round tower is unmistakeable, and the bridleway goes left here (good signpost). Continue straight on along a well surfaced track, and onto a narrow and rutted path. Being slightly downhill, this is quite rideable – very nice! Carry straight on, ignoring any deviations by following the white marks on the trees. Emerging from the wood, we can look across the field to the track running along the Bottom, and the wood beyond extending to the ridge.

Following the extrapolated direction of the track from the wood we run down the field to meet the lower track where we turn right, then left in 100 yards. Follow the bridleway sign, pointing along the track which runs pleasantly up the slope and around the edge of the wood. Along the path, with a brief sortie into the edge of the wood, until we drop off the track when the cottages appear. Shortly, we emerge at the road, marked with the bridleway sign pointing back along our route. There is an alternative of heading uphill into the wood a little earlier, the bridleway then taking one nearer to Hambledon, but there are also several footpaths hereabouts to avoid.

At the road we simply turn right and return to the start in $1/4$ mile, or, better still continue back to Hambledon and explore on foot....

Hambledon

11. Knowl Hill

Route: Knowl Hill – Cockpole Green – Rose Hill – Hurley Chalk Pit – Warren Row – Knowl Hill

Brief Description:
Grading – Moderate
Terrain – 58% off-road
– A pleasant route with some good tracks, occasionally a little tricky. Beware of the Henley road. Passes small Nature Reserve (BBONT) and some nice locations. Can be conveniently combined with the next route. Although south of the Thames, quite a typically Chiltern route in character if not location.

Distance: Total – 11 miles; Off-road – 6.4 miles

Time: 1^1/$_4$ hours

Height Gain: 550 feet

Start/Finish: Knowl Hill/A4 (service road)

Map: OS Landranger 175; start – GR 822794

---

a – b: Knowl Hill to Crazies Hill

Take the lane immediately to the left of the 'Seven Stars' (see Route 12 for details), by the old red telephone box. Ignoring the footpath, press on up the incline, bearing left on the part-surfaced track, becoming a gravel surface. Uphill, but rideable all the way to the top, where a left turn is required into the bridleway. A small sign, almost hidden behind an oak on the right, confirms this. Continue uphill steadily again, a bit muddy, but avoidable at the side of the track, which tempts one into a nice walk! Continue to the top of the hill with evidence hereabouts of double-tracked vehicles badly cutting up the central track, creating some massive holes. Although these can all be avoided by bike, it's a rather vulgar mess in a lovely wood. At the top is a junction of several tracks; we select the right fork, and fortunately the first part of this track is

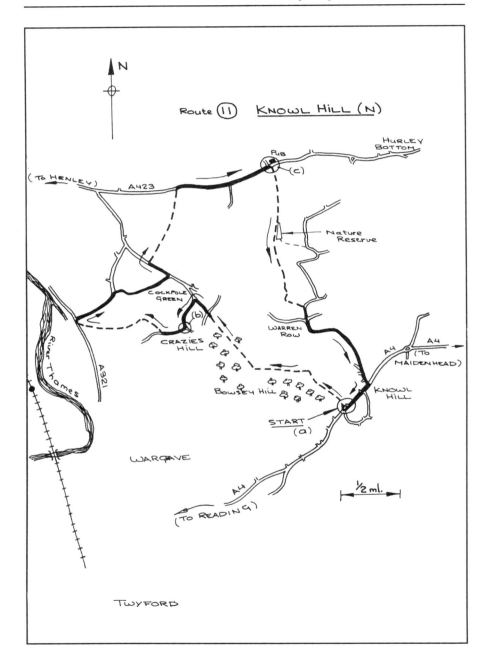

protected from the marauding trucks, permitting good riding past 'Bowsey Manor'. then onto the surfaced track and steeply down (I've seen deer dash across here), and out to the crossroads, signed 'Cockpole Green $1/2$, Remenham Hill 2'.

Straight on at this crossroad for 200 yards and turn left at the turning signposted 'Crazies Hill'.

b – c: Crazies Hill to 'Black Boy'/A423

Continue (if closed!) past 'The Horns' (Breakspears), unmistakable with the magnificent antlers over the door, and timber frame. Pass the white thatched-cottage and go downhill for $1/4$ mile to turn right at the bridleway sign (footpath sign as well as 'unsuitable for Motors'). This leads down an absolutely magnificent narrow track, downhill steadily all the way, but with sufficient flints and sporadic roots to demand attention! At the road turn right, then fork right and up the quite steep hill, regaining the height so readily lost! Past the hill, the lane becomes flat and provides good views, emerging at the T-junction at which a left turn is made. In 200 yards turn right at the unusual triangular bridleway signpost, and across high open ground on a good track to reach the A423 where we turn right (care!)

Once on the road the decline provides sufficient anaesthetic, and the mile to the 'Black Boy' pub on the left disappears rapidly.

c – a: 'Black Boy' to Knowl Hill

Turn right into the bridleway, immediately opposite the 'Black Boy' (care!!). This proves to be another delightful track, rising steadily within a covered grove, but rideable, then steadily downhill. Shortly past 'Hurley Chalk Pit' on the left – a BBONT Nature Reserve, providing a triangular area of $3^1/2$ acres. At the bottom of the track it can be muddy, but only for $1/4$ mile, soon improving to a cinder track and the road.

Turn left then keep right and straight on to reach Knowl Hill and the A4 in a mile. The 'Seven Stars' lies $1/4$ mile to the right, by the A4, and if in the slightest doubt this can be reached by a short push, perhaps taking in the café (see Route 12) if one is fortunate to sojourn on a weekday.

12. Waltham St Lawrence

Route: Knowl Hill – Waltham St Lawrence – West End – Shottesbrooke Park – Knowl Hill

Brief Description:
Grading – Easy
Terrain – 64% off-road
– The unique lack of gradients and delightful off-road going make this a pleasant and short route, with its own charm. A rather atypical route, but OK even in poor weather.

Distance: Total – 9 miles; Off-road: 5.8 miles

Time: 1 hour

Height Gain: negligible!

Start/Finish: Knowl Hill, A4

Map: OS Landranger 175; start – GR 822794

a – b: Knowl Hill to Waltham St Lawrence

On the northern side of the busy A4 road lies a quiet loop of road, providing a useful starting place, with the 'Seven Stars' (Breakspear), a tool shop (for fettling?), and the 'Square Deal', an excellent transport café, unfortunately closed weekends. As the route lies on the other side of the A4, certain life-preserving precautions include the use of the nearby central reservation, or better still, the footbridge which lies 200 yards to the east (Maidenhead) end of Knowl Hill.

Directly opposite the 'Seven Stars', and leading off the A4, take the quiet lane for $^1/_4$ mile and then turn right at 'Michlemas Farm house', signposted with a blue arrow 'RUPP'; this is the first of many encountered on this route. After $^1/_2$ mile bear right at the track entering from the left, generally excellent surface, only occasionally disrupted by horse

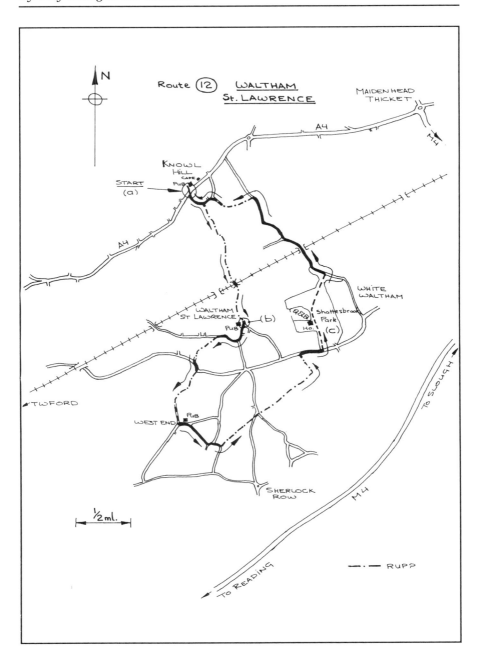

hoof and trials motor-bike – hopefully we can all continue to co-exist comfortably...Out from the covered grove and shortly over the railway bridge, with the line hidden in a cutting below. A gravel track leads to a surfaced road, and a fork where we bear right to Waltham St Lawrence. 'Bell Cottage' is on the right, the flint-faced church behind, and then we reach the picturesque junction with the 14th century 'Bell Inn'.

WALTHAM St. LAWRENCE

b – c: Waltham St Lawrence to Shottesbrooke Park

Turn right here, past a footpath on the left, and after 200 yards left, just past the '40' limit sign. Although not signposted from this end, it is a clear track, and adjacent to 'The Old Press' house. A nice run along what turns out to be 'Nut Lane'. At the road turn left, and after 100 yards right into the RUPP (blue arrow again), and down 'Mire Lane'. This belies its name, any mud presenting few problems. Pass the landfill site on left and 'West End Farm', and onto the surfaced track which leads to a T-junction. Turn left at the junction, and in 200 yards pass 'The Plough' on the left, with its timber beams and thatched barn. Turn right after a further 20 yards into 'Baileys Lane', at the signpost 'unsuitable for Heavy Goods Vehicles'. This is West End.

Follow the road around, past two footfath signs, for $^1/_4$ mile, and turn right at the RUPP (blue arrow) sign, also a footpath sign. There is a clear start to the track, taking one through another delightful covered glade. Occasional patches of mud leads to a fine gravelled surface and onto the road and a turn left. After 100 yards turn right at the junction, past 'Sherlock Row Boarding Cattery' and in 20 yards turn left at the bridleway sign, ignoring a footpath going straight on. Waste tip on the left, and up to the B3024 (care!). Turn right here and then left after 300 yards, at the blue RUPP arrow.

c – a: Shottesbrooke Park to Knowl Hill

Follow the RUPP sign through the gate (muddy here) to the next, similar gate in 200 yards, and straight across the open field, alongside the wood on the left. Pass the pond on the right and head into the middle of Shottesbrooke Park, with the fine church and Elizabethan style brick-and-timber houses and courtyard on the left. On to the short metalled road until, just before the cattle grid where we leave the road and bear right; leaving the wood behind, turning to run parallel with the fence and locked gate. We aim for the wide avenue of beeches, 100 yards from the fence. This soon turns into a well-surfaced track with fine views. At the end of the avenue lies a wide double gate with a massive catch, where we turn left at the road, and so past 'Shottesbrooke Farm'. Over the railway bridge, past a couple of footpaths and a bridleway, on the right, then 100 yards further on turn left at the clearly signed bridleway. Down through another covered grove, very pleasant, and out to a junction. Turn right here, past a timbered barn, ignoring the bridleway on the left, to the next junction. Turn left here, and back to the lane where we began, leading down to the A4; a sharp contrast to the tranquillity before.

Note that this 'back' part of Knowl Hill could make an excellent start and finish, thereby avoiding the A4 entirely.

13. Marlow

Route: Marlow – Chisbridge Cross – Booker Airfield – Ragmans Castle – Marlow

Brief Description:
Grading – Moderate/difficult
Terrain – 55% off-road
– The quintessence of a Chiltern biking route – moderate length, good tracks with flinty base; rising from the busy town quickly into the rolling hills, and back to the town centre and station by the most efficient method – bike!

Distance: Total – 12 miles: Off-road – 6.6 miles

Time: 2 hours

Height Gain: 750 feet

Start/Finish: Marlow (Station)

Map: OS Landranger 175; start – GR 865855

---

a – b: Marlow to Chisbridge Cross

There is, at the time writing, a free car park(!) by the station, which provides the starting point. From here, immediately past the 'Marlow Donkey' pub, and to the roundabout via a left and second right. From the roundabout take the first left on the B482, past the cycle shop on the left and Police Station on right. Take the left fork, at the telephone box, into Berwick Road. After $1/2$ mile turn right into the bridleway, where the sign is almost hidden on the left, by the footpath sign. This proves to be a fine, narrow track, liberally endowed with flints, up an incline that is likely to eventually lead to a push.

At the metalled road head downhill, but after 50 yards steeply down, fork right into the good bridleway track – easily missed as there is no sign and the road soon terminates at a private house. This track is

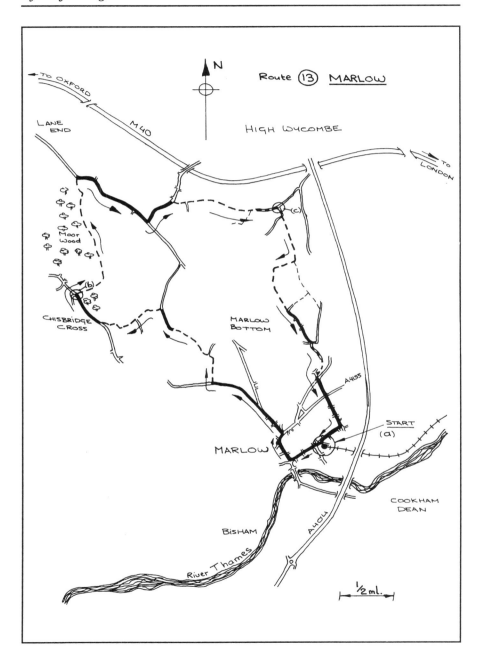

mainly covered, running down past a little mud, then a definite push up over some bigger flints; archetypal Chiltern going! On to the lane at the top. then shortly turn left at the clearly signed bridleway (straight on is 'Copy Lane'). This track rushes down, around banked bends – magnificent – but beware the exposed roots! Continue straight on at the junction of tracks at the bottom, up the hill through 'Shillingridge Wood' (rather cut-up in places) but not far to the road. After 20 yards fork left at the bridleway sign (footpath on right). Continue to the road which rushes downhill, revealing glimpses of fine views through gaps in the hedge, as we head towards the valley bottom, and Chisbridge Cross.

b – c: Chisbridge Cross to Ragmans Castle

Before Chisbridge proper, turn right at the signpost 'Blueys Farm', then right after 20 yards and right again after 100 yards at the own-made bridleway and footpath sign (perfectly clear), and through a small gate. Exhilarating plunge down over the slightly bumpy grassland, making a 30 foot wide route between fences. One is self-arrested by a short rise, ending in a fence and bridleway/footpath junction, where we turn left through the wonderful avenue of yews, providing a complete enclosure to the smooth and dry floor. At the end of this avenue it is possible to go left, around 'Blueys Farm' and through the woods, but we travel right at the fork and up the steep, chalky, well drained track. Emerging from the wood a nice track leads up and over the top, between narrow hedgerows and with superb views, but the final part of the track is mightily overgrown in Summer.

On reaching the road turn right, with the wind-sock of Booker aerodrome flying just the other side of the hedge. Out of 'Beacon Lane', past 'Roundwood Farm', right, then left after 1/4 mile, signposted 'Booker 1, Wycombe 4', (football score?). This is Clay Lane. Turn right onto the bridleway (marked 'Public Waste Disposal Site'), follow the road round until it turns sharp right. The bridleway we require goes straight on (there is a small white arrow on a tree and a tiny blue arrow sign incorporating a horseshoe). Straight on across the field, past the telegraph pole, keeping the wood on our right, and a mile away on the left runs the M40. Keep straight on at the gate, reasonable track improving as it dips gently downhill, and down to the bottom with a line of trees running away to the wood on the right.

Continue straight on and steeply up the track to the house at the top. (An equally pleasant, if shorter, alternative back to Marlow takes a right turn at the bottom).

c – a: Ragmans Castle to Marlow

Evidence of Ragmans Castle there is not, so we take the right turn from the track at the top. After 200 yards the road makes a sharp right turn, but we continue straight on down the well marked bridleway. Initially up a short rise, past a house and down the excellent track, enclosed by high hedgerows, to a fork. We take the right fork, passing another bridleway, on the left, arriving too soon onto 'Hill Farm Road'. On to a junction where we turn left, then right after 20 yards into the signed bridleway.

Through the copse, a little mud, and up a glorious little track, rideable, to Gypsy Lane. Right, then immediately left, down Bodmoor Lane. Straight on at Newton Road, and turn right onto Dedmere Road. Finally, left into the Railway Station. I certainly enjoyed it, *and* returned in time for Sunday Lunch!

MARLOW REGATTA

14. Burnham Beeches

Route: Taplow Station – Taplow – Cliveden – Hedsor – Wooburn
Common – Hedgerley – Farnham Common – Burnham Beeches –
Rose Hill – Burnham – Taplow Station

Brief Description:
Grading – Easy
Terrain – 38% off-road
– All tracks in good condition and incurring minimal Height Gain or loss, making
this a fine route for a less-strenuous day. Something of a record for a number
of potential refreshment stops – at least a dozen pubs and a couple of cafés!
Places of interest abound, including Cliveden, Dorney Court and Hedgerley
Nature Reserve. Altogether a pleasant outing with a maximum of gain for a
minimum of pain!

Distance: Total – 16 miles; Off-road – 6 miles

Time: $2^1/_2$ hours

Height Gain: 500 feet

Start/Finish: Taplow Station

Map: OS Landranger 175; start – GR 916813

---

a – b: Taplow Stations to Wooburn Common

From Taplow Station turn right and almost immediately turn left, at the
crossroads along Station Road. After $1/_4$ mile turn left at the junction
into Boundary Road.

To our left are open fields, with the spire of Taplow church visible above
the woods. Continue along Hill Farm Road (the left turn leads to Taplow
and the Thames), as the road begins a gentle incline. Pass 'Taplow
Vineyard', which may tempt with wine tasting! Continue past the
cottages with 'AD1853' brickwork and then turn right into Hunts Lane,

with its well-marked bridleway. Pass a new sign 'Horses and Footpath', 'Hitcham Glebe House', and the impressive 'Hitchembury Manor'. The surfaced track now continues as gravel, then runs into a woodland path, normally dry and with occasional flints. Through Hunts Wood on this delightful track, rolling slightly up and down and twisting gently, until we are brought out to the road.

Burnham Beeches

Turn right here, and then left after 30 yards, towards 'Burnham Lodge'. This is a charming lane, continuing the predominantly beech tree cover of Hunts Wood, but also with Rhododendrons and Holly in the hedges. Pass Burnham Lodge, another substantial property, and at the end of Parliament Lane left at the crossing of a larger road. On the corner is the 'Montesori School'. Continue for $1/2$ mile along Wycombe Common Road to reach a T-junction, with the entrance to Cliveden straight ahead, and 'The Feathers' (a pleasant stop for lunch) on the right.

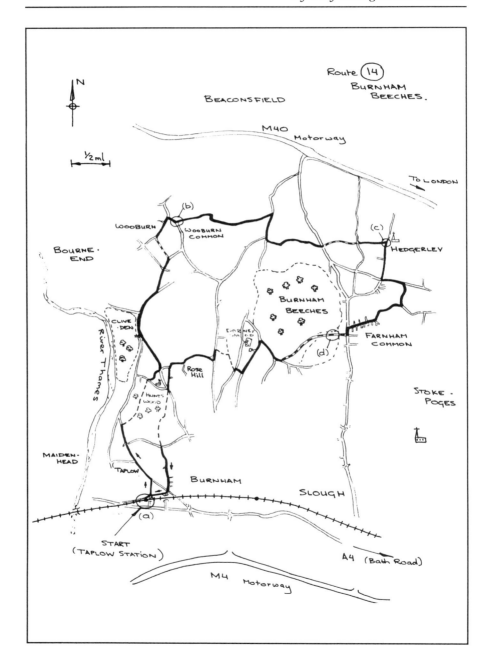

Turn right at the junction, passing Cliveden on our left. Although the house is only open to the public at certain times, the glorious grounds are accessible and provide a glimpse of the splendour of English Country life, with the open lawns and steep woods which run down to the Thames. The setting for many a political intrigue, perhaps the last of which was the first meeting of Christine Keeler and John Profumo which ultimately led to the fall of the Macmillan government; long after the departure of the Astors.

After Cliveden, continue straight on along Heathfield Road, ignoring the first turn to Hedsor on the left, and past 'Hedsor House' (now ICL). Fork left at the next turning, down Sheepcote Lane (signpost 'Wooburn Common 1, Beaconsfield 3, Wycombe 6'). Follow Sheepcote Lane, straight on over the first crossing, then left into the well-marked bridleway (also 'Beeches Way' here). An excellent track, initially part-tarmac, runs into a gravel and dirt path in good condition. Narrow in parts this leads easily out to the road junction. We leave the Beeches Way here and turn right, and past 'Sheepcote Farm'.

b – c: Wooburn Common to Hedgerley

At the first turning after Sheepcote Farm, turn right (signpost 'Wooburn Common, Burnham 4, Taplow 4, Maidenhead 6') along Wooburn Common Road. After 200 yards turn left, just before reaching 'The Royal Standard', another pleasant stopping point! Ride past Lockwards Farm, the duck pond and small fir wood, and along to the T-junction and turn right. Follow the road until it bends around to the right, where we go straight on, following the sign 'Burnham Beeches'. Continue for $1/2$ mile and take the first left along Hare Hatch Lane until the main Slough to Beaconsfield Road (A355) is reached, at the signpost 'Farnham Royal $2^1/2$, Beaconsfield 2'. Carefully cross the road and, thankfully, head towards 'Penlands Farm' on the good bridleway.

'Circular Walk' and bridleway signs show the way, which leads nicely downhill past the farm and its noisy dogs, into an unsurfaced but good–condition track. This leads naturally into Andrew Hill Lane, over the crossing and straight on down Kiln Lane. A delightful lane with a few cottages, this leads down to a T-junction.

c – d: Hedgerley to Burnham Beeches

At the end of Kiln Lane is the 'Brickmould', where we turn right and up Hedgerley Hill. However, if we divert for a short while by turning left, then we will enjoy Hedgerley village with its duck pond, the excellent 'White Horse' (on the Morris Dancers circuit), fine church just behind, and behind that Hedgerley Church Wood Reserve (RSPB).

Returning to the route; continue up the steady incline of Hedgerley Hill to reach the crossroads at the top, with 'The One Pin'. Clearly, this route should be synchronised with opening hours!

Left at The One Pin, (signposted Stoke Poges and Fulmer), along Parish Lane for $1/2$ mile to the first turning on the right, the delightful Gypsy Lane. Along Gypsy Lane for $1/2$ mile to the end where we turn right at the T-junction, into Templewood Lane. Follow this until the T-junction with the A355 is met again, in Farnham Common (at least four more pubs within a few hundred yards!). Turn left here and then first right (care!) after 200 yards, into Beeches Road. After $1/4$ mile we reach the end of Beeches Road and go straight across the junction into Lord Mayors Drive, the beginning of Burnham Beeches.

d – a: Burnham Beeches to Taplow

At this point there is a sign indicating that the Beeches are owned by the Corporation of London, and they have been the site of many a Londoners visit to the country over the past century. Many possibilities exist for the biker hereabouts, and the area is large enough to provide excellent rides without disturbing its other users, even at holiday times. A car parking area provides an alternative start to the route. We take a simple and direct route along Lord Mayors drive to the other side of the Beeches. Passing the 'Glade' mobile café we go over the crossing, past the 'Druids Oak' and down to the T-junction at the bottom of the hill. Here there are toilets and a small café. once there was an open air swimming pool, but now it has fallen to housing as 'Nightingdale Park'. The 'Grenville Lodge' restaurant is just off-route on the left.

Right at the T-junction, past 'Burnham Beeches Sawmill Office', and right at the next junction, along the Hawthorne Lane. Up the short, steady incline of Pumpkin Hill to reach the next junction where we turn left into Green Lane. Hidden away over on the right is the National Trust property of Dorney Wood. After $1/2$ mile we turn right off Green Lane and into Longmead Lane. This is only short and leads to a T-junction where we turn left, and then after 50 yards turn right into the bridleway. Although an obvious track it is devoid of markings. A good, dry track in summer, we follow it for 200 yards keeping to the left, ignoring the gate and bridleway that continues straight ahead. Another pleasant track, it soon emerges at the road, and this time the bridleway is signed.

Turn left along the road and then take the first turning on the right by the golf course and Abbey Rose Gardens, along Nashdom Lane. Continue past the Rose Gardens, ignoring the first bridleway on the left, and also the next bridleway at the apex of the corner. Pass the remarkably fortified property and ride to the small fork at the White gate-house where we turn left. Pass Rose Hill Farm, along Rose Hill Road, to the major road junction. Turn sharp right here (pillar box on corner), and along for only 30 yards, past the bus stop,. and left into the marked bridleway. An excellent path, with only small patches of mud that can be easily avoided. This leads gently downhill, eventually through a covered glade – on going that is very similar to the Waltham St Lawrence route. The hedgerows and tree variety are particularly fine, as we run past Poors Farm, and to the road at Cloverdown House.

Straight on along Hitcham Road, following the sign to 'Taplow Station 1, Maidenhead $2^1/2$'. Gently downhill, past open fields; we are now at the outer reaches of Slough. Straight on at the junction where a road joins from the left (by 'The Maypole') following the sign 'Taplow 1, Burnham 1'. Go past the original phone box and first right, just before reaching the bridge carrying the railway. Along this straight road for $1/4$ mile to the crossing where we go straight over, to return to the starting point at the Station.

15. Jordans

Route: Jordans Station – Hodgemoor Woods – Chalfont St. Giles – Quaker Meeting House – Jordans Village – Jordans Station

Brief Description:
Grading – Moderate/difficult
Terrain – 39% off-road
– Generally good tracks, but less chalk base than usual, and Hodgemoor Woods is prone to being badly cut-up in places. Final path can be rather overgrown. Some particularly interesting places (Jordans with its famous Quaker origins, and Chalfont St. Giles with Miltons Cottage). Jordans Youth Hostel and good pubs en-route.

Distance: Total – 12 miles; Off-road – 4.7 miles

Time: $1^3/_4$ hours

Height Gain: 450 feet

Start/Finish: Jordans and Seer Green Station

Map: OS Landranger 175; start – GR 965901

---

a – b: Seer Green and Jordans Station to 'Magpies'

From the 'pay-and-display' car park at the Railway Station, set off down the slope to meet the road at a T-junction. Note that the bridleway directly opposite is the one that we finally return upon. Turn left at this road (care) and continue for $3/_4$ mile, and turn right up Bottoms Lane. After $1/_4$ mile turn left into the obvious, but unmarked, bridleway. This presents a fine track running across flat, open country with good views.

At the bridleway junction (the trees provide a partitioning of the land here), turn left and through the clearing. On and through the wood, turning left at the next bridleway junction (footpath goes straight on), and up the slightly muddy track to cross straight over the road (A355 – care!). Follow the surfaced bridleway for $1/_2$ mile until it turns right (a footpath goes straight on). Follow this bridleway, open country and slippery if wet, down to the bottom and uphill again, coming out to a surfaced track past the farm, and straight on for 200 yards to the T-junction with the road. Turn right here and pleasantly down for $1/2$ mile to the junction, with the A355 (care!), at the 'Magpies' pub.

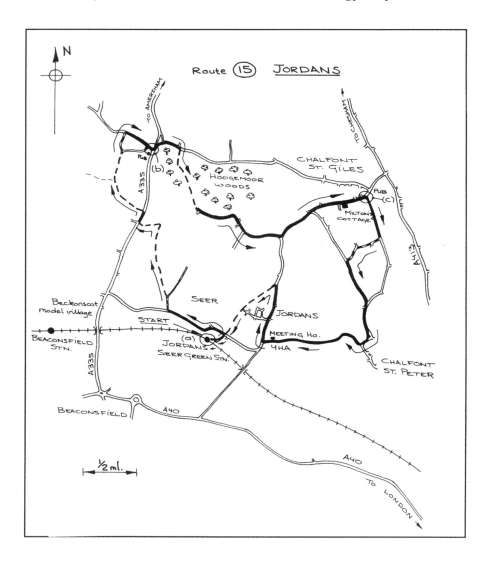

b – c: 'Magpies' to Chalfont St. Giles

Turn left onto the A355 (Beaconfield to Amersham) Road, then immediately right, with signs 'Picnic Area', and then right again and up the hill for $1/4$ mile. Into Hodgemoor Woods on the right at the bridleway sign. There are restrictions on horse riding – a special permit required from the Forestry Commission after January, 1992, and the bridleways were officially closed for a spell prior to July, 1993, an indication of the surface damage that can be wrought on the less well-drained woodland by our equine partners. Obviously, care should be taken to ensure no such damage is attributable to bikes.

Some 200 yards after entering the woods, fork right and follow the orange-painted stumps, with horseshoe depicted. As expected, the wood can be very muddy in places, but it is always simple enough to avoid these areas with a bike. On emerging from the wood, turn left (towards Butlers Cross), and follow Rawlings Lane. At the end of this lane, turn left at the T-junction, and then straight on past the 'Whitehart' pub, ignoring signs to Jordans.

Gathering speed downhill all the way to Chalfont St. Giles, passing the 'Miltons Head' pub on the left then 'Miltons Cottage', on the right. Shortly after, turn right into Bowstridge Lane; just before reaching the village centre with its delightful cluster of church, shops, and pubs around the green, with the remnants of the River Misbourne beside, all worth a visit.

c – a: Chalfont St. Giles to Jordans Station

Along Bowstridge Lane for $1/2$ mile, going up short incline, to turn right at the bridleway (signposted), a gravel track past the houses. Bear left at 'Narcot House', and to the road. Turn left at this T-junction onto Grove Lane. Follow this for 1 mile, and turn right into 'Welders Lane', where Grove Lane bends to the left.

Continue pleasantly along this lane, dropping down and passing the Jordans YHA, then the 'Friends Meeting House', at the corner of the crossroads (care!) where we turn right and up the hill towards Jordans. Pass the village with its large green (just visible on the left) and on for another $1/2$ mile to an acute left turn into the bridleway, marked 'Wilton

Lane'. Gently down the dry and flinty track, over the path crossing which becomes generously endowed with undergrowth, including net- tles, for the last $1/4$ mile to the junction with the road – this is where we began. Straight over the road (care!) and up the station approach.

Chalfont St Giles

16. Great Missenden

Route: Great Missenden – Great Hampden – Parslows' Hillock – Grim's Ditch – Lacey Green – Hillock Wood – Whiteleaf – Pulpit Hill – Hampden House – Prestwood – Great Missenden

Brief Description:
Grading – Difficult
Terrain – 38% off-road
– The bridleways cover the full range from super-muddy and rather trying (first part of Grim's Ditch), to excellent chalk – based uphill (Pulpit Hill), to grassy and flat (Hampden House). The length and variety of terrain make this a reasonably tough exercise that could be easily linked to further routes such as Chesham or Wendover. A good route for the well-prepared.

Distance: Total – 21 miles; Off-road – 8 miles

Time: $3^3/_4$ hours

Height Gain: 1100 feet

Start/Finish: Great Missenden Station

Map: OS Landranger 165; start – GR 893013

---

a – b: Great Missenden to Great Hampden

Turning off the A413 Amersham to Aylesbury road, from the round-about towards Great Missenden, leads past a convenient car park. If we continue straight across the staggered junction then left after the bridge, we arrive at the Railway station to start the route. Although one of the most testing in the itinerary, from the point of view of route-finding, hill climbing, and mud-bashing, it also provides a sojourn through some of the finest of Chiltern country and history.

Pulpit Hill, above Princes Risborough

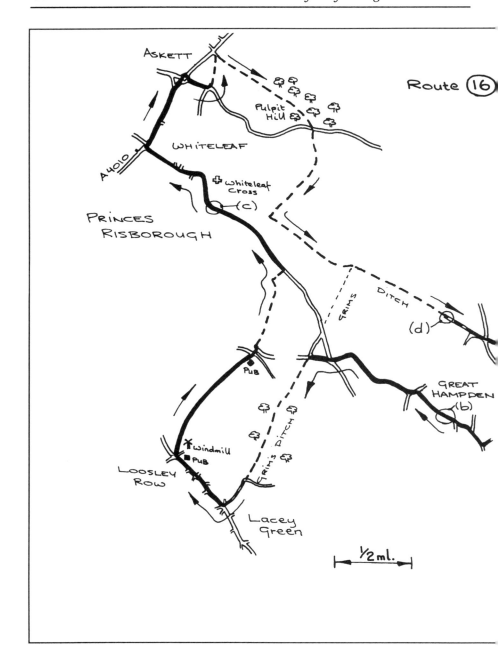

Route 16

Askett

Pulpit Hill

WHITELEAF

A4010

Whiteleaf Cross

(c)

PRINCES
RISBOROUGH

TRIMS DITCH

DITCH

(d)

GREAT
HAMPDEN

(b)

PuB

Windmill
PuB

LOOSLEY
ROW

Trims Ditch

Lacey
Green

½ ml.

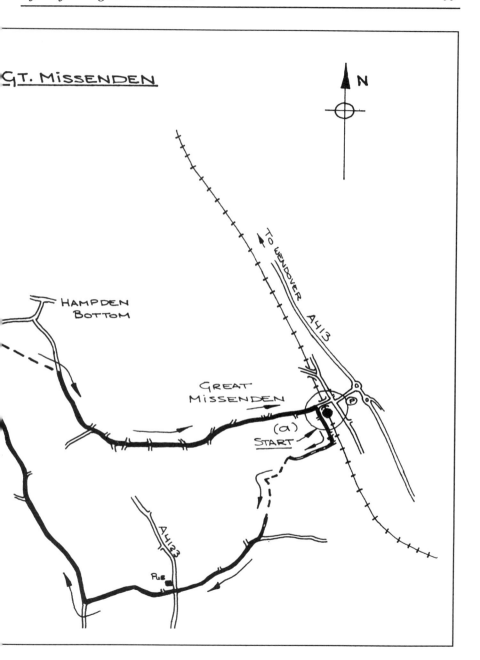

GT. MISSENDEN

N

TO WENDOVER A413

HAMPDEN
BOTTOM

GREAT
MISSENDEN

(a)
START

A4123

PUB

Go past the station, along Trafford Road, which becomes an unsurfaced track to a T-junction, where we turn right and up the hill on a metalled track. Bear round to the left and down a good track past 'Angling Spring Farm'. Follow the track through the wood, with its occasional patches of mud (avoidable), out of the wood and easily along to the road. Turn right at the road and then continue straight on, crossing the A4128, ('Kings Head' on the right).

Down to the next T-junction and turn right and steadily up the ridge for $1^1/_2$ miles, ignoring both a road on the left, then on the right, until reaching the thatched cottage, and bridleway sign tucked away on the left bank. Turn left into the bridleway and follow the track around to the right, ignoring the road to the house. Follow the small white arrows (no other signs), out to the pleasant track that emerges at a secluded thatched cottage and Hampden Common. Follow the sign 'Great Hampden $1/_2$', passing the common with its superbly set cricket pitch, on the left. At the junction, with the inviting 'Hampden Arms' on the right, go left then right on the road to Great Hampden, now no more than a hamlet despite its grand title.

b – c: Great Hampden to Whiteleaf Hill

The next part of the route, along 'Grim's Ditch' is aptly named, and could be easily avoided by continuing straight on past the bridleway turning, to rejoin the route $1/_2$ mile further on; but for the enthusiastic biker or Chiltern bridleway addict, continue across the staggered road crossing (ignoring the right turn to Redland End and Princes Risboro') and up the hill for 200 yards to the bridleway sign. On the right Grim's Ditch is metalled for $1/_4$ mile at a sign, 'Bridland End, Whiteleaf 2'. We turn left into the Grim's Ditch bridleway, through the wood. Grim's Ditch now extends for nearly 2 miles to Lacey Green, and provides probably the most trying, muddy, going in this series of rides; but having started, as in 'Mastermind', we shall continue! At the road crossing continue straight over, following the bridleway sign, up an overgrown track and straight on, to finally emerge onto the lane. A right here leads to Lacey Green in a few hundred yards.

At the end of Kiln Lane turn right past the 'Black Horse', and through Lacey Green towards Loosely Row. At the crossroads turn right, with the 'Whip Inn' at the corner, along Pink Road. This road is at a good height and leads smoothly to the next crossing, where on the right stands the 'Pink and Lily' (famous for its associations with Rupert Brooke prior to the Great War). Over this crossing, then 50 yards later left at the next junction, and then right into the well-signposted bridleway through Hillock Wood. Pleasantly through the wood until near the end where it is muddy (but possible to avoid through the copse on the right), and out to the road. Turn left here down to Whiteleaf Hill, and past 'Whiteleaf Cross'.

c – d: Whiteleaf Hill to Hampden House

Follow the road towards Princes Risboro' which soon shoots one steeply down through the escarpment and high banks of Whiteleaf Hill, then running out at an easing gradient to arrive at the small roundabout where the A4010 Risboro' road crosses. Turn right onto the A4010, passing the Green Hailey Water Tower, en-route for the next roundabout. Turn right here (Cadmore Lane), up the hill past the 'Black Horse' for $1/4$ mile to the golf course where a road runs off to the right, which we ignore. Instead, turn left at the prominent sign 'By-Way, Upper Icknield Way', just before the 'Cadstone' sign.

Easily along the track, until the A4010 is seen again, where we make an acute angle right. This leads delightfully back up the escarpment on a good track, with the stones and camber providing a rideable route all the way to the top (although I resorted, in character, to a push!) Keep right at 'Grangelands Farm' and down slightly to the road crossing. Go straight across and into the track opposite, which is missing its bridleway sign. The wood provides another taste of Chiltern mud and can warrant a carry in places, but to avoid this bridleway would be to miss the next one which is quite a contrast! Then on, and nicely down a superb track, narrow and dry. Uphill from the bottom, across another track to more mud, which fortunately can be sidestepped along the path just to the right, leaving the horses to churn up the main track. This is most pleasant and finally re-connects to run straight on and through the gate and past 'Hampden House'. We have rejoined the upper arm of Grim's Ditch, but this part runs at right angles to the earlier section.

d – a: Hampden House to Great Missenden

From the impressive plastered-facade of Hampden House continue on the metalled track, through the grounds, past the flint covered church, to keep straight on as the road joins from the right. Straight over the crossroads (200 yards) and then as the road bends around to the left in another 200 yards, take the bridleway straight on, signposted. Through the rather overgrown track, narrow but with a good base, and through the gate to open fields. Another three gates, excellent track throughout, lead eventually to the road, Grim's Ditch having vanished from the map.

Right at the road, past 'The Chequers', and bear left to meet the A4128 (Wycombe to Great Missenden) road. Continue straight on along the A4128 to reach Great Missenden in $1^1/_2$ miles, running down the hill, not unpleasantly after earlier struggles, to the right turn into the station just before the bridge. A tour-de-force!

17. Wendover

Route: Wendover Station – Dunsmore – Hampden Bottom – Cobblers Hill – Little Hampden – Chequers – Butlers Cross – Coombe Hill – Babcombe Hill – Wendover Station.

Brief Description:
Grading – Difficult
Terrain – 60% off-road
– The bridleways are well signposted and in generally good condition, with only short stretches of mud, of little hindrance. The off-road work is fairly flat or downhill, until the sting-in-the-tail, from Butlers Cross to the top of Coombe Hill (highest point in the Chilterns). The path back down to Wendover is pure delight. Points of interest include Chequers (passing within 200 yards of the house), Dunsmore hamlet and Little Hampden for their pubs. A reasonably demanding route, but none finer, to be savoured in the cafés or pubs of Wendover.

Distance: Total – 14 miles; Off-road – 8.4 miles

Time: 2 hours

Height Gain: 1020 feet

Start/Finish: Wendover Railway Station

Map: OS Landranger 165; start – GR 865078

a – b: Wendover to Dunsmore

The start point at the Wendover Railway Station is conveniently positioned, just off the main street, and provides a good car park, for parking in side roads is rather restricted. From the station go along Station Approach to the main road and turn left, with the 'Shoulder of Mutton' on the corner. Down the slight hill and straight over the mini-roundabout after 100 yards. The London Road (leading to Amersham) is on the right, with a good café on the corner (bit early for a refreshment stop!).

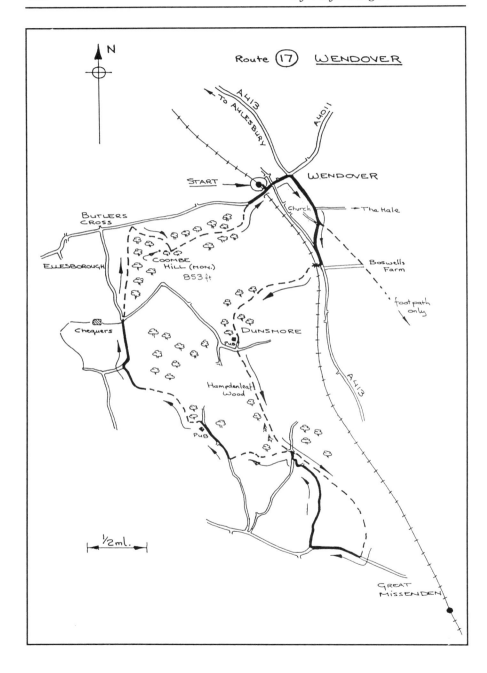

Continue down the hill to a left bend in the main road and then turn immediately right onto the A4011 Tring road, by the clock tower. Then, after 50 yards, turn right again into a small road towards 'The Hale'.

Wendover is soon left behind as we continue straight on, ignoring a left turning signed 'The Hale, St Leonards 2'. On to a crossing with signs to 'St Mary's Church' and the 'Ridgeway', and bear right. Ahead is a fine bridleway, unfortunately it ends in a footpath soon after Boswells Farm, and the obvious lane linking it to the Amersham Road has no right-of-way, so the latter should definately be avoided. If one can afford the time then the ride up-and-back the Ridgeway's bridleway, past Boswells to its end in the wood, is rewarded initially by fine views of the cornfields through the tall hedge as the track climbs gently; and then woods that provide magnificent walking or a site for an early and secluded rest!

Turn left onto the A413 (care!), then first right at the signpost 'Smalldean Scrubwood', along Smalldean lane. Immediately over the (almost hidden) railway bridge and up the lane for $1/2$ mile. As the road bends to the left, with a house on the corner, we take the well-signed bridleway that runs along to the right of the house. Through the gate and up into a delightful covered glade along a magnificent track, steadily uphill but rideable, passing straight over the minor track crossing. The track begins to steepen as it runs between rows of fence posts with wire strands. Possible to ride all the way, although I sneaked in a short push. We finally emerge from the wood, across a clearing, still defined by fencing posts and gently over the crest. The track now eases down as it runs back into the woods after 300 yards, to shortly pass the well-detached houses that mark the start of Dunsmore. A footpath joins the bridleway, as we effortlessly move on to the road crossing.

The village pond lies to the right, with its secluded aspect provided by the tree cover. However, we have just passed the 'Fox Inn' tucked away on the right just before the junction – a bit early for a stop, but highly commended for food and drink.

The Ridgeway path, gained soon after leaving Wendover

b – c: Dunsmore to Cobblers Hill

Back at the junction (signpost 'Wendover 2, Great Missenden 4(L), Kimble $3^1/_2$, Princes Risboro $5^1/_2$(R)') we go straight over and into the bridleway (well signed), and past the pub converted into a restaurant, along the good track. This path is virtually flat, following the ridge for a mile to the next junction. This is, again, an excellent track through the wood – not too simple, with twists and turns and exposed roots and patches of mud, that can all be ridden around with a little cunning; ranking with the best in the Chilterns. As we come out of the wood, the views from the ridge, across to the right reveal Little Hampden amongst a vista of fields, woods and ridges. But now we have three short stretches of mud that demand attention. As usual, these are patches of soft ground churned by horse hooves, and I prefer to push or carry around the edges – in wet weather this could be a bit messy. This is soon passed however, and we return to a good track, finally passing the few houses on the left as we arrive at the lane crossing, then farm on the right. At this junction the prolific signs indicate bridleways (back to Dunsmore, onwards and across) as well as the 'South Bucks Way'.

c – d: Cobblers Hill to Chequers

From this junction it is possible to turn right and go through the farm and straight down Cobblers Hill. However, I'm glad that I couldn't resist the temptation (even in the rain!) to carry on along the bridleway, doing a loop, and returning to pick up the aforementioned track through the farm. Therefore, straight on at the junction, following the bridleway sign along a good track past the houses, that soon becomes quite narrow and then poses some slight muddy patches that can be avoided with little deftness. After $^1/_4$ mile this becomes a gravelled track, past 'Blossoms', keeping right, then straight on to a small track again. Out of the wood, we fork right, following the small (blue) bridleway arrow on a wooden post. This brings us alongside the wood on the edge of corn-fields. A nice track, fairly flat, before running downhill. Through gaps in the trees are revealed occasional fine views, but the path soon demands attention as we run down rapidly to the road at the bottom.

Emerging from this track (Mapridge Green Lane), we turn right, then first right again after $^1/_2$ mile. This lane leads steadily uphill (Kings

Lane). Follow the road around to the right as we near the top, until reaching the farm which we passed-by on the outward leg.

Adjacent to the farm is the crossing of the bridleway and the comprehensive signposts, with one pointing in the direction of the farm-yard. Go boldly through the farm entrance, some 20 yards before the sign, through the gate and along a concrete path. Into the copse and then soon sharply downhill, a magnificent track, demanding care (rain soaked brakes enforced a dismount here). This leads into a lovely field system, and uphill again (not for long), towards Little Hampden. Up to the road, with the unusual little church – part timber framed – opposite. Turn right onto the road here, with a post box immediately on the right.

Keep right at the fork, continue past the 'Rising Sun' (a pleasant stopping point) and then left directly up to the gravel track. After 50 yards, and the end of the houses, bear left following the good signpost indicating the bridleway and 'South Bucks Way'.

Where two staggered posts obstruct the path, this marks the point where we turn left, then right after 20 yards, following the blue bridleway sign mounted on a post. This leads out to the edge of the wood, where we turn right. Continue following the blue signs until a distinct crossing is reached. There is a woodland constriction here, and although it is possible to continue ahead, this route takes a left turn, meeting a metalled lane almost immediately. Swiftly down this lane to the road junction at the bottom, marking one boundary of the 'Chequers' estate, although it is not at all obvious. Turn right here, and directly on the right is a bridleway sign pointing to the route up a wide and obvious track. Up this track, following a slight right fork to meet the obvious bridleway crossing ($^1/_4$ mile from road). Turn left here, back along the South Bucks Way. This good track, although a little muddy in places, provides comfortable riding, and leads shortly to a road. Turn left at the road for 50 yards to a junction, where we turn right (signposted 'Butlers Cross 1, Stoke Mandeville 3, Aylesbury 6, Dunsmore $1^1/_2$'). After only 20 yards turn right into the bridleway directly opposite 'Chequers' gate-house.

d – a: Chequers to Wendover

Although only a few hundred yards from Chequers, we leave it directly behind as we follow the excellent path and bridleway sign (as one might expect!), along the cinder-covered route (initially) with its covering of trees making a fine route. Straight on at the fork, through the gate and past the National Trust sign, 'Coombe Hill', for we are skirting the hill which rises up on the right, and reveals at this point the obelisk (a Boer War Memorial). Gently down, some tree roots to catch the unwary, and out through the gate. A small grass area separates this point from the road ahead, which we avoid, making instead an acute angle to the right. This is the bridleway route up to the top of Coombe Hill. On our left, before making the turn, lies the golf course.

The track up the hill starts steadily and is rideable, but it narrows between steep sides and steepens a bit, which soon had me pushing! As the gradient begins to ease, an obvious footpath makes a diagonal crossing of the bridleway, and it would be churlish not to leave the bike here and nip over to the obelisk a few hundred yards to the right, at about the same altitude. Back on the bike, the top is shortly reached, and besides being at the highest point in the Chilterns we are at the confluence of several major tracks, with our route lying to the left, along a very broad track. Although a bit cut-up in places, there is no difficulty in avoiding the messy parts, the track running throughout within the glorious woodland. This becomes, after $1/4$ mile, an excellent track down a broad avenue of beeches, a superb situation and good surface; and all too soon arrives at the exit from the wood, marked with Forestry Commission signs, onto the road. Turn right here and in $1/2$ mile turn left into Station Approach, downhill all the way! Now, perhaps, the stop at the London Road Café is well earned?

18. Aston Clinton

Route: Aston Clinton – Aston Hill – Forest Trail – Buckland Common – Cholesbury – Drayton Beauchamp – Aston Clinton

Brief Description:
Grading – Easy/moderate
Terrain – 30% off-road
– Although rising through the Chiltern escarpment, it does so on good lanes, and the bridleways are in good condition, although with quite an exciting, if short, descent from the hills. A nice route, that can be easily doubled in length by combining with Route 20 at Cholesbury – a fine place for 'rest and recuperation' at the pub or cricket green.

Distance: Total – 10 miles; Off-road – 3 miles

Time: $1^1/_2$ hours

Height Gain: 700 feet

Start/Finish: Aston Clinton – B489 Lower Icknield Way parking place

Map: OS Landranger 165; start – GR 892124

---

a – b: Aston Clinton to Aston Hill

Start from the lay-by $^3/_4$ mile to the north of the A41 trunk road through Aston Clinton, along the B489. From the lay-by turn right and past the 'Roschilds Arms' (an ABC pub) in 200 yards, and straight on to meet the A41 (T) at Aston Clinton (care!). On the right is the 'Rising Sun' where we turn left, then right after 150 yards into Staple Bridge Road. Over the canal bridge, controlled by traffic lights, and along the B489, uphill, to the T-junction. Turn right onto the A4011 (Wendover) road, a rather busy modern transformation of the Upper Icknield Way. Fortunately we depart via a left turn after $^1/_4$ mile, signposted 'St Leonards 3, Cholesbury $4^1/_2$, Chesham 9'. This is the edge of the popular walking area of

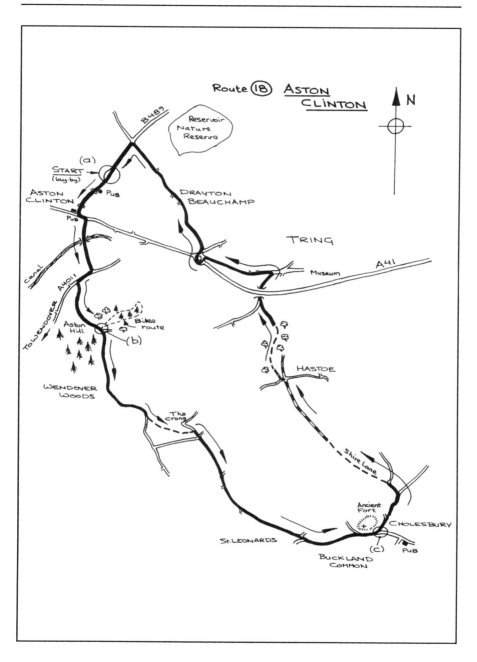

'Wendover Woods'. At present restricted to foot traffic, although it may be possible to obtain permission to ride from the Forestry Commission, whose Administration Centre is in Aston Clinton. Prominent signs depict 'Wendover Woodland Park' at this corner.

We now set off up the rise to the crest of the Chilterns, past the 'Chiltern Forest Golf Club' to reach, near the top, the sign 'Welcome to Aston Hill Wood'.

b – c: Aston Hill to Cholesbury

This is a fine place to pause, for there is an open area with good views and car parking space (an alternative start to the route), and the trail that loops through the woods, dedicated to bike and horse. A map showing the route is displayed here.

Onwards along the road and suddenly over the top and dipping down, round a bend. A footpath sign on the left is followed in 50 yards by the bridleway, with its small sign, alongside 'South Park House'. Left here into the bridleway and through another gate in 100 yards. Straight on across a field, to the gated entrance to the wood on the other side. Through the white gate where the passage through the wood is often muddy but not desperate, pushing is sufficient to avoid picking up too much mud. At the exit from the wood, is displayed information in detail about 'Black Wood' (wildlife and management of the wood), which makes interesting reading.

At the road ignore the bridleway, continuing in the wood, and turn right towards Buckland Common. Gently down, past sign 'Cholesbury' and straight on to the angled T-junction marking the end of Bottom Road. Turn left at the signpost 'Cholesbury $1/_2$, Tring 4, Chesham 5', along Cholesbury Lane.

c – a: Cholesbury to Aston Clinton

Continue to the left turn, just before the Cricket Club and green, and take this left, marked 'Tring 3, Wiggington 2'. Pass the duck pond and turn left into 'Shires Lane' (which marks the boundary between Bucks and Herts). A metalled lane, but pleasantly quiet, this runs through a beech wood, then out of the wood and up a gradual incline. Ignore paths to left and right, until the road bends round to the right as 'Cadmore Lane'.

At the corner we carry straight on and into the track, following the bridleway sign. There is also a Forestry Commission sign indicating 'Parrs Wood', with the Ridgeway footpath running off to the left. Some mud at first is soon left behind as the path begins to drop down on its exciting descent of the escarpment. The familiar flints demand attention, but near the bottom the track smooths. Go left at the fork, past the house and road, continuing straight ahead on the bridleway, now a little bumpy but with a good dry base. Then we find ourselves running parallel to the motorway grade A41(T), separated by only a few yards and hedgerow. Shortly, up a small rise to a junction of tracks, to the left a footpath. We take the right, over the A41 and down the other side.

This, concreted, track leads to the T-junction where we turn left (a more direct route straight across is for pedestrians only). The next $1/2$ mile includes some major roads, but is no problem with reasonable care; so along to the large roundabout where the A41 arrives, right around to take the last exit on the left and pleasantly downhill to Drayton Beauchamp. Over the small canal bridge and past the church of 'St Mary the Virgin', but preferably stop to explore the area which includes a nearby nature reserve. Onwards for $1/2$ mile to the crossroads where we turn left along the B489, Lower Icknield Way, sign to 'Aston Clinton $1/2$', and so back to the start in $1/4$ mile.

19. Chesham

Route: Chesham – Hyde Heath – South Heath – Ballinger Bottom – Herberts Hole – Chesham

Brief Description:
Grading – Moderate
Terrain – 43% off-road
– The early and middle paths are often moderately muddy in parts, but this is more than offset by the magnificent run gently down through lovely country at Herberts Hole. Chesham is a busy and bustling little town, but with a pleasant edge and surroundings.

Distance: Total – 12 miles; Off-road – 5.2 miles

Time: 2 hours

Height Gain: 350 feet

Start/Finish: Chesham centre car park

Map: OS Landranger 165; start – GR 957015

---

a – b: Chesham to South Heath

A convenient start point is the 'pay and display' car park in the centre of Chesham, off the roundabout near the small lake. From the car park turn left, then first left after 50 yards, signposted 'B485, Great Missenden 5'. Pass the Temperance Hall and go up through Chesham village. About $3/4$ mile from the town turn left into the bridleway, unmarked, but a clear track by 'Halfway House Farm'. Go straight on and through 'White Wood'. At the end of the track turn left and follow another track up to the road, a nice track, and turn right at the road. Follow Heath Road past 'The Plough', to the junction with the B485, where we turn left and then right in $1/2$ mile at the 'Barley Mow', along Kings Lane to South Heath.

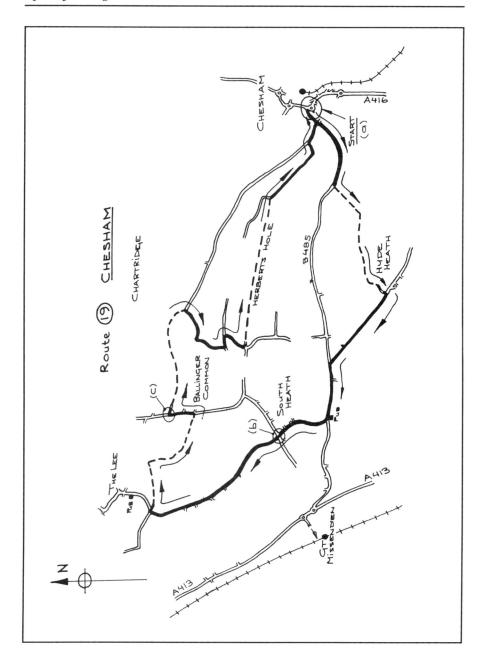

b – c: South Heath to Ballinger Common

At the crossroads in South Heath continue straight on (signed 'The Lee $1^1/_2$') along Potters Row. Straight on to the crossing at Hunts Green, where the bridleway is signposted to the right, directly off the road crossing. The good, stony track, leads down to a semi-metalled crossing of tracks where we turn right to Ballinger Common on the bridleway. Straight on past 'Field End Grange', and then keep around to the left (signs 'FP50') with only white arrows to follow. Generally a good track, with only 100 yards very muddy and where a carry may be appropriate. Out to the lane at St Mary's Church, Ballinger. Carry on past the 'Pheasant Inn' and turn left to Ballinger Common.

c – a: Ballinger Common to Chesham

Down the hill to the bottom and turn right into the well marked bridleway, at 'Rose' and 'Well' cottages. Turn right again after 50 yards, another good bridleway sign. Along a somewhat mixed path, several bridleway signs assisting route following, and around the edge of the field on a rather narrow and overgrown track. Turn left at the junction and down the flinty hill to the bottom. In 150 yards turn right, following a good track along the left edge of the wood, pleasant going with avoidable stretches of mud. Straight on at the junction of paths, followed by a short messy stretch leading to the open, and a nice track to the road.

Turn right at the road, down the hill past Great Pednor Farm, keep left then right after 100 yards and down the short, steep hill, to the junction of roads and bridleways at the bottom. Turn left into the obvious bridleway ('Herberts Hole') signed 'Chiltern Link'. This leads delightfully across open ground, by a fence, gently down all the way to the road leading back to Chesham. A fine run!

On emerging to the road turn right and follow the lane for $^3/_4$ mile to the T-junction, right again leads back to the B485 at Chesham Village. Turn left here and shortly back to the starting point, most easily reached by pushing the last few yards on the pavement.

Herbert's Hole, leading back towards Chesham

20. Cholesbury

Route: Chesham – Asheridge – Chartridge – Buckland Common – Cholesbury – Bellingdon – Chesham Vale – Chesham

Brief Description:
Grading – Moderate/difficult
Terrain – 27% off-road
– The paths are fairly short, but interspersed with good lanes. Downhill from Asheridge on good flint base; later a good stony and well drained track leads over the ridge; and the last bridleway is good but with some muddy stretches. A good, enjoyable route, not particularly taxing.

Distance: Total – 13 miles; Off-road – 3.5 miles

Time: $1^3/_4$ hours

Height Gain: 500 feet

Start/Finish: Chesham centre (as Route 19)

Map: OS Landranger 165; start – GR 957015

---

a – b: Chesham to Cholesbury

Start from the car park, as described in Route 19. Turn left out of the car park, past the park with the boating lake, and straight on at the first roundabout. Turn left after 50 yards, signposted 'Bellingdon $2^1/_2$'. Along Bellingdon Road, pass 'The Griffin', then left at the fork, signed 'Asheridge Industrial Park', following Asheridge Road. Chesham's version of an industrial estate doesn't last long, however, and after $^1/_2$ mile we are in a nice lane in the country. Pass Hazledene Farm, ignoring the bridleway to the right, and go steeply uphill to 'Tile's Farm' where we turn left into the well signposted bridleway and footpath. The good track soon drops steeply, with a small patch of mud in the bottom, and an overgrown track leading up the other side that can be outwitted by keeping just to the right of the hedge, rejoining it soon after. This provides a pleasant flinty track calling for a short push to the metalled lane, past Chartridge Park, and out to the larger road where we turn right.

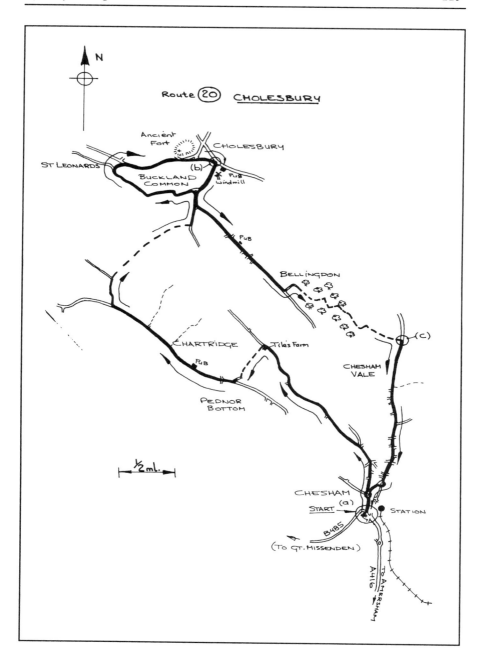

Asheridge, the first bridleway

Through Chartridge and past 'The Bell'. Ignore the first two bridleways leading off to the right, and continue past 'The Chartridge'. In $1/2$ mile turn right into Arrewig Lane (also sign 'Unsuitable for Heavy Goods Vehicles'). As the lane bends around to the left, continue straight on at the apex and into the bridleway, following the signpost. The good track has traces of the brick rubble used to fill some parts. Steeply down then up, through open ground and rolling, flint filled, fields of corn with tremendous views around. Rolling up and down, first along one side of the hedge then the other. Go past the finger of wood with its footpath leading inwards, to the Parish boundary marked with a blue 'bridlepath' sign. Over the rubble-filled section and flatter now to the gate, a fine run! Across the field and in 100 yards through another gate and out to the road.

Turn left at the road towards Cholesbury, and left at the signpost 'Cholesbury 1'. At the next junction, 200 yards on, we turn left and follow the road in a loop around Buckland Common. Keeping right past a couple of turnings at $3/4$ mile, continue straight on where $1/2$ mile later we pass the ancient fort on the left (not actually obvious from the road), and straight on past Cholesbury Cricket pavilion and pitch on the left.

b-a: Cholesbury to Chesham Vale

Just past the cricket pitch is 'The Full Moon' (well worth a pause, as is Cholesbury generally). Fifty yards before the Full Moon is Crays Hill, which runs down to the right. As we go along Crays Hill, a break between the houses reveals a windmill, somewhat surprisingly situated in someone's back yard, backing onto the Full Moon. Down the hill and through Braziers End, past Braziers End Lodge and left at the small triangle of grass. We now retrace our outward route for a few hundred yards to the next turning where we go left, signed 'Bellingdon $1/2$, Chesham 4'.

Continue along this road for $1^1/4$ miles, passing the 'Horse and Hounds', ignoring a bridleway on the left, past 'The Bull' and 'Bloomfield Cottages', finally turning left down Ramscote lane (sign almost hidden).

Along the metalled road with its well-kept high privet hedges, around to the right and past a post marked 'Ramsgate Cottage' where the track becomes unsurfaced. At Ramsgate Cottage turn left. Although there is no sign, the track is obvious enough, running along the edge of the field. The route is defined by fencing on one side and hedge on the other, and the track begins well. Then short stretches of mud appear, but present no great problems as the worst is quite easily skirted by careful footwork. Over the large fallen tree and straight on at the track crossing. Follow the track down hill, an extremely flint-jumbled, dry water course, with no signs apparent. Down to the bottom and some more mud patches, requiring some effort to retain the bikes' transmission in pristine condition, but quite possible. Riding often possible as the track becomes better defined from time to time. At the edge of the wood the track is clear, but rather muddy at first, then improves to a good path descending cheerily to the road. At the time of writing there was a council proposal to uprate this entire bridleway to a 'BOAT' (by-way open to all traffic), although it seems inconceivable that it could be traversed other than on foot, horseback or bike.

At the road, turn right, and down Chesham Vale past a couple of bridleways, to enter Chesham from the north. Pass the cycle shop (L.J. Strannel) to the first roundabout, then go straight on past the second roundabout, and the lake, to the starting point.

21. Aldbury

Route: Tring Station – Marsworth – Ivinghoe – Ivinghoe Aston – Ringshall – Ashridge (Monument) – Aldbury – Tring Station

Brief Description:
Grading – Moderate
Terrain – 33% off-road
– Good tracks throughout, well drained and once located, easily followed. The villages of Ivinghoe and Aldbury should be on any biker's itinerary – the former with a Youth Hostel, both amply catering for R & R!

Distance: Total – 14.5 miles; Off-road – 4.8 miles

Time: 2 hours

Height Gain: 725 feet

Start/Finish: Tring Station

Map: OS Landranger 165; start – GR 951122

---

a – b: Tring Station to Ivinghoe

The railway station lies a mile or two to the east of Tring, but provides a useful starting point. From the station car park turn right and straight on past the left turning, (sign to Ringshall and Aldbury). After 100 yards turn left along the concrete road, signposted 'bridleway' and 'Ridgeway path'. Up to the gate and turn left at the bridleway crossing, following the 'Ridgeway' sign. A nice track, through the grove and out to open ground across the footpath crossing, keeping to the side of the wood. Fine views. Follow the wooden bridleway signs, gently downhill along the delightful track to meet the road.

Turn right at the road, then to the T-junction, where we turn left, sign 'Aston Clinton $4^1/_2$'. The next bridleway takes a little searching out, but is recognised $^1/_4$ mile beyond the railway bridge, and just before the

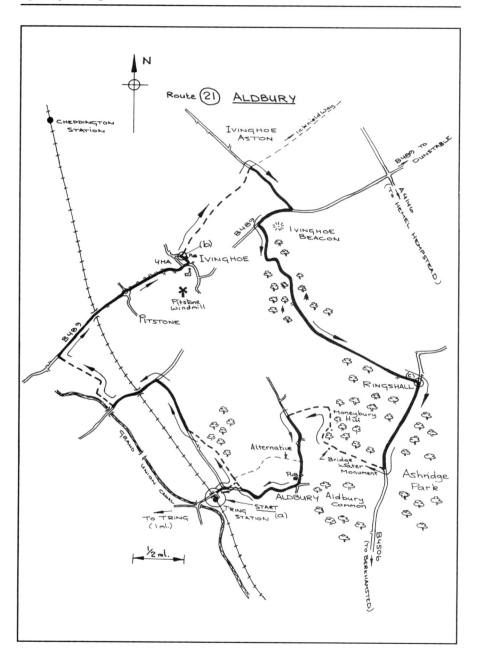

canal bridge (over the Grand Union Canal) and pub. The bridleway is on the right, just after the '30 limit' signs, and although it has a post, no sign exists at present. A good track, dry if a little bumpy in places, following the perimeter fence of the chalk pit easily around a couple of kinks. This runs out to a metalled track for 100 yards, and upto the road at Marsworth,

Turn right here and follow the B489, the Lower Icknield Way, although now a rather fast road. Over the railway line, past the Pitstone Cement Works, following the sign 'Ivinghoe 1', to reach Ivinghoe on this road.

PITSTONE WINDMILL

b – c: Ivinghoe to Ringshall

Pass 'The Bell' then Youth Hostel, and green; then, at the church, turn left along 'Vicarage Lane'. A lovely village. In 150 yards turn right at the 'Rose and Crown', along 'Wellcroft'. Straight on at the end of the metalled road, with Ivinghoe Golf Club on the left. A small bridleway sign points the way down a quite narrow, but extremely pleasant, track which is the Icknield Way. Pass a house a little way off the track, and a solitary old-fashioned street lamp which stands somewhat incongruously by the hedgerow. When I travelled down here in the evening I had a job to avoid an army of slugs traversing the bone-dry track! Pass the track back to 'Crabtree Farm', and follow the small blue bridleway arrow to the metalled road crossing. The path could be followed onwards, but we turn right here, pulling steadily uphill to the B489.

At the B489 turn right, continuing at a lesser gradient, with Ivinghoe Beacon to the left. Left at the first turning, signposted 'Ivinghoe Beacon, Ashridge 4, Ringshall $2^1/2$'. Head uphill, not too bad an ascent, with the summit of Ivinghoe Beacon beckoning (the walker) on the left. Often gliders can be seen, having launched from the Dunstable Downs to enjoy uplifting currents from the hill. In the distance, amid the fine views on the left, is the 'Whipsnade Lion', carved into the chalk hillside. The road now provides a steady decline, enabling the couple of miles to Ringshall to be dispensed with easily.

c – a: Ringshall to Aldbury and Tring Station

At the T-junction, with the 'Coach House' on the corner, turn right at the signpost to Berkhamstead, along the B4506. On for $3/4$ mile, returning to Buckinghamshire, and 200 yards after the road bends left, take the right turn into the drive. There is an 'Ashridge Estate and Information Centre' sign pointing up this drive, towards the monument which can be seen at its end.

Although there are a number of potential bridleways around here, they are not easy to locate, and we simply travel down the drive, keeping to the right of the monument. On past the 'No Through Road' sign into the woods and towards the cottages, down the well surfaced track. This leads down to 'Moneybury Hill', losing quite a lot of height without undue difficulty, running out of the wood and past the farm to the road.

Turn left towards Aldbury, and although there is a bridleway option to the right that connects with the initial bridleway of the route, I choose to carry on along the road to Aldbury. An ideal place for a refreshment stop, surely a tourist marketing-executives' 'typical' English village with its variety of interesting buildings, church and pubs, set around the pond (this could be Ambridge?!). Pass 'The Greyhound' (among others!) and the village pond, to the junction where Toms Hill Road runs up on the left. We turn right here, along Stocks Hill (signposted 'Tring Station 1, Tring $2^3/_4$'). Cycle past the church on the right, and this now becomes Station Road. After $3/_4$ mile take the bridleway signposted to the right as the road curves left. Pleasantly up this to meet the crossing where we came in at the start. And so left here, retracing our steps back to the road where we go right, and so back to the station in 200 yards.

22. Henley on Thames

Route: Henley on Thames – Lower Assendon – Bix – Nettlebed – Lower High Moor – Lambridge Woods – Fair Mile – Henley on Thames

Brief Description:
Grading – Moderate
Terrain – 52% off-road
– Good tracks, easy going, with most of gradient on the lanes. Superb countryside surrounding the busy, but interesting, centres of Henley and Nettlebed. Henley is a good centre for other routes, being almost equidistant from Nettlebed, Stoke Row, Stonor and Hambledon – no wonder it is a popular place!

Distance: Total – 12.5 miles; Off-road – 6.5 miles

Time: 1³/₄ hours

Height Gain: 700 feet

Start/Finish: Henley-on-Thames Station

Map: OS Landranger 175; start – GR 763823

---

a – b: Henley-on-Thames to Bix

Although this route could be started from Nettlebed (as Route 4), it is described here from Henley, in fact from Henley railway station, or the information centre in the middle of this charming Thameside town. It is well worth spending a little time in, providing one is not put off by its hustle and bustle during the day, a place with an interesting past and lively present.

A short way from the station, the roundabout is taken to the Marlow road through Henley centre, past the information centre to the round-about at the northern end of the town.

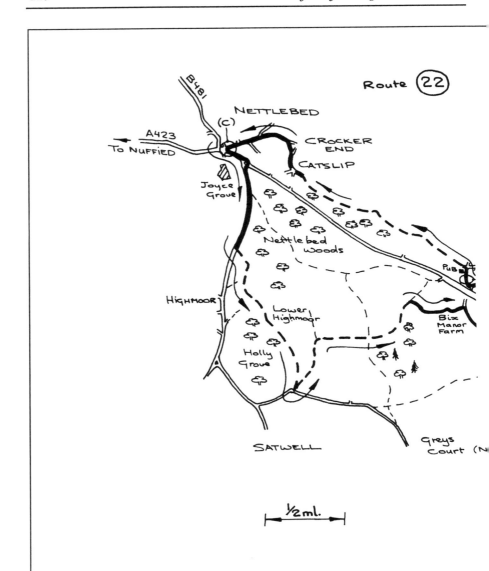

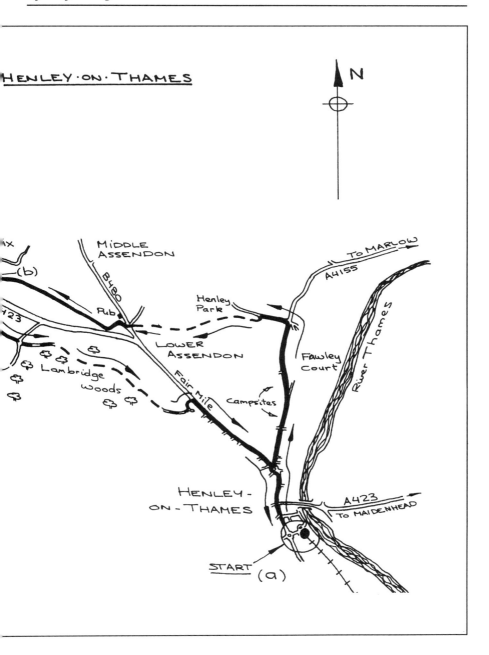

Ignoring the first exit on the A423 (we return here), take the next turn, the A4155 towards Marlow. Along the flat road past a couple of smart campsites for $1^1/_2$ miles. Turn left at the road marked 'Fawley $1^1/_2$ miles'. After 100 yards we pass a 'single track road, passing places' sign, and are treated to lovely views across the rolling countryside back toward Henley.

Steadily up now, towards Fawley, turning left at a fork into the bridleway (good signpost), with 'Dell Cottage' on the left. Continue uphill and pass through the tall wrought-iron gates. Turn left at the bridleway track (no sign, but obvious route), often pigs hereabouts. Track now levelling off and this leads delightfully through high banks to a wood and some welcome downhill. The track improves as we descend, becoming surfaced as we meet the crossing of the Watlington-Henley road (B480) at Lower Assendon, signed 'Watlington 8, Henley $1^3/_4$', just over the small triangular road pattern.

On the right is the 'Golden Ball' (Breakspears pub), but we turn left along the B480, then after 50 yards right to Bix. Follow the magnificent lane steadily uphill all the way to Bix; as we reach the top we can glimpse superb views across the Chilterns towards Watlington Hill.

Bridleway near Nettlebed

b – c: Bix to Nettlebed

We come into Bix at St. James' Church and then turn right. After 250 yards turn left at the small bridleway sign on a fairly open track, straight on through the gateway and toward the wood. Although the track is not terribly obvious the marking is reasonable, leading across a track crossing and into the wood. Although the track degenerates somewhat, the worst areas are avoidable, and being pretty flat, provide interest without excessive difficulty. At the fork bear left, keeping to the track running along the edge of the wood. This leads to a tarmac road passing the house and on to Catslip, where we turn right towards Crocker End. At the junction turn left, passing the 'Carpenters Arms'. I was fortunate to arrive here whilst swallows dashed around in the early evening. Follow the road around to reach Nettlebed in $1/2$ mile, past the brick kiln and out to the main road (A423).

c – a: Nettlebed to Henley

Turn left on the A423, in 200 yards arriving at the roundabout, taking the second exit (B481). Downhill, ignoring the first two bridleways, to the bottom and then slightly up to turn left where the bridleway crosses the road. This turning is just after a miniature memorial to the US Army, 1942. Along the tarmac track, gently downhill to the beautiful beech woods, where I was surprised by half a dozen young deer rushing across the track. At the end of the surfaced track keep left through the bridleway. Through the gate, past the white house, still steadily downhill on a nice, unsurfaced, track through the beech wood. Down past the rhododendrons and a more mixed woodland of not only many broadleaf trees, including yew and holly, but also conifers of several species.

On arrival at the tarmac lane junction two possibilities exist. We could turn right then left along the lane past 'Rockylane Farm', then left at the junction and past 'Greys Court', then left again after $1/2$ mile, past 'Broadplat' to pick up the bridleway $1/2$ mile further on, that turns right into Lambridge Woods.

The other way may require a short push past Bix Manor Farm as, although a surfaced track, it is not actually designated as a bridleway. So, from the original exit from the wood, turn left along the surfaced track (bridleway), through extremely pleasant, rolling, countryside, with clumps of trees providing shelter for the grazing cattle, and plenty of evidence of rabbit burrows. At the bottom of the dip turn right, fairly steeply, up to Bix Manor Farm, where it is judicious to walk, and out to 'Bix Manor', resplendent in its vivid pink plaster and half timber exterior. Turn right along a small lane, down to the junction and straight on at the well-marked bridleway. A broad, stony, track leads into Lambridge woods. Fork right, up the track signposted 'Lambridge House'. Then down through (Spring) bluebell woods, following the arrows on the trees. Fork right, house on the left, down a smaller track, and downhill all the way to the tarmac road – delightful place!

We arrive at 'Spur House', where we turn left onto the lane which, after 150 yards, brings one out to the main Nettlebed – Henley (A423) road. What a contrast with the natural beauty of the woods! Fortunately, however, we can turn immediately right along the service road that runs parallel with the 'Fair Mile' down to Henley, thereby postponing the need to engage with the main road until nearly at the roundabout, passing 'The Old White Horse' (Breakspears) just before the roundabout, where we turn right, retracing our steps back into Henley and, predominantly, the late twentieth century again.

23. Goring to Princes Risborough

Route: (Complete out and return) Goring Station – North Stoke – Carmel College – Icknield Way – Hill Farm – Wainhill – Princes Risborough – Chinnor – Aston Rowant – Lewknor – Hill Farm – Stoke Row – Checkendon – Woodcote – Cleeve – Goring.

Brief Description:
Grading – Difficult (long)
Terrain – 58% off-road
– This takes the line of (Upper) Icknield Way most of the way out, following the 'Swan's Way' in the early part, which is quite flat, delightfully along the Thames. Good tracks all the way.
Return along the line of the (Lower) Icknield Way. Initially metalled, then some mixed tracks, to head up toward the high areas of Christmas Common and Maidensgrove Common, en-route to Stoke Row. Then through the rural lanes to Woodcote and up the last bridleway through the fine wood to emerge overlooking the Oxfordshire Plain towards Didcot. Final flourish downhill to the start. A full day in every sense!

Distance: Out – 29 miles; Off-road – 19.5 miles; Return – 27 miles; Off-road – 13.25 miles; Total – 56 miles; Off-road – 32.75 miles

Time: Out – 4 hours; Return – 4 hours; Total – 8 hours

Height Gain: Out – 850 feet; Return – 1,100 feet Total – 1,950 feet.

Start/Finish: Out – Goring to Princes Risborough (Station to Station); Return – Goring Station

Map: OS Landranger 175 & 165 GR 603806 and 709028.

a – b: Goring to A423 (Wallingford)

From Goring Station head north along the B4009, passing in a few yards the 'Queens Arms', and take the first left and over the railway bridge at the signpost to Streatley. Take the second turning on the right, along Cleeve Road, and continue straight on to Glebe Ride, and so directly onto the first bridleway. This provides a fittingly easy start to a long day in the saddle, for it runs flat and smooth, often within (literally) a stones throw of the Thames. In places well-manicured lawns run down to the river bank, but more often the track runs through lightly-wooded areas familiar in this part of the Chilterns. Soon we arrive at the end of the path, with a road leading on and to our right.

We take the right option, passing under the railway in 200 yards, and slightly uphill to meet the B4009 at a T-junction. Turn left here, past the first crossing, then left at the sign 'Littlestoke $1/2$'. Follow this road downhill, past the house and on until the next bridleway is reached. This is indicated by a bridleway sign, and we go straight on along this as the road bends around to the right.

The bridleway is another fine track which is this time rather more open, leading into Carmel College. Continue around the metalled road and follow the prominent white arrow along the paved track. Just before reaching the underpass, turn right, leading onto the A4074. Turn right (care!) along this road and to the new roundabout in 200 yards. Turn right here, following the A4074 up the hill for 100 yards until reaching the white painted entrance and gate-house of Carmel College. We turn suddenly left here, directly into the Ridgeway path, up and through a small gate and into Grim's ditch. The track rises a little, and the interesting slight twists, turns and roots, make this more difficult to ride in this direction (Route 3 – Stoke Row – comes along here from the opposite direction). This is a fine track, which soon passes the concrete Trig point, and continues as a covered glade until it runs out to the metalled lane crossing. Straight over this and back into similar going along the bank of Grim's ditch – the bridleway is well signed here.

At the next junction, turn left along the metalled lane, and through flat, open country with large fields all around, to the first crossroads, followed immediately by a second crossing. Straight over both, the second being the A423 (left to Wallingford and right to Nettlebed).

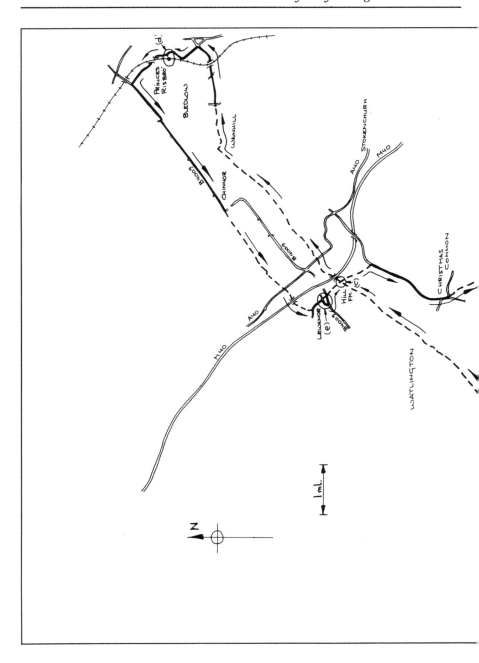

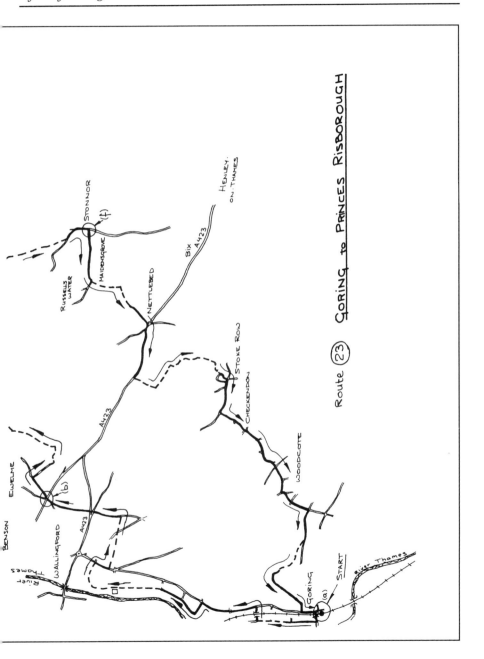

Route ㉓ GORING to PRINCES RISBOROUGH

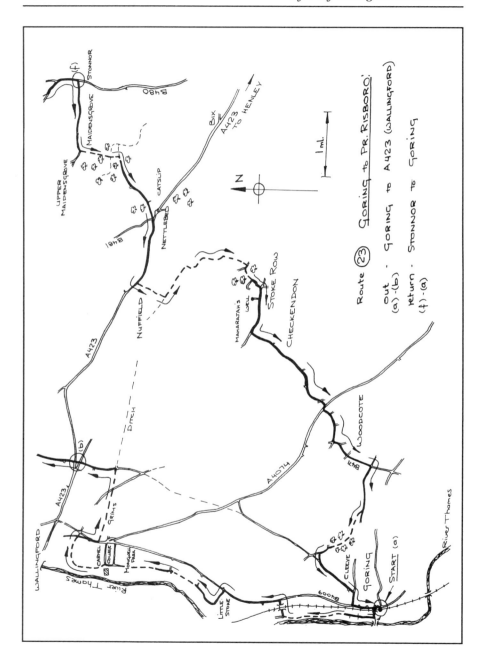

b – c: A423 (Wallingford) to Hill Farm

From the A423 crossing continue towards Ewelme for 1 mile, to the T-junction. Right here, then immediately left. Directly, there is a branch and, ignoring the left to Ewelme, bear right and along for $1/2$ mile to where the bridleway crosses the road.

Turn right into the bridleway here, with its sign 'Swan's Way'. Along the concrete path, past the pig farm on the right until a bridleway sign is reached. Follow this left and shortly fork right, following the Ridgeway route. Out across open ground to an obvious bridleway crossing. Ahead begins the upland Chilterns. Ignoring the right turn (leading eventually to Ewelme park), turn left at this crossing, over the small rise past a track crossing, and down at the edge of the ploughed field to reach the gate at its corner.

Another 'Swan's Way' sign indicates right through the gate, which we follow, along a metalled road for 50 yards, then left into the obvious, broad track, that leads gently up along the ancient Icknield Way. On through a covered grove, and straight over the road crossing, past the track to Dame Alice Farm (see information on Ewelme) along a metalled stretch for $1/2$ mile, over the B480, and $1/2$ mile later the Watlington to Christmas Common road.

This fine track continues its glorious way, shortly crossing the 'Oxford-shire Way' (which leads, on the right, steeply up the hill to Christmas Common as for Route 6 – Aston Rowant). A stretch of a couple of miles now extends with no significant crossings, until Hill Farm is reached. This is soon recognised as just beyond the M40 is carried, remarkably unobtrusively, above the general lie of the land, the route passing through a short tunnel.

c – d: Hill Farm to Princes Risborough

In 200 yards from the crossing we continue under the motorway, with fine views of Beacon Hill to the right. Half a mile later we cross the A40 (care!), well signed, past 'Beacon Cottage', and the great chestnut trees. Out to open country again, with continuous views of the Chiltern escarpment on the right, over the bridleway crossing to Aston Rowant (where Route 6 descends from the hill). This is archetypal Ridgeway/

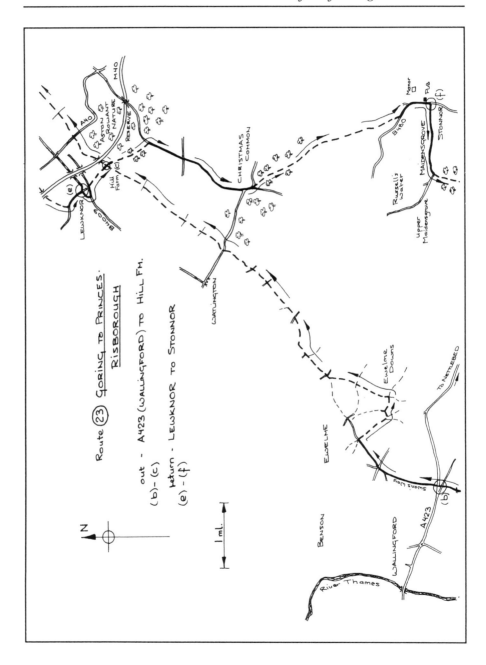

Route ②③ GORING TO PRINCES
RISBOROUGH

out - A423 (WALLINGFORD) TO HILL FM.
(b) - (c)
return - LEWKNOR TO STONNOR
(e) - (f)

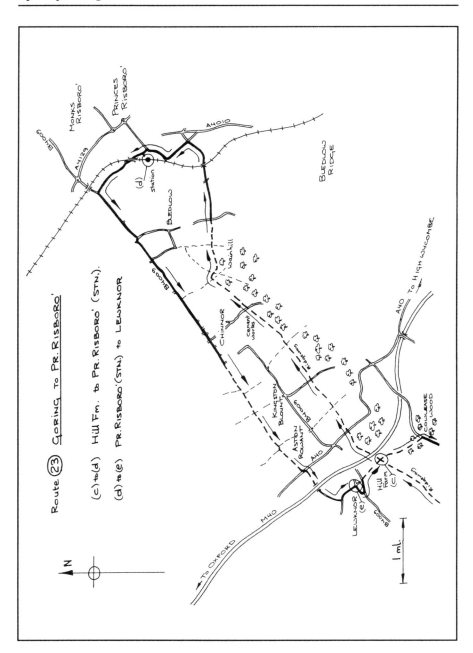

Icknield Way going, a fine broad track, undulating little with generally an almost perfect surface for a mountain bike, in reasonable weather. When I came past here in the early morning sunshine the pheasants out-numbered humans by more than ten to one! Gradually we are nearing the Chinnor Cement Works, having crossed the road to Kingston Blount and then Crowell. The latter is where Route 7 – Bledlow – runs up the scarp to Crowell Hill. The cement works lies over to the left as we begin to run into the edge of the woods, but it is generally hidden by the hedge.

On past 'Stepping Hill' cottage, now running into a fine covered glade, and gaining a little height. Pass the bridleway crossing and along a superbly smooth surface of sand and gravel. At a junction of bridleways one leads up Wainhill on the right, going steeply up a difficult track towards Bledlow ridge. Another goes left and down to Bledlow. instead of these, we take the third option, and continue straight on, close by 'Wainhill Cottage', following the bridleway signs along a ,magnificent broad, tree-covered track, that winds steadily up and past 'Warren Cottage' (a wooden building) to emerge at a further junction of bridleway tracks. Another track from Bledlow joins from the left (the return of Route 7). We carry straight on and pleasantly down past a large puddle at the bottom, to meet the crossing of Bledlow Ridge Road.

Straight on across Bledlow Ridge Road, along the 'Upper Icknield Way', signed 'Princes Risborough $2^1/_2$', High Wycombe 8'. Continue straight on at the next crossing of Bledlow Road (to the left) and Lea Road (on the right); signed to Loosley Row 2, Lacey Green 3. Pass the 'Which Way' house and in $1/_4$ mile go under the railway bridge; a very fine lane leading past the 'Old Rectory' with its tennis court just behind the hedge! A steady rise leads over another railway line, past a bridleway on the right to a crossroads. Turn left here, following the sign to 'Horsenden 1', along Shootacre Lane. This flat region provides views over to the right of the Chiltern hills as they rise from Princes Risborough and the Hampdens. Just before a bridge on the left, we turn right along Picts Lane, signposted 'Princes Risborough 1'. Along to the next junction, the end of Picts Lane, and turn left at the thatched cottage, signed 'Longwick $1^1/_2$, Chinnor 4, Thame 7'. This is the B4444, and after 200 yards we could turn left again into Station Approach, which leads in 100 yards to Princes Risborough Station. One could return home by train here, or preferably, press on along the return journey to Goring.

d – e: Princes Risborough to Lewknor

From Station Approach turn left along Summerleys Road. We soon pass a bridleway sign to the left, which also forms the road to 'Princes Industrial Park' (Trading Estate), complete with Café. Continue along the B4444 (past another bridleway on the right) to the T-junction, which marks the end of Summerleys Road.

This is the crossing of the B4009, at the signpost to 'Bledlow 2, Chinnor $3^1/_2$, Watlington 9'. Turn left here, along the Lower Icknield Way. A good, straight road which soon disposes of the miles to Chinnor, having passed the turn-off to Bledlow – with 'The Lions' of Bledlow only $^1/_2$ mile distant. This becomes 'Chinnor Road' as it passes Bledlow village hall and runs into Oxfordshire again. Superb views of the Chiltern scarp are offered to the left as we travel along this flat region at its foot. Into Chinnor, following the B4009 past the 'Red Lion' and then 'Royal Oak', and along Mill Lane at the signpost showing Lewknor and Watlington. We continue straight on along Mill Lane, past the timber frame and thatched cottage, to another crossing. On the corner is the 'Bird in Hand' (Moorlands Pub), and we continue straight on along Mill Lane again.

Pass 'Mill Lane Primary School', and where the road bends left, go straight ahead into the bridleway, although it is not marked yet and is metalled for the first 150 yards. After this, the surface begins to loose its tarmac cover and in 200 yards a bridleway sign points the way straight on, to 'Aston Rowant 2', as well as an 'Unsuitable for Motors' sign. The track now leaves behind the few houses and runs directly through flat, open country. The Post Office tower can now clearly be seen atop the scarp, and we soon cross a small stream by a small bridge. A delightfully tranquil place to pause – even being provided with a slab of concrete nearby for a rest (seems comfortable to lie on after being in the saddle....!). On towards Aston Rowant the track is more susceptible to retaining water, but the resultant patches of mud and puddles are easily skirted around, in the more awkward places being provided with planks or ways around the edge, ideally sited for bike or foot travellers.

Finally, we arrive at the junction where the track from Aston Rowant joins from the left (as for Route 6). We turn right here, then left in 50 yards, setting off on the last half-mile before reaching the A40. This bridleway crossing does collect a lot of mud, but a short push or carry soon disperses with the mess, and the track is clean, if very bumpy, to the A40.

At the A40 we turn left then right after 20 yards and into the bridleway, via a gap beside the gate; although the gate is often the regrettable receptacle for rubbish. Along the flat track with a good, fast surface that soon runs down under the A40, and in no time we bear left at the metalled road towards Lewknor. At the T-junction (with 'The Manor' ahead), we turn left. This leads up to the junction at 'The Leathern Bottle', where we turn right, bringing us up to the T-junction where the B4009 crosses.

e – f: Lewknor to Stonor

At the T-junction we turn left (signed 'Chinnor, Princes Risborough'). First right after 200 yards at the sign to Hill Farm, leads up the slope along the good track to the bridleway crossing. Here we cross the Icknield Way of the earlier part of the route to Princes Risborough. A fine refreshment stop is afforded at Hill Farm, proclaimed by its sign – 'Teas, open 10 to 6 Weekends and Bank Holidays'. Immediately after this take the right fork, past the blue sign 'Unsuitable for Motors'. Steadily up the rough track, running from the open country into the wood, and up Bald Hill to Cowleaze Wood. A fine track that maintains its steady, but not excessive, gradient all the way and provides an opportunity to select the lowest-of-low gears, for those intent on pedalling all the way (I chose to enjoy the scenery on foot, again!). Heavy rain coursing down this track has provided deep runnels, removing the top-soil and exposing the chalk and flints, but still with sufficient surface for riding.

At the top the track flattens as it runs to meet the road, where we turn right. This spot is also a good one for walking and provided with a parking and picnic spot in the woods across the road. After the climb the road runs gently down, enabling one to go from bottom to top gear in a short distance. We are now back on the Oxfordshire cycleway, and soon arrive at Christmas Common where we ignore the first turning to the right (to Watlington Hill). On for 200 yards, and then left at the fork, signed 'Northend ', Turville 3'.

After 50 yards the road bears left, but we continue straight on, following the bridleway sign down the obvious path. Continue straight on, part-metalled surface in places, as the track eases down all the time, finally steepening a little to provide an exhilarating run down through high banks and hanging trees to the road. Straight on at the road, ignoring the turning off to the left, and past Stonor park (open April to September) and into Stonor.

f – a: Stonor to Goring

Take the first turning on the right, at the 'Dover House', and signpost 'Maidensgrove 1, Russell's Water 1'. Up this fine little lane, where now we pay for the downhill from Christmas Common; rising all the way, past several bridleway and road crossings through the wood. Emerging from the wood, the road leads out to Maidensgrove Common, a broad clearing. It then approaches some more woodland at this high point, and bends right in the direction of Russell's Water. Instead of following the road right we go straight ahead, through a gap in the hedge, following a 'Public Right of Way' sign which gives access to the excellent bridleway. This becomes a covered grove and leads pleasantly down the flinty and fairly steep path, into the BBONT Warburg Nature Reserve (visited on Route 4 – Nettlebed).

At the bottom is an obvious track crossing. There are no signs here, but we go straight across and uphill to meet the track further on. Turn right here, and steadily uphill on a chalky, flint-covered surface, that is well drained. Finally out from the wood, leaving the Nature Reserve and passing Souness House on the metalled road. At the crossroads, turn right towards Nettlebed, past the cottages, and then the Brick Kiln (start of Route 4), to reach the busy A423 Henley to Wallingford road.

Turn right onto the A423, past the White Hart Hotel, along High Street and soon out to the country, albeit on a busy road. Pass the fine church and go down Port Hill. Continue past 'Brambles', the flint cottage, up a slight rise and then left at the sign to 'Hayden Farm', and the small green bridleway marker. Go past a few houses and the lane leads out to open country, providing good views from this high ground. A quarter mile past the farm we run into an unsurfaced track and, almost imperceptibly, join the bridleway that comes in from the right from Nuffield – we're now following Route 4.

A truly magnificent bridleway, gently down all the way, passing the isolated farm with its unusual barn, and its unusual carved wooden post some 4 feet high. At the small fork, keep right and then straight over the lane, following the bridleway sign. After 100 yards across another lane at the bottom, and up the flinty track to the edge of the wood, where the entrance is barred to motors by the fallen tree.

At the road turn left along Newlands Lane, leading to a crossing in Stoke Row. Turn right here, past the 'Cherry Tree' in 100 yards, then the 'Farmer Inn', Stoke Row village stores, the church and, of course, the Maharajah's Well. Turn left at Uxmore Road following the sign to 'Checkendon'. Straight on through Checkendon, with its fine old timbered buildings and cricket green. Pass the 'Four Horseshoes' (Brakespears Pub) and follow the signpost 'Woodcote $1^1/_2$, Whitchurch $4^3/_4$'. Continue past the road to the left marked 'Exlade St. $^1/_2$', still along the Oxfordshire cycleway. At the T-junction with the A4074, turn right, signed 'Crowmarsh 6, Wallingford 7'.

Fifty yards along the A4074, then turn left at the signpost to 'Woodcote $^1/_2$', and past 'Woodcote Stores'. On reaching the junction by Woodcote Village Hall turn left (signpost 'Goring $3^1/_4$, Whitchurch $3^1/_2$') along Goring Road. Straight on over the first crossroads to the next where we turn right (signpost 'Cleave, South Stoke', and Oxfordshire cycleway). Nicely downhill, but watch for the bridleway that leads off on the right, indicated with a green signpost.

Gently up this chalky, cambered track (familiar from Route 1 – Mapledurham), ignoring the track that later departs over the hill to the right. Keep straight on along a narrow track, with barbed wire fence on left and tall hedge on the right. Superb views across to left. Into the wood, nice track, and at the fork keep right, bringing us suddenly out from the wood and providing a magnificent vista – across to the Berkshire Downs beyond Goring, and out to the Oxfordshire plain with Didcot in the distance.

From here it's just about all downhill, so glide off left, then left again and down to Cleeve, past the Fire Station, to the end of Icknield Road. Turn right here and shortly to the crossroads where we turn left along the B4009. Slightly uphill (gradients are readily-noticed by now!). And so in $^1/_2$ mile past the 'Queens Arms' and a final roll into Goring Station. Who could ask for more?

Ridgeway crossing of the A40, heading north

Places of Interest

The following are places of interest on or near each route, worthy of a visit in their own right.

Route 1 – Mapledurham

Mapledurham House and Watermill – Built 1581-1612, patterned red brick; Mill last corn-and-grist watermill on Thames.

Reading Museum and Art Gallery – Natural history, local archaeology, Roman collection, metalwork pre-historic and medieval.

Museum of English Rural Life, University of Reading – English countryside collection.

Child Beale Wildlife Trust, Church Farm, Lower Basildon, on A329 South of Goring – Rare and exotic birds in Thameside setting of walks and playground.

Basildon Park, National Trust, near Pangbourne, on A329 – 8 miles north or Reading – fine house, built 1776, in park.

Route 2 – Wallingford

Wallingford Castle – Destroyed in Civil War – only rampart and moat remain.

Castle Priory, Wallingford – Can be viewed by arrangement.

Ewelme Church – Tombs of Thomas Chaucer and Alice, Duchess of Suffolk. Almshouses and School.

Benson Veteran Cycle Museum, 61 Brook Street, Benson -Cycles from 1818, seen by arrangement.

Route 3 – Stoke Row

Maharajah's Well, Stoke Row – Restored well, built 1863.

Ipsden House and Memorial, Ispsden – Traditional home of Reade family, associated with Maharajah's Well.

Wellplace Bird Farm, Ipsden – Wide variety of birds and some small animals.

Route 4 – Nettlebed

Brick Kiln, Nettlebed – Last remaining kiln at previous centre for brick and tile making, supplying Ewelme and Stonor House, since 15th century.

Bull Inn, Nettlebed; **'Pudding Stone'** – Sarcen Stone, as used for signposts in ancient Britain.

Nature Trail and car park, between Nettlebed and Maidensgrove, on bridleway – (BBONT managed trails and wood).

Route 5 – Christmas Common

Watlington Hill, Christmas Common – National Trust, focal point for walks.

Town Hall Watlington – Originally built as Grammar School in 1655, Watlington also has other fine buildings.

Route 6 – Aston Rowant

Church of St. Peter and St. Paul, Aston Rowant.

Wormsley Park (on route).

Beacon Hill Nature Reserve, adjacent to M40 – Wide range of flora, by Nature Conservancy with nature trails.

Route 7 – Bledlow

Church and 'The Lions', Bledlow.

Bledlow Cross, Bledlow – Cross carved into chalk, recently cleared of undergrowth.

Chinnor Hill Nature Reserve, Bledlow – BBONT reserve with noted flora and several warblers.

St Botolphs Church, Bradenham – Memorial to Isaac Disraeli and old bells of 1250 vintage.

Route 8 – Stonor

Stonor Park, Stonor – Home of Camoy family since 13th century, fine house and deer park.

Turville Village and Windmill – Charming village with church and pub; mill now a private house.

Route 9 – West Wycombe

West Wycombe Park – National Trust; 18th century Palladian House and grounds with temple and lake.

Hell-Fire Caves, West Wycombe – Across the A40 from above Park, associated with Sir Francis Dashwood. Also mausoleum, and church with famous 'Golden Ball' adjacent.

Hughenden Manor, on A4128, $1^1/2$ miles north of High Wycombe – National Trust home of Benjamin Disraeli and park.

Wycombe Chair Museum, High Wycombe, Priory Avenue – History of local furniture making and crafts.

Bottom Wood, Studley Green – Chiltern Society.

Route 10 – Hambledon

Hambledon Mill, off A4155 along Thames – Mill, lock and weir; outside only, dates from 17th century.

Hambledon Village – church and pub.

Fingest Village – church and pub.

Route 11 – Knowl Hill (North)

'Courage' Shire Horse Centre, on A4, $1^1/_2$ miles west of Maidenhead. Brewery heavy – horses, and their world, displayed.

Hurley Chalk Pit; north of Knowl Hill – BBONT Nature Reserve, passed on route – small area off bridleway.

Route 12 – Waltham St Lawrence

Village, church and pub of Waltham St Lawrence.

Shottesbrook Park – Fine mansion, exterior only, set in parkland traversed by bridleway.

Route 13 – Marlow

Marlow town, including the suspension bridge and 'Compleat Angler' restaurant.

Bisham church, on the river 1 mile from Marlow – Norman tower and Hoby family memorials.

Winter Hill, Cookham Dean – Fine views from across the river to Marlow.

Cookham Church – By the river with origins in the 8th century, and Stanley Spencer painting 'Last Supper'.

Stanley Spencer Gallery, Cookham High Street – Display of the work and artefacts of the artist.

Route 14 – Burnham Beeches

Cliveden, Nr Taplow – National Trust property, limited access to house, leased as college, with superb gardens rolling down to the Thames. Previously home of the Astors and with many early and recent associations with politics.

Dorney Wood garden.

Burnham Beeches – Large area of ground with good access and paths, owned since 19th century by City of London.

Dorney Court – National Trust.

St Giles Church, Stoke Poges – Basically Norman, church with fine grounds and inelegant memorial to Thomas Gray of 'Elegy in Country Church-yard' fame.

Church Wood Reserve, Hedgerley – Interesting nature trails, situated by the village of Hedgerley with two good pubs, and church, on route.

Route 15 – Jordans

Near Jordans: **'Old Jordans, Mayflower Barn, Meeting House'** – Interesting centre of Quakerism, with the barn containing the famous ships' timbers; William Penn's grave, and YHA in Welders Lane.

Milton's Cottage, Chalfont St Giles – Contains relics of 17th century Chalfont, and Miltons work and times; open most of the year, lovely garden, easy access and parking.

Chiltern Open Air Museum, Chalfont St Giles – Covers large area with fascinating displays of Chiltern past, from Neolithic huts to Victorian conveniences! Wide range of items and periodic displays and re-enactments.

Bekonscot, Beaconfield – Famous model village, started in the 1930s, still going strong and recommended.

Beaconfield Church and Old Town – Previously an important coaching stage between London and Oxford, and well endowed with refreshment opportunities!

Bulstrode Park, Gerrards Cross – Previous home of infamous 'hanging' Judge Jefferies, and by the large ancient 'fort' behind the exclusive Camp Road.

Route 16 – Gt. Missenden

St. John the Baptist Church, Little Missenden – 13th century wall paintings in 10th century surroundings.

Amersham Museum, High Street – Opened in 1991 in the towns oldest building, 15th century, recalling local history.

Smock Mill, Lacey Green – Oldest of its type in the country, circa 1650.

Princes Risborough Manor House – National Trust, off Market Square, fine 17th century house, open by arrangement.

Whiteleaf Cross, Whiteleaf, Princes Risborough – Passed on route, large cross in chalk on the hill.

Gt. Hampden – Church and private house. Family home of Hampdens, with John Hampden buried in church-yard.

'Pink and Lily' pub, Parslows Hill, Princes Risborough – Frequented by Rupert Brooke before the First World War.

Route 17 – Wendover

Wendover town – Recorded in Doomsday book, still has many fine buildings around a busy thoroughfare.

Coombe Hill, Wendover – Highest point in the Chilterns at 852 feet, with memorial to Boer War; National Trust property. Fine views across Vale of Aylesbury, with Chequers nearby.

Cymberlines Castle, Gt. Kimble – Hill fort attributed to ancient Britons, with good walks around.

Route 18 – Aston Clinton

Tring Nature Reserve – Artificial lakes now provide habitat for wetland wildlife.

Tring Zoological Museum, Akerman Street, Tring – Wide range of species and part of British Museum.

Wendover Woods – Forestry Commission, developed leisure area in woodland for walking. Also trail for bikes/horses.

Buckinghamshire County Museum, Church Street, Aylesbury – presently undergoing renovation, but with an extensive range of exhibits of Chiltern times.

Route 19 – Chesham

Chesham town, including 'The Bury' – A mansion dating from 1712.

Berkhampstead Castle – Ruins of earthworks and moat remain from this earliest Norman Castle.

The Lee – Pleasant village, with the figurehead from the last British wooden warship, some of the timbers of which were bought by the Liberty family at the Manor house and used to clad 'Liberties of London', in Regent Street.

Route 20 – Cholesbury

Cholesbury – Village, common, pubs, and ancient fort earthworks with church within.

Route 21 – Aldbury

Aldbury village – St. John the Baptist Church, Almshouses, Manor house and duck-pond along with pubs and shops range from Tudor to modern buildings.

Pitstone Windmill, Nr Ivinghoe – Owned by National Trust, dated 1627, and oldest of its type.

Pitstone Green Farm Museum, Vicarage Road, Pitstone – Rural and domestic artifacts from the area.

Ford End Watermill, Ivinghoe – Probably older than the recorded 1798, in use until 1963, recently restored and only working watermill in Buckinghamshire.

Ivinghoe Village – Church, pubs and YHA.

Ivinghoe Beacon – National Trust, end point of the Ridgeway, fine views , footpaths only.

Ashridge Park, Berkhampstead – Although used as a college it is open to public on selected days, and there is a nature trail with good access.

Bridgewater Monument, Nr Aldbury – Possible to climb 100 feet up this to get splendid views of Chilterns.

Whipsnade Zoo, Dunstable – large open spaces for the animals.

Dunstable Downs – Chalk hills that are very popular for picnics and gliding!

Route 22 – Henley On Thames

Henley on Thames – Early July visitors can glimpse the Regatta, or explore the town, with the Kenton Theatre, 4th oldest in the country.

Greys Court, Rotherfield Greys – National Trust, fine Manor house and gardens, with remains of 13th century fortifications.

Rotherfield Greys Church – 13th century in parts, and good brasses such as Robert de Grey, local land-owner.

Route 23 – Goring to Princes Risborough

This is an amalgam of many parts of the previous routes, basically following the Ridgeway, north-bound, and looping back (Upper Icknield Way, out; Lower Icknield Way, return). The routes involved include:

Mapledurham
Wallingford
Stoke Row
Nettlebed
Christmas Common
Bledlow
Aston Rowant
Stonor
Gt. Missenden
Henley on Thames

Refer to these routes for a substantial list of places of interest.

Information and Accommodation

Perhaps the widest range of accommodation is sourced from the English Tourist Offices, and those in the area are:

Aylesbury – County Hall, Walton Street. Tel: 01296 382308

Dunstable – The Library, Vernon Place. Tel: 01582 471012

Hemel Hempstead – Pavillion Box Office, Marlowes. Tel: 01442 64451

Henley on Thames – Town Hall, Market Place. Tel: 01491 578034

High Wycombe – 6 Corn Market. Tel: 01494 421892

Maidenhead – The Library, St Ives Road. Tel: 01628 781110

Marlow – Court Garden, Leisure Complex, Pound Lane. Tel: 016284 3597

Oxford – St Aldgates. Tel: 01865 726871

Reading – Town Hall, Blagrave Street. Tel: 01734 566226

Wallingford – 9 St Martins Street. Tel: 01491 35351

Wendover – The Clock Tower. Tel: 01296 623056

Windsor – Central Station, Thames Street. Tel: 01753 852010

Youth Hostels

There are several YHA hostels in the region, providing ideal bases for a cycling holiday in the area:

Bradenham – The Village Hall, Bradenham. Tel: 01494 562929

Ivinghoe – The Old Brewery House, Ivinghoe. Tel: 01296 668251

Jordans – Welders Lane, Jordans. Tel: 01494 873135

Streatly on Thames (Nr Goring) - Hill House, Reading Street, Streatly. Tel: 01491 872278

Useful Addresses

Forestry Commission (Chiltern Area) – Upper Icknield Way, Aston Clinton. Tel: 01296 625825.

Grand Union Canal – Watery Lane, Marsworth. Tel: 0144282 5938.

National Trust – Hughenden Manor, High Wycombe. Tel: 01493 528051.

Also of Interest:

OFF-BEAT CYCLING IN THE PEAK DISTRICT – Clive Smith *(£6.95)*

MORE OFF-BEAT CYCLING IN THE PEAK DISTRICT – Clive Smith *(£6.95)*

CYCLING IN & AROUND MANCHESTER – Les Lumsdon *(£6.95)*

CYCLING IN THE LAKE DISTRICT – John Wood *(£7.95)*

CYCLE UK! The Essential Guide to Leisure Cycling – Les Lumsdon *(£9.95)*

CYCLING IN THE COTSWOLDS – Stephen Hill *(£6.95)*

50 BEST CYCLE RIDES IN CHESHIRE – Graham Beech *(£7.95)*

CYCLING IN OXFORDSHIRE – Susan Dunne *(£7.95)*

CYCLING IN SOUTH WALES –
Rosemary Evans *(£7.95)*

CYCLING IN NORTH WALES –
Philip Routledge *(£7.95)*

CYCLING IN DEVON & CORNWALL –
Philip Routledge *(£7.95)*

CYCLING IN SCOTLAND &
NORTH-EAST ENGLAND –
Philip Routledge *(£7.95)*

CYCLING IN LINCOLNSHIRE –
Penny& Bill Howe *(£7.95)*

CYCLING IN NOTTINGHAMSHIRE –
Penny & Bill Howe *(£7.95)*

CYCLING IN THE WEST COUNTRY –
Helen Stephenson *(£7.95)*

All of our books are available from your local bookshop. In case of difficulty, or to obtain our complete catalogue, please contact:

**Sigma Leisure, 1 South Oak Lane,
Wilmslow, Cheshire SK9 6AR
Phone: 01625 – 531035
Fax: 01625 – 536800
E-mail: sigma.press@zetnet.co.uk**

ACCESS and VISA orders welcome – call our friendly sales staff or use our 24 hour Answerphone service! Most orders are despatched on the day we receive your order – you could be enjoying our books in just a couple of days. Please add £2 p&p to all orders.

Your Towns and Cities in th

Newport
in the Great War

Your Towns and Cities in the Great War

Newport
in the Great War

Julie Phillips

Pen & Sword
MILITARY

First published in Great Britain in 2015 by
PEN & SWORD MILITARY
an imprint of
Pen and Sword Books Ltd
47 Church Street
Barnsley
South Yorkshire S70 2AS

ISBN 9781473828179

Printed and bound in England
by CPI Group (UK) Ltd, Croydon, CR0 4YY

Typeset in Times New Roman

Pen & Sword Books Ltd incorporates the imprints of
Pen & Sword Archaeology, Atlas, Aviation, Battleground, Discovery,
Family History, History, Maritime, Military, Naval, Politics, Railways,
Select, Social History, Transport, True Crime, and Claymore Press,
Frontline Books, Leo Cooper, Praetorian Press, Remember When,
Seaforth Publishing and Wharncliffe.
For a complete list of Pen and Sword titles please contact
Pen and Sword Books Limited
47 Church Street, Barnsley, South Yorkshire, S70 2AS, England
E-mail: enquiries@pen-and-sword.co.uk
Website: **www.pen-and-sword.co.uk**

Contents

Dedication

The First World War was an incredibly difficult time, not only for the soldiers who fought in it but for those left behind who fought the war, in their own way, on the home front. This book is dedicated to the fallen of Newport and the surrounding villages and for the gallant effort of their communities in keeping the home fires burning. The world they knew may have changed, but the compassion and support from their local communities and the memorials built to commemorate their fallen friends and comrades ensured that their sacrifices would never be forgotten and that life would carry on.

Due to the vast numbers of servicemen from the Newport area that fought in the Great War and the activities and events that occurred, it has been impossible to include every detail here. Nevertheless, all those who paid the ultimate sacrifice and those who stood strong on the home front are remembered and sincerely thanked.

Acknowledgements

As always, grateful thanks are due to many people involved in the production of this book. I am indebted to the following in particular: David Adams, author, researcher, historian; John Alsop & Stenlake Publishing; Julie Brook (Alumni Archivist, Harper Adams Agricultural University); Chris Deaves, Discover Shropshire Website/Newport History Society SNAP; Linda Fletcher, Archivist, Newport History Society; Allan Frost, author, researcher, local historian; Elizabeth Kosinsky, Librarian & Archivist, Adams' Grammar School, Newport; the Newport Advertiser; Newport History Society; Newport Library; Dorothy Nicolle; Christopher Owen; Radio Shropshire, 'Eric & Claire Show'; Clifford Smout; the *Shropshire Star*; Fred Tipton; Mr Brian Watson Jones; the *Wellington Journal and Shrewsbury News*; Wellington Library; Malcolm Williams; Stanley Williams.

All images featured in this book are the author's own unless otherwise stated. All reasonable efforts have been made to ascertain the correct copyright-holder of other images used.

Abbreviations used:

AGS: Adams' Grammar School
HAAC/HAAU: Harper Adams Agricultural College/University
KSLI: King's Shropshire Light Infantry
NA: *Newport Advertiser*
NHS: Newport History Society
VAD: Voluntary Aid Detachment
WJSN: *Wellington Journal & Shrewsbury News*

Chapter One

A Brief History of Newport

Originally Newport was a small township that bordered the manor of Edgmond, given to the Earl of Shrewsbury by William the Conqueror. It reverted to the Crown in 1102. In the twelfth century Henry I founded a new town adjacent to the old settlement. Here, the long High Street emerged with narrow burgage plots coming at right angles to the main road.

This new town was called Novus Burgus, meaning new self-governing settlement. Although the original charter is missing, it is known that the town was confirmed by Henry II in 1163 at Brewood. The name was changed to Newport circa 1221.

Newport crest. *(Author)*

The intriguing crest of the town with its distinctive three fish comes from when King Henry II, King Edward II, Queen Elizabeth I and King James I confirmed the charter, enabling its privileges to be expanded. The burgesses kept their privileges by giving a quantity of fish from the vivary to the royal household.

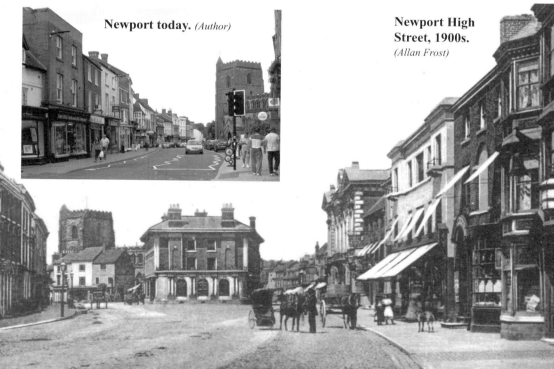

Newport today. *(Author)*

Newport High Street, 1900s.
(Allan Frost)

Newport railway in the 1900s. *(John Alsop, Stenlake Publishing)*

Geographically, Newport sits on the boundary of Staffordshire in north-east Shropshire, close to the villages of Edgmond, Church Aston, Chetwynd Aston and Lilleshall. The nearest large towns are Telford and Stafford. Newport currently has a population of around 15,000.

The town – a natural conduit for trade and travel – boasted a railway line that operated between Stafford, Wellington and Shrewsbury.

Newport railway in the 1900s. *(NHS)*

Newport Station, however, was a casualty of Dr Beeching and closed in 1962. The town is also serviced by the A41 which runs north-south between Chester and London.

Newport was not lacking in large, wealthy estates that surrounded the town, offering employment to the local townspeople. The estates would also play key philanthropic roles during the coming war. The lack of imports would lead to food shortages and utilizing some of the estates' land as well as people's back gardens to increase food production would stand them in good stead.

There were five estates bordering the area: **Lilleshall**, belonging to the Leveson-Gowers, also known as the Dukes of Sutherland; **Woodcote** of the Cotes family; **Longford** – the estate of the Talbots – related to the Earls of Shrewsbury; **Chetwynd** – estate of the Pigotts and later the Burton-Boroughs; and the **Aqualate** estate of the Bougheys.

The largest of these estates was Lilleshall with over 1,380,000 acres and a rent roll of £141,000 a year. They were also mine owners, forge and furnace operators. Their main operations were with the Lilleshall Company. Also the biggest employers of the local area, the Lilleshall estate employed an estimated 150 people in 1879, including those employed for seasonal work. They also contracted many services from the town of Newport, including plumbing, leather goods, groceries and household furnishings. At the time of the First World War they had almost 4,000 workers on their books.

Lilleshall Hall in 1903. *(Allan Frost)*

Not only did the estates support the local economy, but they also were great benefactors to the town and part of the local community, including funding schools and churches and the building of the workhouse. The economy in Newport was booming with its busy, industrious High Street with many skilled and professional workers living and working within the community.

In July 1914, however, the *Newport Advertiser* published an advert showing that 2,400 acres of the Lilleshall Estate were being sold between Wellington and Newport.

The dukes were very much involved in the local community's affairs, particularly Salop Infirmary, Shropshire Rifle Association, Shropshire Archaeological Society and in 1912 they became presidents of the Newport Agricultural Society.

Unfortunately their wealth was not to last. In July 1914, the total acreage sold between Wellington and Newport was 2,400. In January 1917, a dark cloud descended over Newport as the Duke of Sutherland announced to his tenants that he was to sell the rest of his estate and he gave them notice to quit, which was to be on Lady's Day in 1918. The combination of the war, the resulting loss of skilled labour and the blow to the economy may have had something to do with the sales. The official line from the duke was the rise in tax and death duties which had crippled his finances. He was not the only member of the landed gentry to find himself in this position. Across the nation, similar estates

Lilleshall visitors in carriage, 1900s. *(Allan Frost)*

The Aqualate Estate, 1900s. *(NHS)*

were to hear the bang of the gavel at the auctioneers.

The Aqualate estate, bordering both Staffordshire and Newport, was originally bought by John Fenton Fletcher who changed his name to Boughey. Another member of the family, T.F. Boughey, helped to found the Newport Literary Society and was a great supporter of many recreational assets to the town, especially sports and the Horticultural Society. They even organized transport to church, which was dubbed 'the Aqualate Bus'! In March 1909 the Revd George Boughey sold some of the estate and there was, unfortunately, a big fire at the hall in 1910.

As with most of the great estates, the families who owned them, their tenants and workers would soon feel the heat of war and be sending their sons and workers to fight.

In Shropshire between 1918 and 1923, 80,000 acres of land were sold as the estate owners tried to reduce their outgoings and raise capital. Ralph Leeke of Wellington made his fortune with the East India Company and bought the Longford Estate, which would also do its bit for the wounded soldiers of the First World War by part of it being used by the VAD as an auxiliary hospital.

A common occurrence in the war was for more than one family member to enlist. This was certainly true of the Leeke family. When

Newport Church, Salop

St Nicholas Church, Newport, 1900s. *(Allan Frost)*

St Nicholas Church, Newport as it is now. *(Author)*

Colonel Leeke's two sons were both killed there was no one to take over the estate and so when the colonel became too old to manage it, it had to be sold in 1935, all 1,635 acres of it.

Religion also featured highly in the lives of the people of Newport. There was a church first recorded in Newport during the reign of Henry I, 1100–1135.

In 1904 Lady Annabelle Boughey of Aqualate Hall paid for the addition of a south porch to St Nicholas Church and for the rebuilding and furnishing of the sanctuary.

St Nicholas Church, Newport: building of new porch. *(NHS)*

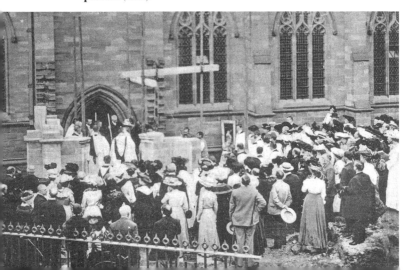

Lady Annabelle Boughey. *(NHS)*

In Newport's early years the main industry was agriculture, although it was also close to the mining areas of Lilleshall, Donnington and Oakengates in Telford. As a bustling market town it was independent and had a variety of shops serving the rural and industrial needs of the community. They had everything from doctors, chemists, clothes shops, food and drink, inns and public houses, tobacconists, dairies, leather goods, a timber

Davies brazier's shop, Newport. *(NHS)*

yard and a printing press, alongside farriers and a company that manufactured valves.

In fact, local farrier Mr J. Williams of the Stafford Street forge won second prize in the 'Roadsters Class' at the annual Birmingham and Joint Counties Horse Shoeing Competition in July 1914. Little did he know

Local farrier J. Williams, 1916. *(NHS)*

Newport Show, 1906. *(NHS)*

that war was about to break out and he'd be making a prize effort to produce 150,000 horseshoes for the army.

One of the biggest events of the year for Newport was the Newport Horticultural Show. Many of the town's eminent inhabitants and benefactors were involved in this, including J.S. Burton Burough, who was the president, the Reverend Sir Robert Boughey, the Reverend W. Budgen and Colonel Leeke.

The show included dancing, sports, bees and honey displays as well as the usual vegetable and flower displays and competitions. Newport was very much a rural town with accompanying rural traditions such as these agricultural and horticultural shows and maypole dancing.

Life in Newport was by no means easy but little did its people know, as they went about their daily lives, what was to come as the volatile situation escalated elsewhere in Europe.

Local maypole dancing, 1900s. *(NHS)*

Chapter Two

The Call to Arms

'If there is ever another war in Europe, it will come out of some damned silly thing in the Balkans.' Prince Otto von Bismarck, 1890

Assassination

Considering the potential disaster the events that led up to Great Britain's entry into the war were about to cause, the local newspapers made very little fuss about the assassination of Archduke Franz Ferdinand on 28 June 1914. In fact, the small article was placed above an advert for Bird's Custard!

It explained that a bomb was thrown at the car in which the Archduke was travelling on a visit to Sarajevo in Bosnia. This was the first assassination attempt, foiled by the Archduke who deflected the missile away from the car. It was the second attempt when they were leaving the town hall that accomplished the deed and sealed Britain's fate. The Archduke was very much regarded as the 'dark horse' of international politics and Germany in particular with concerns about what would happen when he ascended the Austrian throne.

Little would the people of Newport know that the actions of the assassin Gavrilo Princip, a Serbian sympathizer, would see their sons, brothers, fathers and uncles march off to war to a place they might have read about but would most probably never have seen had the war not broken out.

Breaking the News

The events of the war, the 'breaking news' of the assassination and the declaration of war failed to make the front pages of either the *Newport Advertiser* or the *Wellington Journal and Shrewsbury News*. Advertisements and local event items covered the front pages, usually consigning the war news to pages 4, 5 or 6. It is in the *WJSN* 1 August issue that we see the headline 'Austria Fights Serbia – All Europe may be Involved – A Grave Crisis'. The people of Newport had their interest piqued.

Could Great Britain be dragged into the war across the water? There was certainly nothing yet in the local news to suggest the sacrifice and horror that was to come. The people were so used to hearing about little spats between the Balkan States and Europe that it was thought this was probably just another tiff that would more than likely fizzle out to nothing. The Second Boer War of 1899–1902 in which some family members may have fought was already becoming a distant memory and surely nothing like that would ever happen again?

Unfortunately, despite the best efforts of Foreign Secretary Edward Grey, he failed in his attempt to form a peace conference between the ambassadors of Germany, France, Italy and Great Britain. The general consensus of opinion was that Serbia 'deserved chastisement' and that 'the powers should be content to stand aside until the Austrian military measures against Serbia are completed.'

However, standing aside was not in the moral code of Great Britain. Even at this early stage we were already implicated, and when Germany decided to invade Belgium – with whom we had a treaty to protect their neutrality – it was only a matter of time before Britain would be joining France in the trenches.

Life, at least for the moment, would carry on as normal in the town of Newport. The council would continue to meet and discuss its roads and its water supply; the guardians would look at the numbers of vagrants and out-relief payments; children would still be in school, not one of them for a minute thinking that within a few years of leaving they might be soldiers fighting in the biggest and most devastating war the world had ever seen. Their teachers and headmasters would never have imagined their old boys being sent to war and ending up dying in Flanders or Loos.

The Best-Laid Plans

While life carried on at home, the Schlieffen Plan was beginning to come into force abroad. The idea was for German armed forces to advance to the west through Belgium and northern France, while other flanks would close in and Paris would be encircled. The plan was supposed to take no more than forty days, which is why it was thought the conflict would be over by Christmas.

When they read that 'extreme activities' were taking place in the dockyards of Great Britain 'in making preparation against any untoward result of the European situation' and that on the whole leave was being stopped, the people of Newport, as indeed in many other cities, towns and villages across Great Britain, may just have been thinking that war was not as far away from their rural farms and front doors as they had hoped it might be.

When a telegram from Berlin confirmed that Germany had declared a state of war and Belgium announced that it had mobilized its troops, it is a wonder how many Newport residents remembered the little treaty that their country had signed. However, the official line from the government was that regarding its financial situation caused by the initial rumblings of war in Europe, there was no need yet for 'emergency action'.

The British government was, initially, going all out for peace. The government also pledged its support to France should Germany push through the Channel into the North Sea in a hostile manner. Germany even offered not to attack the coast of France if Britain 'pledged itself to neutrality', but it was not to be. It was here that Britain's earlier promise, the Treaty of London signed in 1839, came into play and her entry into the war became inevitable.

The order of the day was very much to stand up for one's convictions, honour, values and integrity and this would stand the people of the Empire, Great Britain and towns like Newport in good stead during the coming years. The early realization was that Britain was at war and the British public would have no option but to support it.

Yet not everyone agreed with the government's plans. Sir William Byles, a newspaper owner, MP for Salford North and a pacifist, stated that the defence of its people was the first duty of the government and that by going to war the rights of the British people would be violated. He would be a key supporter of conscientious objectors when the issues of enlistment and exemption were raised.

The government, nonetheless, carried the nation forward into war with calls for councils to place restrictions on aliens, the detention and removal of spies and the then Prime Minister Herbert Henry Asquith read out a message from the king who wanted to provide more for the military services by way of the army reserves being called up on permanent service. The subject of the insurance of shipping against war risk was also discussed and an agreement reached with insurance companies.

The Government takes Control
As news of the war sank in, the government enacted several new laws that meant they would be providing for men who were wounded in the war and their dependants; registering aliens and controlling the 'too

many' Germans living in Great Britain; increasing the amount of coins, providing paper money and making postal orders legal tender. Measures were also being put in place for the regulation of retail prices and groceries to prevent extortionate future price rises.

When news reports came in from other parts of the country that some 'needlessly alarmed' customers were making 'excessive purchases', they were vilified and the British public was warned that their 'unreasonable conduct cannot be too strongly deprecated'. Within government ranks, the rousing speeches and rattling of swords were designed to instil confidence in the British public and rouse their patriotism in the face of adversity.

'In its hour of trial and danger the country has the supreme advantage of unity,' said Mr Bonar Law. He was the one-time Conservative MP for Glasgow Blackfriars in 1900 and then Parliamentary Secretary to the Board of Trade in 1902. A straightforward and charismatic speaker, he earned respect, becoming leader of the Conservative Party in 1911 but he conceded to Lloyd George's premiership, playing a key role in his new War Cabinet.

The railways were also now controlled by the state and the latter would be controlling food supply distribution. Even the bank holiday was extended by three days to prevent panic buying and a run on the banks.

Your Country Needs You

The British army in peacetime was relatively small at around 750,000 men and it was well-documented that there was initial difficulty with enlistment. The media of the time did link this apathy to the Kaiser's invasion plans as he knew the British army was so small. When it is considered that the German army had around 4,000,000 men, it's no wonder the Kaiser was laughing. However, when the latter's plans became apparent and Belgium was invaded, Great Britain and the Empire were given a rude awakening and the men were galvanized into action.

In a regular section of the local newspaper, 'Local War Items', it was claimed that it was possible Shropshire was leading the way in its recruitment of men. It was estimated that in the first few weeks of the war the King's Shropshire Light Infantry (KSLI) had 1,200 men; the Shropshire Yeomanry 1,400 men; the Shropshire Royal Horse Artillery 220 men; the Royal Army Medical Corps 250 men; Shropshire men belonging to other units 500; and Lord Kitchener's New Army 300 men, giving a total of 4,500. Nationally, by the middle of August 1914 Germany had 1,077 battalions in the field while the British had only 48; therefore drastic recruitment measures were required.

The boys from Newport were no exception. In the week of 29 August National Reservists from Newport, Ernest Allen and A.L. Brotherton, among seventeen in total, proceeded towards Newport Station, following the town band to board a train to Shrewsbury. Their departure was a great event in the town, with a large crowd gathering to see them off. They certainly wouldn't be the last to go.

Even the local sexton, John Scott from Church Aston, answered the call to arms. These were ordinary men living ordinary lives who had to leave their families behind, wondering if they would ever see them again.

In response to the call to arms, Newport formed a volunteer force at a

Local sexton John Scott from Church Aston with his daughter.
(NHS/E. Dicker)

meeting called by Captain James Foster of Woodcote, which was held in the parish church room. There were over 100 men present, many of whom could not offer themselves for active service through being too old, too young, suffering from illness, disability or other reasons but still wanted to help in home defence. On 4 August 1914 the Newport Volunteers, later incorporated into the KSLI, marched proudly up the High Street amid the cheers and admiration of the town.

There was talk of finding a rifle range on which to practise shooting, and the local rector, although not willing to offer his services in a fighting capacity 'owing to his office', was happy to act as the chaplain. The volunteer force would be separated into two different classes: Class 1 for men aged 30 and above, and Class 2 for men aged less than 30. The force would be open to eligible men who, for whatever reason, were not able to join the regular army or the Territorials.

Unfortunately, soon after it was announced that the force had been set up, it was revealed that its formation had been suspended due to fears that it might detract from Lord Kitchener's appeal to form his New Army. Nevertheless, by January 1916 the Volunteer Training Corps of Newport had moved into new headquarters from 9 High Street to 24 St Mary's Street and they were using the Chetwynd range for musketry practise.

A full advert in the local paper identified, together with any police station, recruiting officer or the barracks at Shrewsbury, Mr Keight of Newport as the point of contact for those men 'desirous of joining the army'.

The *NA* was also keen to keep the fire of volunteering alight but they didn't feel there was much to celebrate yet. The people of Newport respected their local paper and the following extract from the 29 August 1914 issue would have hit home hard: 'They didn't much talk of the "magnificent response" to Kitchener's appeal... but if the facts are examined closely, there is not much cause for congratulations...'

They were referring to Field Marshal Kitchener's campaign to raise his New Army. Kitchener became Secretary of State for War in 1914 and he realized that if the allies were to have any chance of winning the war a great number of extra volunteer men would be needed. His face and pointing finger adorned many a poster stating 'Your Country Needs You.'

'The 100,000 has taken far too long to raise .... and is miserably inadequate.' The paper bemoaned the country's attitude of assuming that the British armed services would be victorious without any great effort and spelled it out to readers that victory would not come easily. '...Nor is it [victory] to be reached by the singing of patriotic songs and raising of 100,000 men.'

However, by 15 August 1914, in the eyes of the editor, things had begun to improve. The overall response 'has been no more than could confidently be expected of the manhood of Great Britain.' The paper also took offence at the 'business as usual' attitude. 'We want men, we want them badly and we want them quickly.' This was the overriding message, and an urgent one at that. 'Business as usual by all means, but there are enough men of 30 and 40 and over to see to that.' The paper's opinion was that if conscription had to be brought in and men forced to go to war it would be a 'standing disgrace'. They were keen for the local lads to show the enemy and the world the 'stuff Britons are made of'.

Up until the end of August 1914, the Shropshire Territorial Volunteers totalled 623 members of the 4th Battalion KSLI. The Shropshire lads, including those from Newport and the surrounding area, certainly did

Soldiers from Newport marching through the streets. Notice the leading soldier: it is sexton John Scott. *(NHS)*

their towns and villages, their county and their king and country proud, as was mentioned in the *NA*. 'In no part of the Kingdom has greater interest been taken in the war than throughout Shropshire ... All classes are united in rallying round the flag.'

The main military depot for the county was in Shrewsbury and was regarded as one of the most important military organizations in the country. It formed the headquarters for five districts – Wales, Cheshire, Shropshire, Herefordshire and Monmouthshire – as well as being the headquarters for the Welsh Territorial Division, Shropshire Light Infantry, Cheshire Regiment, Royal Welsh Fusiliers, South Wales Borderers, the Welsh Regiment and the South Lancashire Regiment.

As soon as the conflict broke out, it was already known that Shrewsbury barracks would be playing a key role in the war effort. The order to mobilize was given at Shrewsbury at 5pm on the Tuesday and they were more than ready with posters and orders posted on all public buildings and places of worship.

In the week that Britain engaged in the war, the local Territorials were at their annual camp in Aberystwyth and had to return to Newport early on the Monday where they awaited further instructions. They didn't have to wait long as the orders came that day to mobilize and they entrained to Shifnal for medical examination where, if they passed, they moved on to Shrewsbury and then to Barry in Wales.

Similarly, the Yeomanry were mobilized on the following Thursday and some local chauffeurs who were also members of the Mechanical Transport (Special Reserves) were ordered to report to Avonmouth and some to Liverpool by 6 August 1914.

As Newport was largely agriculturally based with a high proportion of working horses, there were also high-class waggoners to work those horses. Some waggoners from Salisbury, part of the Royal Army Service Corps, came through Newport on their way to Liverpool. It wouldn't be long before the highly-skilled waggoners from the farms in and around Newport would be enlisting and joining the war effort.

These were not the only army personnel who marched through the town en route to their various destinations. On the Sunday, members of the 3rd Mid Royal Army Medical Corps (Territorials) also came through the town and encamped at Bletchley on their way to North Wales, but on Monday night they had orders to return and they made camp in the Adams' Grammar School grounds for the night.

For the townspeople watching all this coming and going, it must have been a tremendous sight. Due to Newport's exceptional positioning, it was a good thoroughfare for troops to reach their destinations.

The local papers were soon full of reports about what was happening in the war. In the 15 August issue the paper reported on the 'vast proportions' of the war already, with around 2 million men opposite each other covering 250,000 miles along the German and French lines. There was news of the allies causing serious problems for the German troops.

However, this was only the beginning. The call to arms had been well and truly sounded and Newport, as the rest of the country, was bracing itself for a war that most definitely would not be over by Christmas.

Invasion of Britain postcard.
(Clifford Smout)

Chapter Three

Who Fought?

'But wives and mothers wept, their tender ken, prophetic, saw the red blood poured like wine.' Cresandia

One such son of Newport who answered the call to arms was Patrick Kilcoyne. His father was an Irish immigrant from County Mayo and a general labourer, harvester, farm labourer and nurseryman on the Lilleshall estate, on Mutton Grange Farm which is now the golf club. He married a Newport woman, Honor. They had eight children, Patrick being born in 1887. According to the 1911 census the family was living in a house with four rooms with Patrick's occupation at that time being listed as a moulder's labourer at the ironworks.

Patrick, Service Number 11356, was one of the first Newport lads to enlist with the KSLI in Shrewsbury and on 29 August 1914 he became a lance corporal in 'D' Company of the 5th Battalion.

He had fought in the Battle of Loos but was badly injured in the Hohenzollern Redoubt in September 1915. This was one of the worst sectors of the Loos battlegrounds for casualties as it was a strongly-defended area within the German lines.

Sadly, Patrick was not to survive. He died, aged 28, in a hospital in Manchester on 24 June 1916 of wounds received on the battlefield, and

Funeral cortége of Patrick Kilcoyne (1). *(NHS)*

Funeral cortége of Patrick Kilcoyne (2). *(NHS)*

was the first serving soldier from Newport to have his funeral in the town. His cortège included members of his family and some of his colleagues from the Audley works where Patrick was employed before he enlisted. He was buried in the town's cemetery.

As well as being a Catholic and a keen sportsman, he was well-known and liked in the town, so it was only fitting that on the night before the funeral, as his body was brought home by train, many of his family and people from the town – his friends, colleagues, team-mates, old school friends, a crowd of 200–300 people – were there to meet him as the train rolled in at 11pm, having been expected at 8.20pm, from Stafford.

Patrick Kilcoyne's grave in Newport Cemetery. *(Author)*

This being so solemn and important an occasion, he had a military escort through the town's streets, lined with people paying their respects. Reverend Giles of the Catholic Church in town received Patrick's body through the entrance of the church, where he remained throughout the night. His funeral procession on the Thursday afternoon was headed by the Grammar School Cadets with his old headmaster Captain J.W. Shuker in the lead.

The townspeople of Newport were immensely proud of the fact that their sons, brothers, fathers and uncles were joining up in their droves. Initially there was a great rush of willing volunteers, and often brothers or several members of the same family or friends and work colleagues would join up together; these were referred to as Pals' battalions. Even farmers' sons and labourers marched into town to answer the call of their country. Sadly, Patrick would not be the only Newport man to die in this bloody conflict as the names on the town and nearby villages' war memorials show. By the end of 1914, 1,186,337 men had enlisted in Britain. Of these, there were around 89,000 British casualties.

Families of deceased servicemen were given commemorative discs known as 'dead man's pennies'. On the front of each penny was engraved the words: 'He died for freedom and honour.'

Frank Cooper's family received one. Frank was one of three brothers who enlisted in the British army in 1914. Within days of each other, Frank and his brother Fred were wounded and sent home to recover. Unfortunately, two weeks after they returned to the front both were killed.

As the body count increased, the initial national shows of bravado and courage soon gave way to despair and anguish over the bleak and grisly reality that was the Great War. As reports of the huge numbers of casualties came in via the pages of their local papers, the population would have been only too aware of the sacrifice their menfolk were making.

Many prominent families in the area saw some of their members enlist. The Reverend Budgen, for instance, originally from Lichfield, Staffordshire, was married to Elizabeth and two of their sons enlisted and both saw active service.

Frank Cooper's commemorative penny. *(NHS)*

The Budgen brothers. *(NHS)*

Gordon (left in the photo), born in nearby Church Aston, was a former captain at Adams' Grammar School in the town. He joined the 5th Battalion KSLI and was killed at Ypres aged 21. Ypres (now Ieper) in Belgium is close to the border with France. At the time of the war it held a prime central position of road and rail and was a key transport centre for both the French and British armies. It was attacked three times during the war – October 1914, May 1915 and July 1917 – which indicates its importance as a key area.

Many of the old boys from Adams' Grammar School also fought in the war, including the Budgen brothers. Douglas (right) initially joined the Leinster Regiment but transferred to the Royal Flying Corps, was badly wounded and lost a leg.

In the years before the war he had been a popular and gifted pupil with celebrated success on the sports field and the school enjoyed a visit from him in a rest period from the fighting. However, they were soon announcing his wounding, as published by the editor of the school's *Novaportan* newsletter: 'We regret to announce that W.D. Budgen [Douglas], who holds a commission in the Prince of Wales' Leinster Regiment (Canadian) was severely wounded – shot through the lungs – near Lille, but we are glad to hear he is progressing satisfactorily. We wish him a speedy recovery.'

Another old boy who fought was Dr George Elkington MB ChB, Birmingham, a member of a prominent medical family in the town of Newport. He earned the diploma of a member of the Royal College of Physicians and was immediately commissioned into the Royal Army Medical Corps (RAMC) and sent on active duty.

The war wasn't just confined to the Western Front in Europe. It was also being fought in Africa

Lieutenant W.D. Budgen. *(NHS)*

where Britain, Germany, Belgium and France also had colonies and it was inevitable that the war would extend to these areas.

Many Newport lads also saw their bravery being rewarded. Second Lieutenant (Acting) Albert Gittins KSLI was rewarded for his bravery with the Military Cross. He had attended both the C of E infants' school and the boys' school in Newport and was also in the town band.

Albert had quite a reputation within the KSLI as an expert bomb-thrower. There were reports that in the trench where he was situated the enemy managed to detonate a mine; the results of this saw him immediately

George Elkington. *(NHS)*

elevated to the most senior officer available. He quickly took control of the resulting crater and held the Germans off.

Missiles and Malaria

However, those who did not survive the war didn't all die from wounds received in battle. It wasn't just the machine-gun fire, bayonets and shells that the soldiers had to worry about. Diseases such as typhoid,

Three First World War medals known as Pip, Squeak and Wilfred.
(Fred Tipton)

tuberculosis and gastritis were prevalent; body lice, malnutrition and the cold were also a problem for the British forces in the battlefield. Not surprising when you consider the living conditions that the men were forced to endure in the trenches, their close proximity to each other and the wounds they may have had.

Frederick Allman from Newport, a sergeant in the RMA (Royal Marine Artillery), died of malaria in a hospital in Dar es Salaam on 16 October 1917. Another Newport lad, Albert Bently, a private in the 8th Battalion KSLI, died of dysentery on 14 September 1916 in a hospital in the Greek port of Salonica.

Lieutenant George Harold Newbold, who is buried in Newport Cemetery, died at home aged 33 from pneumonia which was aggravated through having been gassed. Gas warfare was first used in the First World War and could render those exposed to it immobile within seconds. It was highly toxic and aimed to disable the enemy. Various toxins such as chlorine were used with varying effects such as breathing or visual difficulties. However, it was unpredictable and often blew back into the users' lines if the wind changed direction. On the first day of the Second Battle of Ypres 168 tons of chlorine gas were used.

George saw action in Belgium, France and Italy. He was the son of Mrs G. Newbold, an old boy of Adams' Grammar School and prior to enlisting was headmaster of Abbey School, Shrewsbury.

Major Robert Henry Leeke, one of the Leeke brothers of the Longford estate, was with the Rifle Brigade (Prince Consort's Own) attached to the King's African Rifles and died of blackwater fever on active service in British East Africa on 5 November 1915.

All at Sea

The war wasn't just to be fought on land and the sea would be soon become a battleground in its own right. Newport men supported the naval offensive too.

John Edward England was an ordinary seaman who sailed on HMS *Defence*, a Minotaur-class cruiser (1907).

George Newbold's grave in Newport Cemetery.
(Author)

Unfortunately, as with many ships defending the seas, *Defence* was destroyed under German gunfire at 6.20pm in the dusk of the Battle of Jutland.

The Battle of Jutland took place in the North Sea off the coast of Denmark on 31 May 1916. Proving to be the biggest engagement at sea during the First World War, the battle brought together the world's two most powerful naval forces of the time: the British Royal Navy's Grand Fleet and the German High Seas Fleet. Britain had the larger fleet with 150 vessels to Germany's 99 and it was Britain that was to suffer the heaviest casualties with 6,097 men killed to Germany's 2,551.

One of those casualties was Allen Perry, son of Mr and Mrs B.C. Perry of Beach Grove, Newport and an Adams' Grammar School old boy, who was a boy telegraphist on board HMS *New Zealand*.

Another Newport sailor was James Wright Evans, stoker first class, who sailed aboard HMS *Good Hope* (1889). *Good Hope* sank at the Battle of Coronel, off the coast of Chile. Rear Admiral Sir Christopher Cradock added the armoured *Good Hope* to his fleet which had just come out of reserve with inexperienced hands, some of whom had never fired the ship's guns. The British fleet was outnumbered, the ships slow and woefully armoured, whereas the German fleet was more modern and robust. The result was no surprise.

Wedding Bells and Funerals

Despite the call to arms, for many in Newport life carried on pretty much as normal: babies were born, children went to school, people died, and many soldiers decided it would be prudent to marry. One Harborne Reservist soldier from Eccleshall, just a few miles from Newport, was married one day at 9am. The wedding party sat down for breakfast at 10am, but five minutes later a policeman called with papers ordering him to Portsmouth. Exactly one hour and forty minutes after the wedding he was on his way to join his ship. Soldiers and sailors had a duty to perform and that was that.

The local schools and colleges provided a wealth of old boys who were only too willing to enlist for their king and country, but these were not the only sources of soldiers. A letter read out and recorded in the minutes of the Newport Rural District Council (15 August 1914) was from Lieutenant Colonel H.P. Sykes, reporting that he had been called away on service and wouldn't be able to attend any further council meetings. The call reached far and wide and to every corner of the community.

One man, Lieutenant B.W. Philipps, was unfortunately killed in a

B.W. Philipps in uniform. *(NHS)*

LIEUTENANT
B.W. PHILIPPS
ROYAL GARRISON ARTILLERY
AND ROYAL FLYING CORPS
14TH NOVEMBER 1917 AGE 2

B.W. Philipps' grave in Newport Cemetery. *(Author)*

flying accident on 14 November 1917. He was due to return to his medical studies but was instead buried at Newport Cemetery with military honours on Saturday, 17 November 1917.

His school was saddened by the news: several members of it attended his funeral and a wreath was sent. His father was the Reverend Dan Philipps.

Readers of the local newspaper became no strangers to bad news as more and more of their men's names appeared in its pages as either missing, wounded or killed. Sadly, many would never discover the true fate of their loved ones or the whereabouts of their bodies.

The Reverend Philipps, having lost his own son, would soon be presiding over the funerals of other local lads. One such service at the Congregational Church of Newport in March told of a double tragedy. In a crowded church the town paid their respects to two of their men: Charles Ward and James Alfred Latham.

Charles, known locally as Charlie, had been a member of the Boys' Club but was killed in action in Salonica on 17 January 1916. James was a former choirboy and had sent letters to the Reverend while on service. Unfortunately, as he was taking part in the siege of Aubers, France on 9 May 1915, he was listed as missing and there had been no trace of him since. It was, perhaps, a coincidence but one of the last choruses he took part in while in the choir was Crossing the Bar. The address given by Reverend Philipps centred on 'Greater love hath no man than this that he lay down his life for his friends.'

Another local man, Alaric Borough, was killed in France in 1917 and his service was held at St Michael and All Angels Church in nearby Chetwynd where he was buried.

To show their support for those men going off to war, many industries and professions pledged to keep the soldiers' and sailors' jobs open for when they came back. The Shropshire Education Committee meeting held in August 1914 made it clear that any officer or servant of the council would be allowed a leave of absence with 'no loss of position or emoluments' as well as

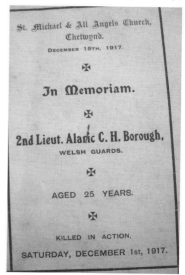

St. Michael & All Angels Church, Chetwynd.

DECEMBER 15TH, 1917.

☩

In Memoriam.

☩

2nd Lieut. Alaric C. H. Borough,
WELSH GUARDS.

☩

AGED 25 YEARS.

☩

KILLED IN ACTION,
SATURDAY, DECEMBER 1st, 1917.

Alaric Borough's church service sheet. *(NHS)*

agreeing to make up their wages from what they were paid by the government.

It was difficult for families to get news of their loved ones who were engaged on the battlefields. A notice issued by the Shropshire Territorial Force Association in the *WJSN* requested that families and friends wishing for information about their relatives should supply their regimental number, rank, full name, the company or squadron of the regiment in which they were serving and warned that if these details were not included they could not give out any information.

While things at home were beginning to change, there was much going on with news of the war abroad. The *NA* carried a piece on the Declaration of the Allies, which outlined a formal agreement that Britain, France and Russia were not to establish peace individually and not to request any terms of peace unless mutually agreed.

They blamed Germany's 'attempts of misusing the original defensive Triple Alliance' of Germany, Russia and Italy, and utilizing it for offensive reasons to demolish that alliance and forming a new alliance opposed by the Entente Cordiale, uniting France and Great Britain and the dual alliance of Russia and France. It truly was a hotbed of mistrust, old rivalries and jealousy.

Home Rule

Prior to the commencement of the Great War the only conflict on the minds of Newport people was the thorny subject of Home Rule for Ireland. There were, after all, a number of Irish workers in the town. However, the British government and those in Ireland against Home Rule were united in fighting against a common enemy: Germany and her allies.

Nevertheless, not all were happy. Sir Edward Carson set out his manifesto to the Loyalists of Ulster early on in the war, accusing the English government of taking advantage and using the war as leverage to 'inflict upon us this degradation and humiliation'.

For the war to be won, it was imperative that Great Britain came to the battle showing a united front. Any dissention or fighting among the ranks would potentially be seen by the enemy as a weakness, bolstering their campaign while whittling away at the confidence and patriotism of the English soldiers and those left behind on the home front. However, some in Ireland were of the opinion that it should be 'our country first'. The general agreement was that the mutual enemy must be defeated and the Irish issues dealt with later. Unfortunately, the unrest did not remain long on the back burner with the Easter uprising of 1916 not far away.

Conscription

As more soldiers and sailors fell on the battlefields and at sea, the government knew that they were running out of men. Fewer volunteers came forward; partially, no doubt, due to fear and not wanting to become another statistic. These men were seen by many as cowards and shirkers for failing to do their duty for king and country. They, alongside men who had previously been exempt from active duty, would soon find themselves being hunted down or their appeals and exemptions turned down at the local tribunals. Conscription, under the Derby Scheme, was to be introduced in 1916.

Conscription was deemed a necessary evil as there were 651,160 unstarred single men who had not enlisted. (Some occupations and employees of certain industries were exempt from being called up and these were starred.) They were being blamed for the situation the country now found itself in. If they weren't prepared to fight voluntarily, then they would need to be forced to.

It seems, though, that the government and those facing conscription couldn't do anything right in the eyes of certain quarters. A cartoon titled 'Recruiting for the Imp Army' featured in the *NA* of 8 January showing various imps in uniform with captions such as 'Just the fellow for Black Watch', 'I'll be all right at taking cover' and a section of the cartoon showed two imps wearing signs reading 'totally deaf and blind'. The cartoon was poking fun at the fact that it appeared they'd take anyone into the army now whether they were up to the job or not because the need for men was so desperate.

The Military Service Bill stated that all British males (except Irish) between the ages of 18 to 41, unmarried or widowers without dependants would have to enlist. The only exceptions would be those not usually resident in Great Britain, members of the forces (Reserve or Territorial) when liable for Foreign Service, men in the navy, Royal Marines, or those recommended for exemption, the Admiralty, or men of the church.

Exemptions would be those with dependants who would not be able to care for themselves if the man went away to war, workers whose jobs were of national importance, those incapable of fighting through ill health or injury, and conscientious objectors. As a footnote, however, conscientious objectors would be encouraged to serve in a non-combatant role.

Conscription was not welcomed by many members of society who saw it as a strike against freedom and democracy. However, if the war was to be won, men had to be found from somewhere with which to fight it.

It is clear that many of the men of Newport and the surrounding villages played their part in fighting for king and country, far too many to mention here, but what of the fight on the home front? The next chapter will look at the biggest industry of the area at the time – agriculture – and the fight of the farmers, the government and, eventually, every household in the town to feed the nation.

Chapter Four

Agriculture: Feeding the Nation

One of the major industries and employers in the town was that of agriculture. With the vast acreage of arable land in the area, it was both a profitable but back-breaking concern. The land was laid open to cereal crops such as corn and wheat, and the farming of livestock, particularly cattle. There was also a thriving market catering for the local community.

A letter published in the *WJSN* on 8 August 1914 detailed the plight of agriculture. The writer was concerned about farm labourers' wages and claimed that agriculture was the only industry that had been subject to so many unrestricted free imports. Little did they know, in a few months' time, how drastically this was to change. One thing the conflict did do was force Britain to step up its agricultural output as it could not rely on such imports during time of war.

The rural idyll that many seek today bears little resemblance to the hardships faced by farmers, tenants and farm labourers during wartime. Farming was hard work and they were at the mercy of the elements. A wet, cold summer was bad news for the farmer as it affected the quality and quantity of the crops, subsequently leading to shortages and price increases for the consumer.

Local ploughing in the 1900s. *(NHS)*

Local farmers and their cattle, 1900s. *(NHS)*

In the year preceding the war, agriculture, according to an article in the *NA* on Saturday, 5 July 1913, was doing well: 'The haymakers have been having a good time. Most of the clovers and mixtures have now been secured in the south of England, and also many good stacks of meadow hay have been put up in first rate condition.' However, due to less than expected rainfall the weight per acre was not expected to equal the average over ten years. 'If all are secured without damage, however, the quality will fully make up for the small deficiency in quality.'

The dependency of the farmer on the land and the weather would be

Aqualate staff sawing wood, 1900s. *(NHS)*

A traction engine belonging to the North Shropshire Saw Mills, 1900s. *(NHS)*

all the more crucial in the years to come. The state of the harvest was critical in wartime, especially for an island nation such as Britain.

In the 'Market Review' section of the paper local farmers were urged to know the prices across the country. The fluctuation in prices could affect their profit margin and sales, especially in wartime. There was much speculation about supply and demand and the quality of food and rumours of increased prices. These were quashed by the Board of Agriculture and Fisheries but where there is smoke, fire is usually to be found.

Potato-growing in the 1900s. *NHS)*

Just before the war, the Boards of Agriculture and Education produced a white paper which was the report of the Rural Education Conference, detailing the recommendations for developing the skills of those employed in agriculture. Older boys and girls attending rural elementary schools were to be instructed in manual work in agriculture. The school holidays were scheduled so as to allow the boys to work the land and help get the harvest in. There was agreement that the manual instruction would be provided by the local education authorities. The problem would be, in the years to come, that many of the local lads working the farms would be off to war, leaving a deficit of skilled labour.

In Newport, the annual Horticultural Society Show was a popular affair, as it still is today. It was announced in the *NA* that it was to be held on 19 July 1913 at the old cricket field. The usual showing of plants and table decorations would be taking place but there was also to be a physical training display and a Swedish drill display by the King's Shropshire Light Infantry. No one could have predicted that in little over a year, instead of enjoying and taking part in this important centre of community life event, they would be waving their men off to war.

It appears, however, that the situation with the harvest around the time of the declaration of war was fortunately good: 'It seems nothing but providential that the declaration of war finds us with a harvest of seven million quarters of wheat ready to our hand.'

The Plight of the Farmer

Yet all was not well. This letter, printed in the *WJSN*, dated 11 July 1914, gives some idea as to the plight of the farm labourer at the time:

> Although £1 a week cannot be called good wages ... every able-bodied farm labourer ought to get £1 a week and his cottage and garden free and may I add that it might be quite possible to arrange for each man to stop work at one o'clock once a fortnight, but how can this be done as long as under our present system our farmers are unfairly treated by the importation of duty-free agricultural produce from all over the world, whilst our own products are so heavily taxed?

'Rusticus', the agricultural correspondent of the *WJSN*, had this to say on the connection between war and agriculture:

> There is an intimate association between war and agriculture. Anomalous as it may appear that the most peaceful of all industries should bear any relation to the horrors of modern warfare, it is

A tractor from Harper Adams Agricultural College at Edgmond. *(NHS)*

nevertheless a fact that great campaigns can only be waged by means of fruits and products of the agricultural industry.

Already the seeds of what was to come were being planted in the farmers' minds. If only they could have predicted its scale and the implications this would have on their tenants, their workforce and their livelihoods. Serious changes to the level of home-grown food were already on the cards.

Food Shortages

At the onset of war the issue that concerned farmers and people in the street was the potential for food shortages should Britain go to war, but the government had reassured them that the country had enough wheat to make flour to last four months.

Rusticus continued to point out that the farmer had the initiative to 'strike a powerful blow for the maintenance of the nation as a whole in its hour of trial'. He also issued a warning that whether Britain went to war or not, 'we are on the eve of a winter of high prices'. This was a new call to arms, and one that could not be ignored by farmers.

Contrary to government reassurances about sufficient food being available, the general public was not so sure. In fact, in the week of 22 August the Higher Education Committee discussed the possible shortage of food for that winter and advised that it would be 'desirable' to encourage cottages and other homes to produce what they could. In order to make sure the quality of food was good, plans were laid for 'practical cookery instruction' in every parish and hamlet across the country.

The Lord Lieutenant of Shropshire (the Earl of Powis) also tried to reassure the people of Shropshire regarding a potential food crisis due to the war. A committee was appointed to oversee food production and was further divided into smaller local committees for the day-to-day business; these were to comprise three or four 'prominent' ladies, one of whom should be a 'lady of influence and position'.

The Board of Agriculture and Fisheries also appointed an Agricultural Executive Committee for food supplies looking at the status of supplies across the country. Although they fully understood that farmers were at a disadvantage due to their skilled workers going off to fight, something had to be done to increase food production. They had plans to help alleviate the deficit by trying to obtain suitably skilled workers via the Labour Exchange.

In the early months of the war harvest time was fast approaching and if the country wanted to avert a potential disaster for the war effort they were going to have to address the lack of skilled workers in the fields. Because finding the right skilled labour was difficult, local landowners were asked to second some of their workers to help the farmers gather in the harvest. The Newport estate owners were involved in this scheme.

Ever ready and eager to help, the Scouts took up the call to assist and were asked take messages between farmers and landowners and could also be a potential source of labour.

Horses
Another way in which farmers were asked to support the war effort was the commandeering of their working horses. There was a local depot in Newport where the horses were taken. However, farmers were warned that not all those purporting to be working for His Majesty and the armed forces were to be trusted. There were unscrupulous people claiming to have a right to take horses on commission when in fact they did not. Impressing, as it was referred to, could only be undertaken by constables who had a warrant. Unfortunately, even with this knowledge, the procedure wasn't always followed. People were so enthusiastic about their offers of help that they assumed everyone seeking assistance was as patriotic and upstanding as they were.

The Backbone of Britain
Even Lord Kitchener recognized the value and importance of rural districts such as Newport and was eager to engage their support: 'I rely

confidently on the rural population of all grades, to perform its share of the national duty at this crisis in our history.'

The government recognized that farmers and landowners were the 'backbone' of Britain and the Empire and that they were being relied upon in their nation's hour of need. This was a tall order when it is considered that farmers were already on the back foot through losing their workers and they were, essentially, at the mercy of the weather and the government. How the crops grew now and throughout the war would be key to the war effort. Food was effectively as important as munitions. There would be little from abroad to help if the harvest failed – with the fighting going on in France, Belgium and other areas – and with our own farm workers engaged in the fighting the home harvests would also be affected. Once the Germans laid their mines and engaged their U-boats, supply cargoes would be lost at sea.

Local Farmers to the Rescue

The Jones family farmed in the Newport area before, during and after the First World War. In 1914 Mr Edward Jones and his father John worked a 480-acre tenanted farm at Whitley Manor near Newport. Throughout this time Edward wrote a farm diary which gives a valuable insight into what farming was like during the war years.

The issue that concerned Edward, as indeed it did the whole farming community both locally and nationally, was the increase in wheat values. 'Wheat made £1 per bag (224lb this autumn). Other grain and stock prices did not make any appreciable rise but showed a gradual hardening. Barley sold at 38/- shillings per quarter, bullocks made to £24 each and Tegs to 55/- shillings each.'

When the need for more horses for the army arose, Whitley Manor complied when the government sent their representatives out twice to the manor and commandeered suitable horses for good prices. On their first visit in September they chose four horses aged between 5 and 8 years for which they paid £200. Their subsequent visit in October saw them take one horse, a 6-year-old gelding that fetched 60 guineas. They were trucked, via Newport Station, down south of the country where they were broken in and trained.

The loss of such valuable horses to the farming community occurred nationwide and was a blow to the farmers who relied heavily on horsepower for many aspects of their working life. However, John used his initiative and embraced new technology and engineering, meaning that the loss of some of his farm horses was not as disastrous as it might seem.

Local horses at a farrier's in the 1900s. *(NHS)*

Early in August 1914 he had been entertaining the idea of buying a tractor for use in ploughing and cultivating. This would be a brave and bold move as no one else in Shropshire had one. In fact, many in the area scoffed at the very idea of getting such a new-fangled machine and were convinced it wouldn't work.

Unperturbed by the naysayers, Edward and his father travelled to Bedford to see a new Saunderson tractor being demonstrated. The version of interest was a two-cylinder, 20hp machine that weighed 3 tons and cost around £260.

The demonstration included the tractor pulling a three-furrow plough on a stubble field but it was a different story when they got one back to Whitley Manor and realized that it was all very well pulling the 21cwt plough on a dry stubble field in August, but would be a trial when it came to winter when the ground would be unsuitable for the combined weight of tractor and plough. However, as more horses and the waggoners that drove them were taken by the army, this resulted in higher prices and due to a lack of skilled waggoners the tractor and plough were bought.

Buying the tractor despite criticism from the neighbouring farms was not the only hurdle Edward and his father had to jump. The farm workers were less than enthusiastic about driving the new tractor, with two flatly

Maud Jones driving the Saunderson tractor. *(Brian Watson Jones)*

refusing to have anything to do with it. So it was Aunt Maud, John's sister who would learn to drive it. This would make them independent of outside help which was also in scarce supply. The manufacturers of the tractor came to Whitley to help instruct Maud on how to drive the tractor and how it worked and they stayed for just over a week.

As they had feared, there were difficulties in the fields with poorer drainage. The main problem was that if the tractor became stuck in the boggy fields, there wasn't another tractor to pull it out and horses would have to be relied on. However, after a while Maud became an expert driver, silencing their critics.

As the rain fell that winter, the tractor was put away until the weather improved and the land became drier in the spring. Despite the tractor only being of use in dry weather, it did help to clear the land remarkably quickly, land that would otherwise not have been arable due to the shortage of skilled farm workers because of the war.

By 1917 it became clear that the only way Britain could produce enough food would be to start a campaign to plough pasture land. When two local committee members went to the farm they decided that a 44-acre field would be ploughed. With the scarcity of skilled labour there were concerns as to how they would get this essential work done. However, help was at hand with soldiers being available to assist.

Whitley had five soldiers, three billeted in the main house and the other two in the cottages. Also they took advantage of the fact that the nearby Harper Adams Agricultural College was now training Land Army girls and they received the help of three of them. Although grateful that their farm worker shortage was now somewhat alleviated, unfortunately the combined efforts of the relatively unskilled soldiers and Land Girls could not replace the specialized skilled farm labourers.

As the conflict continued the War Agricultural Executive Committee commandeered the tractor, ordering for it to be worked around the clock in eight-hour shifts. The team that undertook this monumental task included three soldiers and the local doctor's chauffeur. Everyone was doing their bit for the war. John was paid 7/6d per acre for undertaking ploughing on other farms as well.

Whitley farm was not just useful to the army and the government for its tractor, agriculture and food production. The two cottages on the farm were also used to house prisoners of war. In July 1917 ten German prisoners were there with two guards. Five of these men were put to work on the neighbouring farms and their work, give or take a couple of problems, was deemed satisfactory.

The War Agricultural Executive Committee demanded to be paid the going rate for the use of the prisoners on the farm but the government did supply their food. However, this was not sufficient for men undertaking such hard manual labour and so the farm subsidized this.

Eventually the tractor was released from army/government control and the farm continued as it had previously.

Grow Your Own
Of significance to farmers early on in the war was the notice that the military authorities would be looking out for large amounts of market garden and farm produce for use by the troops. Farmers were once more called upon to help the government and the war effort by declaring how much they could offer and sell at a fair price.

There was a meeting at the Parish Rooms in Newport on 21 April 1916 at which they discussed how they would motivate the wives and dependants of those in active military service to grow vegetables. It was decided that they would grow as many vegetables in their gardens as possible, something they were more than willing to do. Everyone was encouraged to do their bit.

As the war progressed, farmers would come to play an increasingly important part in food production on a much larger scale than ever before. Early on in the conflict, there was much talk about the utilization of allotments to help prevent food shortages. The Board of Agriculture and Fisheries planned to encourage more use of allotments to help relieve any future problems. There were to be technical advisors from agricultural colleges to assist in instruction of how to get the best yield from allotments, what to plant, etc. With Harper Adams College just up the road, it was inevitable that they would play a big part in this initiative.

Apart from working hard to increase food production, farmers were also engaged in charity work, raising money via jumble sales. By April 1916 they had raised £65,000 for allied farmers.

Landowners were also asked to donate land for the allotments, tax-free and rent-free for a year. The local committees would contribute seedlings and see to it that any person with free time would assist in the maintenance and running of the allotments.

As the country grew increasingly concerned about food production, the *NA* started to receive letters to the editor regarding the matter: 'Sir, Everyone now admits that the weakest point in any defence of our nation is her dependence upon countries overseas for four fifths of her food supply … The more food produced at home, the less need for importing …' The reader certainly had a point.

One of the biggest campaigns in the feeding of the nation was egg-collecting. The eggs were to be used for soldiers recuperating in the local VAD hospitals. Various collection points were set up, one of which was at 9, High Street, Newport. Numbers of eggs collected and their sources were regularly published in the *NA*. In the issue of 22 January, it was reported that four local schools had collected 100 eggs.

The Show Must Go On

Despite the hardships and reduction in workforce faced by farmers, the 27th Newport Agricultural Show still took place at Victoria Park in the summer of 1916 and enjoyed a big write-up in the local paper. People needed something to look forward to; a distraction from the atrocities occurring overseas. Farmers were also under a lot of pressure as the agricultural show was far more about business than pleasure. The show was also about fund-raising and there was a marquee in the grounds where flowers could be purchased, the proceeds going to the Red Cross.

As the war continued through 1917, the need to increase production of home-grown food became more urgent. The Newport District War Agricultural Committee turned their attention to how ordinary gardens, allotments and waste ground could be cultivated to help food production at a local level. They also considered the manpower that would be required to do this, suggesting that German prisoners of war could be used. In fact by 20 July 1917, it was known that German POWs would be coming to work in the Newport district and that the War Agricultural Committee would be inviting applications to use their services.

The *NA* also carried a series of short articles giving tips on how to reduce waste and buy/grow food responsibly and effectively. The articles encouraged everyone to do their bit and food production was promoted as being key to the war effort. Those who couldn't fight could grow food. Even local schoolchildren became involved by growing potatoes at the C of E School. However, this was not enough to prevent the government considering instigating voluntary rationing.

Save or Starve
The Food Controller stated in April 1917: 'Every crumb should be saved, and the person who eats a slice of bread more than he needs, the servant who throws away a crust, the housewife who fails to exercise the most careful supervision over the rationing of her household is helping the enemy.'

By December 1917 'Save or Starve' had become Great Britain's motto with a whole week devoted to encouraging people to make further sacrifices to reduce food consumption.

In January 1918 the Food Control Joint Advisory Committee met to look at the price of butter, milk and bread and how these items would be distributed. It was decided that butter would be fixed at 2s 6d per lb. Due to the flour shortage, potatoes would be used in the bread-making process and the committee had bought 4 tons. Those producing and selling milk were finding times hard but the committee decided to keep to the going rate of 5½d per quart delivered, 5d if not delivered. Bread was to be weighed.

The Shropshire War Agricultural Executive Committee was also coming down hard in January 1918. It threatened that if those who had already been given notice to plough and cultivate their land did not commence before the following week, enforcement proceedings would begin. However, the task would not be easy in the cold, snowy weather.

Meat rationing was to come into force on 25 March 1918 and the Newport Food Control Committee warned that the rationing of margarine and butter was to follow. In June 1918 new ration books were available and the people of Newport were told to apply for them. From 18 June margarine and butter were rationed.

If it hadn't been for the colossal effort of farmers, the local community growing their own vegetables, good fortune with the weather, and the bringing in of rationing, the outcome of the war might have been very different.

Chapter Five

Industry: The Wheels Keep Turning

The Audley Engineering Company

Probably the next biggest employer of the town, after agriculture, was Audco. They manufactured valves for over 100 years up to 1996. In 1906 it transferred over to the Audley Engineering Company Ltd.

Their employees were not slow to join the war effort and in August 1914 one of their directors, N.B. Saunders, was first in the queue to enlist. Luckily for him the company kept his position open and he still received a generous two-thirds of his usual salary. Records from the time show the company's 'appreciation of the manly spirit exhibited' and they wished him 'Godspeed'.

Of the fifty staff employed by the firm, twenty-six volunteered to fight and the management of the time took the decision to pay 5/- to 10/- per week towards assisting the families of those employees who had gone to war.

As the war progressed and skilled men became scarce, the company advertised for women workers in October 1915. They had around eighty on the payroll and even had a Mrs Kate Saunders employed as a director; she even chaired meetings there. This marked considerable progress for women at the time and was excellent news for the suffrage movement.

However, as the war raged on, the company's thoughts changed from the making of high-quality valves and iron cocks to the manufacture of anchor plummets for mine-sinkers. The conflict made them realize that they would need to focus their efforts and the only way forward would be to specialize, meaning an injection of capital and new, more modern premises. The year 1917 saw a tax increase, so the need for a revamp came to the fore. In 1918, for the princely sum of £2,110, a steam laundry in Wellington was purchased but high prices and the economic boom following the war soon bent to the 1920's slump.

The Lilleshall Iron Company

Another big sector of industry was the Lilleshall Iron Company that had iron merchants in Lilleshall, near Newport, and they too played their part in the war effort. The company owned vast areas of land, collieries, and engineering factories and foundries just down the road in Oakengates, Snedshill, Donnington Wood, Coalbrookdale and Ironbridge. In their heyday they controlled just about everything locally, even the water supply. They were also major employers in the area.

In the early 1900s, when there was no sign of war, the company began to diversify and improve their management team. Between 1904 and 1905 they brought in three eminent German managers: Rudolph Bechtel, J. Schmidt and C. Bauer. In 1906, the company managed to purchase a licence to manufacture from the German Nuremberg Company which was to prove a profitable move.

However, with the outbreak of war things changed and Bechtel was recalled to join the German army. Yet he did not go and was incarcerated as an enemy alien upon the introduction of the Alien Registration Act and British Nationality Act in 1914 through which those over the age of 16 were compelled to report to local police stations and register. This came about partly due to the government's fear of spies infiltrating Britain's war effort from inside the country.

His fellow German Schmidt fled to his home country. The company could ill afford to lose two such highly-skilled engineers in wartime and things began to fall apart.

At the beginning of the war the company had been in a good position but this was not to last. Their relationship with their workers had also begun to break down with the miners' unions showing their displeasure and a miners' strike affecting the whole of Shropshire being held just prior to the war in 1913. With the advent of war the company was busy in every department – coal, iron and steel, supplying the country's and the war's needs – but their overriding problem, as in most industries and professions, was

A 37.5mm infantry cannon round. *(NHS)*

Two First World War standard-issue rounds. *(NHS)*

one of a lack of manpower due to many of their employees enlisting and, as the war dragged on, they were to lose more and more men to the trenches.

Although prosperous in certain areas, other areas of the company, most notably the brickworks, were struggling most as more men enlisted. This was partly alleviated by the employment of women. The company was also to be engaged in munitions, having received an order for shells to be manufactured in batches of 50,000.

So prolific was this war work that the board were made aware in 1914 that 183 male employees had enlisted and the management requested permission for female workers to work the night shift in order to fulfil their orders.

Along with many other companies and landowners in the area, they also made a commitment to help the dependants of those employees who were engaged in the war. They did this by allowing such people to remain in their cottages rent-free and also allowing them a certain amount of free coal to heat their homes.

In 1917 the company paid for an ambulance and some surgical equipment for its own hospital. Members of the Shropshire Miners' Federation along with officials and workmen from the Lilleshall Company also gave two motor ambulances to the Red Cross Society in

1916, each vehicle costing around £600.

The local businesses and employers were by no means immune from the effects of the war effort; there were expectations of charity and Newport certainly did its bit. For example, Messrs Walker's employees were giving two pence in every pound from their wages each week to contribute to the relief fund. Similarly, a pit manager Mr Taylor organized two collections at the pit and raised £15.

Chapter Six

Women's Work is Never Done

'She bears up as best she can, patiently and without complaint.'

The war was both a blessing and a curse for women. Many of them had jobs in service or families to care for but the war suddenly saw them being thrown into the spotlight, changing how they were viewed by society and their roles within it.

Many of their menfolk had gone away to war and they had no idea if or when they would see them again. News from the battlefields was scant at the best of times, subject to rumour and confusion, and many women felt the pressure of the risk of losing their only income and, potentially, their homes. Who would take care of their interests with the main breadwinner gone? This may explain why so many men were reluctant to answer the call to arms when one considers what they had to lose.

However, this then put women in a difficult position. They were expected to encourage their men to enlist and, judging from several letters in the local newspapers, they did this with aplomb, often attempting to shame those men still at home into signing up. It was seen as their patriotic duty, and their biggest movement – the suffrage movement – came under fire and was expected to stop its quest for the vote and equal rights at the outbreak of war.

The Suffrage Movement
In early July 1914 the women's suffrage movement organized a pilgrimage from 'the four corners of England' to a meeting in London. There were reports of huge crowds assembling, 'working towards the vote by all legal means available to them'. Although none of the four routes passed by Newport, those suffragettes from the town and across Shropshire who were able would have gone to show their support as the pilgrims marched down Watling Street in Wolverhampton.

An open-air meeting was held in Newport in August 1914 where Mrs Harley of Condover and Miss Knight, the organizer of the West Midlands Federation, gave an address on the subject of women's suffrage. The meeting was well supported but the suffragettes, particularly as our country entered into war, were not admired by everyone as shown by a letter in the local press:

> May I express my regret that so many women of my old country in the form of militant suffragettes should in their demand for the vote behave in such a deplorable way… It seems to me that if these English women desire to help to make laws they would be more successful if they were more law abiding.

Hopefully, by the end of the war, women had more than regained the writer's respect by their patriotic and charitable conduct during the war years.

Immediately after Mr Asquith announced that Great Britain was at war with Germany, the suffrage movement wasted no time in its call to arms. A meeting was called in Wellington 'to make arrangements for organising help for those who will suffer from the effects of the war'.

Soon women would be taking on many more duties as the arm of employment swept in a different direction during the war and women took the place of men in the fields and the factories. The First World War was, in many ways, the catalyst that sparked a change in opinions and attitude across many sectors of British life, including the way women were perceived in the workforce and at home.

A poster in the local paper highlighted that a woman's work was never done. It ends with a poignant line, showing a woman's lot during the First World War: 'She bears up as best she can, patiently and without complaint.' No doubt this was a precursor to the patriotic and 'can-do' attitude of women on the home front during the conflict.

The newspaper also spelled out the role and expectations of women as war broke out: 'Not only have they seen their sons, sweethearts and brothers don the khaki and vanish into the fighting ranks without murmuring, or more than tears shed in secret perhaps; but they have inspired their men-folk to do their duty.'

In August 1914 Mrs Henry Fawcett made a 'stirring' appeal to the National Union of Women and the suffrage societies to join together in order for them to better organize the aid that the country would need if it were to get through the war. The suggestion that they should lay down their arms and cease working towards their own goals of greater women's rights and gaining the vote and concentrate instead on the plight of the country and alleviating the distress caused by the war was met with open arms.

A week later the women had made a prompt response to Mrs Fawcett, with more than 1,000 applications for work being registered. Many of those who applied, however, were professional and seeking paid employment; this was not within the remit of Mrs Fawcett's wishes as she wanted volunteers. Those women who did want paid work were referred to the Labour Exchanges instead.

Do Your Duty

The women of Britain were now expected to put down their 'votes for women' banners and engage in the war, but the question was how? Some of the suggested suitable activities included helping on farms with the harvest, field work, boarding out young children, distributing government stores and money to Reservists' families, Red Cross work, medical work, and clerical work in offices set up for the emergency services. With Newport sitting amid prime agricultural land it was inevitable that their attentions would soon be turned to working the land, as we shall see in a later chapter.

With the numbers of men signing up – most of them being the sole breadwinner of the family – it was natural for the women left behind to have to find work to keep their families going. Assurances from the government and some of the local landowners and employers that they would keep the soldiers' and sailors' jobs open until their return and help ease the financial burden of the families left behind were viewed with suspicion. Most people's minds were on the potential threat of the workhouse if they failed to keep their heads above water. For many it was already hard enough to make ends meet and the war was just another added financial pressure. It wouldn't have taken much to break many families of that era.

A Nudge from Abroad

The local newspapers of the time also carried a story of the bravery of Belgian women who were under attack from German forces at the munitions factory where they worked at Herstal, near Liege. Their men had enlisted in the army and so it was left to the women to defend their town. They used their initiative and whatever they had to hand, including boiling water, leading to 2,000 Germans being wounded and scalded.

Reports such as this encouraged the women of Newport to do their bit for the war effort. If the Belgian women could do it, so could they, especially as they had Belgian refugees living in the town; a reminder of what some women in other parts of the world were enduring.

In another report of the time, in contrast to the admiration of Belgian women, there was a warning issued to parents living in rural areas who let their young girls 'loiter' in the streets of many Shropshire towns 'inviting the attentions of young men'. This was deemed improper and counter to the war effort.

In some ways the war was a double-edged sword for women. Not only did it offer them opportunities in the workplace not normally open to them, but it also caused problems with more traditional types of employment. Domestic service was one of the occupations to suffer as the war began to bite and the gentry were forced to let some of their staff go. However, there was a remedy to this problem and it came from the government of New South Wales offering work to British domestic servants who were well thought of over there. They were offered paid passage overseas and good wages, the more experienced earning 12/6 to £1 a week. They used the premise that Australia was part of the Empire and was a healthy and 'attractive' place to live. There were also adverts enticing British farmers to work in Canada, aiming to eventually own their own farm and settle there.

Yet were these offers as good as they appeared? The former was certainly taking women workers away from where they would soon be required in unprecedented numbers to work the land and take over other traditionally male-orientated occupations such as driving buses, working on farms and in offices.

The efforts of women across the country, particularly in agriculture, caught the eye of the Earl of Selbourne who was so impressed that he thought a Women's Roll of Honour should be set up to acknowledge their achievements. The idea of giving them a badge was considered. He was keen for women's efforts to be acknowledged in the same way that their menfolk fighting in the war were honoured.

However, there would have been another greater benefit for women and that was to be given the vote, so long denied them. This point was highlighted in the 5 August 1916 issue of the *NA* by a letter from the suffragette movement. They pointed out that both men and women had been working hard throughout the war and 'if service in His Majesty's forces during the present war is to be regarded as a voter's qualification it is quite impossible to leave them [women] out.' This could have been seen as an attempt to use war service as leverage to get the female vote, but the author was keen to point out that they did not see voting rights for women as a 'prize' for their war efforts.

Despite the hardships of the war and the government having more pressing concerns than votes for women and the locals pulling out all the stops to engage in the war effort at home, on 2 March 1918 a public meeting was held at the Foresters Hall, Newport by the Reverend Prebendary Talbot (rector) and the Reverend W. Tingle (Primitive Methodist minister). The meeting was titled: 'Votes for Women; How to Use Them.' Miss Roddam, the local stalwart of charity in the town, was present as chair.

The Reverend Tingle was extolling the domestic side of women's lives but also their public side. He said that a woman's influence began in the home but was not solely confined there. He saw women's work outside the home as in helping the needy of society and that now, with the vote, was a good opportunity for women to bring Christian values into society and 'make for the greater happiness of mankind'. Education, improving housing and temperance were some of the ways in which Reverend Tingle thought the women's vote could do good.

Women would eventually be given the vote, albeit it in a restricted fashion to begin with. It cannot be denied that the effort women had put into keeping the home fires burning for the duration of the war played no small part in winning them the vote.

Women's work during the war years was unprecedented and the women of Newport certainly had their mettle tested in many ways. Unfortunately for them and their counterparts all over the United Kingdom, many of their roles reverted back to the pre-war days as soon as the conflict ended and the men who had survived came home. However, their lives and their standing in society would never be quite the same again.

Chapter Seven

Charity Begins at Home

'If there is one place in the world where the light was needed it was Newport. They wanted to send a searchlight and remove the shame and disgrace of that town. They all knew what the morality of Newport was.'

This was the disparaging opinion from William Latham of the town before the idea of war was even conceived. William's family had strong ties with the Salvation Army in the nearby town of Oakengates and he was a leading light in trying to do the best for the poor people of Newport.

The area was known for its mining industry with various pits being situated in Oakengates and Donnington, owned and managed by the Lilleshall Company. By the time William was 11 years old he found himself working in one of these pits and he rose through the company to eventually become an agent of the Shropshire Miner's Federation.

He was also deeply interested in politics and became a Labour Party member, a local preacher for the Methodist Church and a Sunday school superintendent. His interest in politics and the church soon saw him elected onto the Newport Rural District Council where, presumably, he thought he could do some good as he was opposed to the Poor Law and was of the opinion that it was the state's duty to care for its poor. He was often scathing of Newport's pitiful attempts at providing for its poor.

The 1834 Poor Law Amendment Act had seen the formation of the Newport Board of Guardians and the workhouse which was situated in the then Workhouse Lane (now Vineyard Road). At the start, the owner of Woodcote Hall, Mr Cotes, was elected chairman and Thomas Boughey was vice chair. The parish that had traditionally been responsible for the poor could no longer cope with demand due to the increase in population and the expansion of industry. There followed the election of guardians, of which Miss Roddam was one, and the formation of the Rural and Urban District Councils.

Prior to the war, the Board of Guardians records show that in January 1913 the number of persons in the district receiving out-relief for that fortnight was 175 against 181 in the same period the previous year. The master also reported that the number of indoor poor was 73 compared to 75 the year before. The number of vagrants relieved was 127 in that fortnight in comparison with 163 in the same period in 1912. This demonstrates the numbers of poor and destitute living in the district at the time.

The Workhouse

Despite being surrounded by wealthy landed gentry on their vast estates, Newport was by no means immune to poverty and the social and health problems this entailed. In many ways the war was a catalyst for huge social and economic changes, as well as the geography and balance of power in Europe.

One way in which the government tried to help was with the Poor Law. The Board of Guardians was set up as a result of this and its purpose was to take care of the running and upkeep of workhouses and provision for the poor. Newport had its own workhouse, which as well as providing for the poor also helped the local economy.

The Newport Board of Guardians, in its meeting of 28 March 1914, recommended that several tenders received from local tradesmen be accepted, including Mr J.C. Lloyd to supply flour, sharps, bran and oatmeal; Mr F. Shropshire to supply meat and milk; and Mr W. Wheat to supply coal and slack. Medicines would come from Mr F.H. Slynn; the undertaker would be Mr J.B. Wiseman; and stationery would be supplied by Mrs A.S. Hall.

Also just prior to the war the Mental Deficiencies Act came into force which was billed as ensuring the needs of the 'unfortunates' were catered for and they were protected and controlled. Provision for such people was to be improved. This had been a long time coming and was much needed.

The Newport Rural District Council also held regular meetings and just before the war one of their concerns was the Working Classes Act. They had received a letter from the Local Government Board requesting details of how far they had got with the schedule for the inspection of houses in the borough.

Not all the houses were fit for habitation, with varying degrees of decay and issues regarding sanitation and overcrowding. Disease and ill health were prevalent in such areas of poor housing and the local government committees and local MPs were doing their best to redress this.

Children from the workhouse attended the local schools as this entry in the Newport Junior School Logbook of 13 September 1918 shows: 'Have just been informed that Philip Barker, a child living at the

Workhouse, will not be able to attend the school again as he is to be transferred to a home for the feeble minded boys.' Another boy, Samuel Felton (of Church Aston), became an inmate of the workhouse for fifty years. He was a sickly infant and was admitted to the workhouse when it was situated in Workhouse Lane. When Audley House was built and he was transferred there, he became blind and could do very little for himself but knit. He died, for that period, at a great old age of 69.

There is also the sad tale of Emma Scragg who died at the age of 74 in March 1919. Unfortunately, as was not uncommon at the time, her

Newport workhouse. *(NHS)*

mother died when Emma was only two months old. Her father, who was a sailor at the time, full of grief and not knowing what to do with Emma, decided to take her to friends who would look after her but on the journey he became ill and entered the workhouse where he died, leaving Emma an orphan and she remained in the workhouse.

The situation for those townspeople who were poor or destitute was not good, and this was a problem nationally. There was very little in the way of financial, housing and health aid for them as is abundant nowadays, but fortunately for those in Newport there were many more affluent members of the community who were trying to improve the poor man's lot.

However, they were swimming against a tide of opposition at a time when begging in the street was an offence and it wasn't uncommon to see paupers in the local police courts being fined or given hard labour for trying to stay alive and simply not wanting to enter the local workhouse.

At the time, the workhouse was seen by many as a last resort: they were reluctant to enter for fear that the only way they would get out was in a box. Conditions inside were hardly cosy and even the authorities tried to make it clear that the workhouse was no picnic and they openly encouraged people to find work and some means of supporting themselves rather than enter their doors. For many, however, they had no other option.

William Latham must have been delighted when, eventually, the Poor Law was abolished and things began to change for the better. The Newport Guardians – a committee of local people set up under the Poor Law to care for the needs of the town's poor – disagreed with what was happening at a national level and how parliament was interfering in their affairs and they resigned.

Mary Roddam

Mary Roddam's social work within the town began with the church from which she became associated with the Girls' Friendly Society which trained and helped to find employment for working-class girls in the area. So prolific and proficient was she in her charity work that she soon became the first woman guardian, seeing that the work of her fellow guardians and the Poor Law was implemented.

She founded a home at Chetwynd End for girls who came mostly from the workhouse but in 1898 she had her own house built to accommodate the girls in Newport Road, Edgmond, now known as Moorfield House. The girls left school and went to Mary's home to train

Mary Roddam in later life. *(NHS)*

in domestic service and, hopefully, be placed in service at the various manor houses or in similar situations. The home closed in 1922.

This was not Mary's only enterprise. When the war came, as soft toys could no longer be imported from Germany, she founded her own cottage industry – initially in Newport and later in Edgmond – producing soft toys that were made by local women and girls. Mary's new enterprise certainly heeded the government's request for British companies to grab every opportunity to take trade away from Germany.

For her relatively small concern orders came from London, and many other manufacturers around the country followed Mary's lead. When the war ended, so did her business when the imported toys returned from foreign shores.

An article in the *NA* on 2 October 1915 extolled Mary's enterprise: 'The Shropshire toy industry which was initiated by Miss Roddam ... has made wonderful progress since it was started and may now be said to be on the highway to success.' 'The original idea of the founder was to find profitable employment for young people in the town and villages, especially in the making of the best style of soft toys...' '... The young women proved to be apt pupils, who quickly realised the necessity of the co-operation of brains, hands and eyes with the result that they may now be said to be skilled workers.' There was even an exhibition of the girls' work that was well attended with the 'flocks of farmyard fowl, rabbits, crows and rooks, bulls, teddy bears, and Humpty-Dumpties' favouring a special mention.

Interestingly, although Miss Roddam's initial premise had been to find work for local girls and women, their skills and determination would be all the more in demand after the war. Not only did she care for the welfare and employment prospects of women and girls, she was also concerned with childbirth. Her work for the

Edgmond Girls' Home. *(NHS)*

Roddam House today. *(Author)*

guardians at the workhouse was the catalyst for her wanting to improve childbirth issues, as well as her realization that the main causes of poverty were old age and ill health.

Mary founded the Newport Benefit Nursing Association in 1893 which looked after women who were pregnant or nursing in their own homes. Her pioneering efforts to train nurses became the Newport & District Nursing Association. She died aged 80 in 1931.

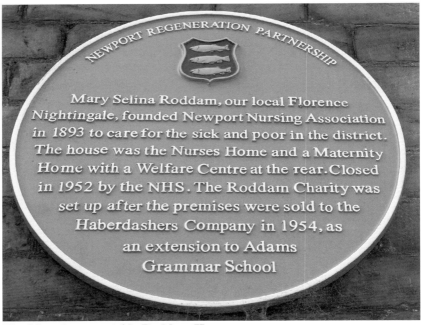

The blue plaque outside Roddam House. *(Author)*

Before the Great War, the people of Newport were generous in their charity towards their own poor but they faced a never-ending challenge. Even Lloyd George said that the people of Britain and the government were fighting an implacable war against poverty and squalor. In 1914–18 they would be fighting another war, one that might mean the townspeople's charity would be diverted elsewhere and their resourcefulness and resolve tested to the limit.

Chapter Eight

War Charities

The advent of war caused many problems for the people of Newport. Not only did they have their own poor to care for, they now had the added pressure of raising money for the war and wars don't come cheap. What little money they had was being stretched further and further. Charity and relief of distress caused by the war went hand-in-hand with patriotism and doing one's duty. Those who could not fight put in every effort they could through fund-raising, donations or making items for the war effort. During the conflict around 17,899 British war charities were set up.

The Prince of Wales' National Fund
Newport was no exception in this respect and when it came to the Prince of Wales' National Fund, Mr J.C. Capper of the National Provincial Bank in an advert in the *NA* of 15 August 1914 stated that he would be pleased to receive subscriptions to this fund from local people.

The fund was set up by the Prince of Wales to provide financial help to the dependants of servicemen while they were away fighting and the cause was taken up enthusiastically. The people of Newport threw their efforts wholeheartedly into raising money for the Prince's War Fund, including Edgmond which held a united meeting with the Brotherhood Society and the Church of England's Men's Society at Foresters Hall with forty to fifty men present.

The men decided that the two societies would offer their help to the farmers during the evenings to help gather the harvest and other jobs that were required with proceeds being given to the fund. They were also keen that provision should be made for the families of Reservists who had gone to fight and that a 'vigilant' eye should be kept on food. However, one attendee, Mr P.H. Foulkes, wasn't satisfied that the meeting was representative and that local people might pledge their support if they knew what was planned and so a further meeting was called.

The town and its surrounding areas were generous in their response to the Prince of Wales' Relief Fund with Captain James Foster donating the handsome sum of £500. Other local donators included the Reverend

Sir Robert Boughey (£200) and the Duke of Sutherland (£1,000). Up to the week of 29 August 1914 they had over 115 contributors. It wasn't just the rural landed gentry's workforce that they wanted for the war effort but their money too.

Even the local shopkeepers and businesses were involved. One patriotic shopkeeper, Mr G.H. Sidebotham, resident on several committees, dressed up one of his windows displaying 'materials suitable for Red Cross requirements' which also included a life-size model of a nurse; possibly helpful to the townsfolk who might have been wondering what they could best supply to help the war effort.

Another of his window displays showed Britannia holding her trident and shield as she ruled the waves. To show our alliance with France and Belgium, their flags, alongside the Union Jack, were also on display.

Mr G.H. Sidebotham. *(NHS)*

Patriotic concerts were held on a regular basis, one being held in the Assembly Room at the Town Hall. Whist drives were also held: one in the nearby Adbaston School cost 2s to enter including refreshments, all in aid of the Belgian Relief Fund.

Men who enlisted from the Chetwynd Estate. *(NHS)*

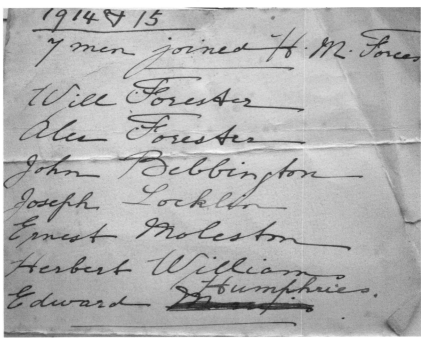

The local landowners did much work to help the war effort: not only did some of their workers enlist, but many of their sons went off to fight too. Those left at home also organized fund-raising. Mrs Borough promoted a sale of work in the grounds of Chetwynd Park in association with the Women's Home Mission. The proceeds went to the Prince of Wales' National Relief Fund and the Women's Home Mission.

Committees and charities set up to help with the war effort and those in need of help at home were in abundance in the Newport area, including the

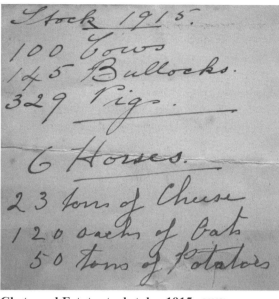

Chetwynd Estate stock-take, 1915. *(NHS)*

Queen's Work for Women Fund and the Soldiers' and Sailors' Families Association whose representatives in the town included Miss Liddle for Church Aston and Chetwynd Aston and the Reverend W. Budgen, father of two sons who fought and died in the Great War for Newport.

Many reforms were also expedited in the face of the war, including the formation of a Ministry for Labour in 1916 and a Ministry of Health in 1919. In the years before the start of the war, nationally there were over 300,000 applicants for relief but by 1922 this figure had risen to 2,000,000 despite government intervention and unemployment insurance.

Nationally, Princess Mary, the king's 17-year-old daughter, decided she would like to do her bit for the war effort and make life a little more comfortable for those fighting. She sent out specially-designed brass gift boxes to soldiers and sailors serving abroad. Each box contained her photograph, a writing set with a pencil in the shape of a bullet, cigarettes, lighter, pipe and pipe tobacco or sweets for non-smokers and a Christmas card. At Christmas 1914, 426,724 of these boxes were sent out.

A local committee for the

Princess Mary Christmas gift box, 1914.
(Malcolm Williams)

prevention and relief of distress was also formed, asking for applications for assistance from the community to go to Mr R.P. Liddle at 60 High Street.

In addition, the people of Newport held sales, concerts, and purchased blankets for soldiers. The sewing society in one of their many charitable turns held a public tea raising £1 10s and a subscription of £1 for the Belgian Relief Fund. The Congregational Church also became involved and held a fruit sale that raised £2 for the same fund.

The Belgian Refugees
When the government announced plans to help the thousands of Belgian refugees who had been forced to flee their homeland by German troops, Newport was only too pleased to play its part. The refugees were to become the responsibility of the Local Government Board; a letter had been sent to every such board's chairman of each County Council, including Shropshire.

It was hoped there would be many suitable volunteers to take in the refugees, particularly those who could take whole families. There were, however, concerns that the refugees may be viewed as cheap labour and great pains were taken to ensure this did not happen. There was also a particular concern that the women and children were placed in appropriate homes where they would be safe. All refugees were to be checked by a doctor before being placed. It was Mr R.P. Liddle who would be representing Newport in this matter and he sent out enquiries as to who in the area could help: 'We hope to hear that proud Salopia is ready to do her bit in the duty of extending hospitality to the unfortunate refugees who have been aptly styled "our guests of honour".'

Newport Rural Council met and decided to suspend the closing of some houses in Mill Street so that they could be made habitable for some of the Belgian refugees. The Board of Guardians at the workhouse were also asked to allow part of the workhouse to be used as a distribution centre for the refugees.

The Catholic Church was keen to ensure that anyone housing the refugees, most of whom were Catholics, would let them know so their spiritual needs could be catered for during their stay in Newport. There were concerns in the nearby village of Tibberton where some of the refugees were to be accommodated as they were 4 miles from the Catholic Church in Newport. The locals came to the rescue, offering them lifts to and from church.

In fact, Newport accommodated a few Belgian families throughout the war. In October 1914 the council rushed to find homes for two more Belgian refugee families of around fifteen people of the tradesman class. They were hoping to be able to have No. 117 High Street made ready to house them more permanently. This house had previously been occupied by the Boughey family. The Belgian family residing in the Boughey Brothers' Saddlers shop were the Vanonkelens. They were a family of five: a grandfather, his son, the son's wife and two children. They were estate and land surveyors but had been forced to flee their home in Tirlemont. One of the sons attended Newport Grammar School. There were also Belgian refugees housed at Merevale College, with more expected in the town.

Those responsible for finding places for the refugees relied on charitable donations and local volunteers to help finance them and provide furniture, etc., for the houses as well as food. The Belgian refugees were appreciative of the people of Newport's help and wrote a letter of thanks to the *NA*:

> … We venture to hope that our armies will obtain a speedy victory, when we shall be able to give final expression to the feelings, continually on the minds of every Belgian, in admiration and honour, and gratitude to England for her generous hospitality… No Belgian is ignorant of, or fails to render homage to their organisation and disinterestedness and each one individually testifies his profound gratitude, and will carry away an unforgettable remembrance of his stay at Newport.

Some of the refugees left the town in June 1916 and one of the houses where they were staying, near the grammar school, was being given up. Unfortunately one refugee who would never see his homeland again, Mr M. Vanonkelen who was staying at 7 High Street, died aged 81 in July 1916 before he could be repatriated. He was buried at the Roman Catholic Church in Newport.

Anything Goes

In May 1916 Newport received a rather unusual object. It was a German 77mm field gun that had been seized at Loos on 25 September 1915. The gun went on a national tour and would, it was thought, boost recruitment. It also helped to raise money for the VAD hospitals.

War Savings Bonds

Charities were not the only organizations in pursuit of money. The government was too. In 1914 the gold reserves of Great Britain amounted to around £9 million. Worried that the war would trigger panic, initiating a run on the banks, the government immediately extended the Bank Holiday to three days to allow for the Currency and Bank Notes Act to be passed.

Wars are expensive and so the government introduced a scheme in which people were encouraged to buy war bonds. These comprised a loan to the government that would be paid back to the purchaser in the 1920s. They were launched, with various interest rates, in 1914, 1915 and 1917. Again, it was billed as patriotic to buy them. The government couldn't finance the war without them. Shropshire certainly took it all on board, buying bonds worth a respectable £230,810.

In July 1916 the town met to try to appoint a representative for the local War Savings Committee and form an association. They were disappointed by the turnout as they felt this committee was important if they wanted to raise enough money to fund the war. It was thought that the war savings fund would help keep the cost of living down, reduce unemployment when the war ended, and have the potential to provide benefits for those who needed them.

War Pensions
In January 1918 a Naval and Military War Pension meeting was held in the town, owing to several applicants having come forward for relief under this scheme. It appeared that most of those applying were looking for compensation for the rise in living costs which was not within the committee's remit. It was felt that applicants thought the committee could give them funds to provide a better standard of living than they had had prior to the war.

After the war, those servicemen who had seen active service but did not remain within the armed forces were expected to retrain and take up some form of occupation, wounds and disabilities allowing. It was mentioned at this meeting that even though two of the applicants knew that training would be free of charge, they had still refused to undertake it.

As well as catering for soldiers and sailors still on active duty and POWs, the people of Newport also formed a group for discharged soldiers and sailors that met in the Oddfellows Hall, Market Square.

The Discharged Soldiers' and Sailors' group met again in August 1918 with the topic of discussion being pensions. They voted in favour of their colleagues in Wolverhampton's adoption of a resolution urging that all the political parties should work together to ensure a good pension for soldiers and sailors and that the pensions should be administered correctly and quickly.

Food Parcels

It was discussed in January 1918 that food parcels should be sent to British prisoners of war in Germany. There were some Newport men who were in this unfortunate position, including Corporal C. Williams, 7th KSLI who had been chauffeur to Mr Morris Lynton before enlisting; his mother lived at 7 Station Terrace, Newport, and so the people of Newport were only too eager to help. This saw the formation of the KSLI War Fund that was registered under the War Charities Act 1916. There had been a total of forty-five KSLI POWs since the war started, three of whom had died and two that could not be found.

There would be three food parcels a fortnight for each prisoner and each parcel would weigh 10–11lb when packed and would cost 7s 6d to post. There would be one bread parcel plus cigarettes per week. The parcels contained essential items such as margarine or dripping, meat, tinned fish, soups, tea and milk; a welcome gift for those prisoners.

Our Day, another fund-raising exercise for the VAD and Red Cross, took place in the town in October 1918 and it was reported in the *NA* that there were 'adverse' conditions that they could not mention in the paper due to DORA (Defence of the Realm Act) restrictions but they raised £46 2s.

Sewing for Soldiers and Sailors

Prior to the onset of war, there were several women- and church-dominated societies including the Girls' Friendly Society that would have a big impact on the war effort in Newport in the years to come.

Immediately after it was announced that Great Britain and the Empire were to enter the war, the Newport women wasted no time in setting to work. Following a highly fruitful meeting presided over by the rector in the Parish Rooms, voluntary aid began with the first consignment of garment-making for those soldiers and sailors going to fight. The sum of £10 was collected at this particular meeting to buy material to make the garments and it was to be the first of many.

Queen Mary herself issued an appeal to the women of the Empire, urging them to supply 300,000 pairs of woollen socks and 300,000 knitted or woven body belts for the 'gallant soldiers' to see them through the winter months.

Several sewing parties were set up in Newport and the surrounding villages where women could go to sew items for soldiers and sailors. Many items would be made during the course of the war including bed-jackets, socks, bandages, mufflers and shirts. The effort was phenomenal and much appreciated by the receiving servicemen.

One of the leading lights in the area of the women's war effort, the Duchess of Sutherland, made several appeals for women volunteers to help make items for soldiers and sailors and made it clear that her association 'knew no religious or political party' and that she just wanted help from whoever was willing to give it. This was another example of how the community of Newport pulled together to help a common cause.

The Hon. Mrs Lindley, Chairwoman of the Work Committee of the Shropshire Voluntary Aid Organisation, reported that between September and October 1914 4,046 articles had been received with 3,994 of these being despatched. This included 1,058 pairs of socks, 1,000 day shirts and 253 bed-jackets. They were distributed between the Red Cross, the KSLI and St John's Ambulance with provisions also distributed among the Belgian refugees in local areas.

There was no shortage of willing helpers, with lists reproduced in the newspapers regarding what was most needed. Some of these items included handkerchiefs, bootlaces, newspapers, chocolate, sweets, peppermints, dried fruit, briar pipes and tobacco pouches, cigarettes and papers, small tins of boracic ointment, borated Vaseline for sore feet, antiseptic powder, pocket knives, postcards, lead pencils, soap, leather soles for boots, toilet paper, and thin woollen sleeveless vests. It took a lot to keep a man at the front line and a few home comforts were most definitely welcome. Something familiar and comforting such as chocolate could improve the morale of the soldiers, even in the direst of environments.

Had it not been for the efforts of the various charities, the war would have been far worse for everyone. Those fighting in the conflict had their morale boosted every time they received something from these charities, as did those at home who sewed, donated and raised money.

Chapter Nine

The Role of Education: Adams' Grammar School

Newport was lucky enough to have good schools because it was geographically placed within a good road and railway network. There was also a wealth of townspeople and housing suitable to cater for the educational needs of the town. One local school that was to play a big part in the war, both abroad and at home, was Adams' Grammar School.

The school was established in 1656 by local man William Adams who was already a tremendous benefactor to Newport. It was run by the Haberdashers' Company, who in the Middle Ages were a group that was formed to protect their industry.

The headmaster at the time of the war was Mr J.W.M. Shuker (1903–26) who pushed the school forward to become a modern institution. After the end of the war, in 1919 there were 225 pupils on its books. Over time the school had become an excellent breeding ground for future officers who would go on to fight in the war. By July 1915

Adams' Grammar School interior, 1900s. *(AGS)*

Adams' Grammar School exterior today. *(Author)*

there would be 165 old boys serving in the Great War, and at least three of them had already died with many more wounded.

As well as giving its students a solid grounding in education at the time, even during the war years the school's prowess and enthusiasm for sports continued unabated. The Shropshire Inter-sports Competition was held at the school in 1915, in which six schools from around Shropshire – Bridgnorth, Coalbrookdale, Oswestry, Wellington, Wem and Newport – took part.

However, sport was not the only activity in which the school excelled. Their literary and debating society, formed in 1909, would have a lot to think about in the war years. Before the war, subjects that most occupied members were contemporary and topical issues such as Home Rule, the nationalization of the railways and, as an inspired omen, they concluded in 1910 that Britain was in danger of invasion from Germany!

The debating society, not one to forgo the issues of the day,

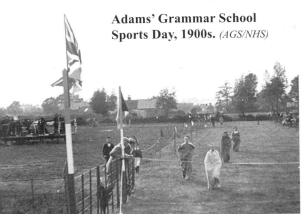

Adams' Grammar School Sports Day, 1900s. *(AGS/NHS)*

also raised interesting and sometimes heated comments on a range of topics, dominated by issues of war. On 18 October 1915 the topic was 'The German submarine blockade is a failure', while on 25 October 1915 it was 'Conscription is now necessary for the welfare of Great Britain', whereupon it was commented by R.B. Lane that it was 'a common sense way of defending our country and upholding our tradition and freedom'. This was challenged by J. Corbishley, who said in reply 'One volunteer was worth twenty pressed men.'

In response to the war a school cadet corps was formed by the headmaster. It was the 8th Company of the Secondary Schools' Cadet Battalion, which was attached to the 4th Battalion of the KSLI. Eighty pupils enlisted and were divided into two platoons: juniors and seniors. They 'drilled assiduously' and embarked on field days, route marches and flag-signalling. The rifle club was also part of the corps. This training would prove to become all-important in the coming years.

One shining star among the dreadful war news was the fact that in 1918, after coming second twice, the cadet corps had finally won the coveted Lucas-Tooth award for the best company in Shropshire. The school was to be recognized again in 1920 when they were in receipt of a German howitzer gun from the War Office. The gun had been pulled from the railway station and came to rest on the grass outside the school, where it remained during the Second World War. The corps was eventually disbanded in 1920 when the boys took on the more serene recreational activity of dramatic arts.

Even before the war, the school was already playing a major role in producing the calibre of officer required by the British military. They would go on to play a similarly significant role in the war effort for Newport, making a great sacrifice by way of the old boys who fought and died in the war. One of its previous pupils, the rector's son Lieutenant W.D. Budgen, helped the corps with its drill practice. Later he would be promoted and appeared in a 1918 Roll of Service in the school magazine as 'Budgen W.D., O.B.E., Major, Leinster Regiment (S.O. [Staff Officer], Royal Air Force)', having been invested with the OBE.

R.G. Budgen. *(NHS)*

When war eventually did break out the old boys enlisted in their droves. The school magazine published a list of 122 ex-pupils who had answered the call to arms by 22 December 1914. Of that number, only eight had already been in the regular forces and the rest were volunteers. The ensuing war years saw the numbers of enlisting Novaportans steadily rise. By April 1915, 141 old boys had enlisted and there were 200 serving by December 1915. Some 162 of them, out of a potential 240 who could have signed up, were pupils of the school between 1905 and 1914.

When conscription finally became law in January 1916 and all men between the ages of 18 to 41 were required to enlist, the effect on the school's enlistment rate was negligible. By April 1916, 217 were serving their county, rising to 255 in December 1916. By the end of the war it was estimated that 362 old boys had seen active service.

As news of the casualties and fatalities began to filter through, the impact on the school and town that had seen so many of their men go to war was immense. A couple of the school captains were to lose their lives in the war; Clifford Grail was killed at Gallipoli and the numbers of dead slowly rose. By July 1916 10 had been killed, by the following year it was 21 and by 1918 40 had died. The final total of Adams'

Lieutenant J.W. Bocking. *(AGS)*   **Lieutenant B. Bocking.** *(AGS)*

Grammar School fatalities would be 45, with a further 77 having been injured and probably more as yet unknown. All that intelligence and the promise of successful careers wiped out by the bullets and shells of the Great War.

Sadly, the pupils' success and skill on the sports field in the years prior to the war was all too frequently followed by news of their untimely death on the battlefield.

The reports of the deaths of brothers John and Bernard Bocking, sons of the rector of nearby Gnosall who were killed within four months of each other in 1918 at the ages of 22 and 20 respectively, came as a shock to the school community.

The Battle of the Somme saw the single highest number of old boys die, with eight losing their lives. Others were lost at sea and at home, in the Middle East, and during RAF training. The age range of those killed was 21 to 25 years, with most of them being infantry – 11 belonging to the KSLI – plus 19 officers and 6 NCOs.

On the first day of the Battle of the Somme (1 July 1916), more than 19,000 British soldiers were killed and by the time it ended in November 1916, British casualties would amount to a staggering 420,000. Many of the old boys fought in this infamous battle.

In a letter to the school dated 4 April 1918, one of them, A.L. Jones, wrote the following, although judging by the date he appears to be referring to another action in the Somme area rather than the aforementioned main battle:

> One morning, March 23rd, opened out with a terrific bombardment. We were expecting it, and therefore ready to leave, marching full pack and three blankets to a place nine km distant. There we dug ourselves in and fought a rear-guard action to enable the infantry to retire to positions further back. We succeeded in holding him about four hours. Then he broke through on the right and left of our positions. We thought ourselves surrounded, but we managed to escape by wading neck high through the Somme … I am very thankful to be alive.

He added: '… the life is full of adventures and narrow escapes.'

As well as supporting their old boys in the war, the school did its best to assist in matters closer to home. With regard to the arrival of the Belgian refugees in the town, three of them attended the school: G. Cambier, R. Bayet and A.M. Vanonkelen. Bayet was a boarder at the headmaster's house and Vanonkelen left early to study at the Birmingham Academy of Arts.

THE NOVAPORTAN.   51

War Relief Fund Account.

FROM WEEK ENDING OCTOBER 2ND, 1914, TO WEEK ENDING APRIL 3RD, 1915.

RECEIPTS.	£	s.	d.	EXPENDITURE.	£	s.	d.
From the Headmaster and the Staff	12	16	2	Pipes and Tobacco for Soldiers and Sailors	2	15	6
,, Mr. E. H. Wadlow	0	5	0	Christmas Treat to Wives and Children of Newport Soldiers	2	17	5½
,, The Boys	15	10	7½	To Red Cross Fund	2	0	0
,, The Literary and Debating Society	1	0	0	,, Serbian Relief Fund	2	0	0
				,, Montenegrin Relief Fund ...	1	0	0
				,, Polish Relief Fund	1	0	0
				,, Mine Sweepers' Relief Fund	1	0	0
				,, Indian Soldiers' Relief Fund	1	0	0
				,, Queen Mary's Work for Women Fund	1	0	0
				,, Princess Mary's Christmas Gift Fund	0	10	0
				,, Y.M.C.A. War Emergency Fund	1	1	0
				,, British and Foreign Bible Society	1	1	0
				,, Newport Belgian Fund ...	5	5	0
				,, Gnosall Belgian Fund ...	1	2	0
				Stamps	0	3	1
				Total	23	15	0½
				Balance	5	16	9
Total	29	11	9½	Total	29	11	9½

P. MAMLOCK, Hon. Treasurer.

The Relief Fund accounts entry. *(AGS)*

Among their other charitable concerns was the formation of the school War Relief Fund which received generous contributions from both staff and boys. They also donated to other war-related causes, including pipes and tobacco for soldiers and sailors, the Red Cross and the Serbian Relief Fund. They also treated the wives and children of Newport servicemen to a special Christmas. They even deprived themselves of the traditional annual prizes during the war years, preferring to receive certificates and money, most of which the boys donated to the War Relief Fund.

A.M. Vanonkelen in Belgian Volunteer Army uniform. *(AGS)*

There was also a scheme set up that allowed pupils to take War Savings Certificates whereby they promised to buy a set amount, the staff would purchase them on behalf of the boys and the boys could repay them in weekly instalments.

Despite their tremendous war effort, the burden of shortages caused by the war began to make itself felt in the school. In 1917 they grew vegetables in the school's paddock, railway services were reduced and the national shortage of paper began to bite. In April 1917 the editor of the school magazine, *Novaportan*, published this piece that gives some idea of the state of the school's morale at the time:

> It seems more than ever difficult, in looking back upon the school life of this term to see, through the obscuring mists of wartime tension and anxiety, even the remnants of the happy, irresponsible life, the wholehearted work and play of pre-war days. Call-up papers, medical examinations and tribunal appeals are disturbing factors; and the taste for school sports and academic successes is inevitably dulled by the wormwood draughts which all, to varying measure, have to drink today. At the time of writing, the science of the school is at a standstill because the War Office has withdrawn all exemptions of school masters classed in the higher medical categories ... We do not complain, but an editorial which is honestly to convey the spirit of the school to readers of today or the future could not ignore such disquieting elements.

The editor was also disparaging regarding tribunal appeals because the government had changed the rules regarding the age of those who were to enlist. Men were obliged to enlist at the age of 18 years, seven months sooner than before if taking exams. Those hoping for a postponement so that they could continue their studies would be disappointed as it wasn't always allowed. Even the scarcity of paper did not escape the school, with the magazine being issued once every two terms instead of each term.

Along with all this misery the school could well have done without their outbreak of measles in April 1918, causing no issues of *Novaportan* to be published for a term. The sudden lack of the magazine was certainly noticed by those old boys serving overseas who wondered if they had been overlooked for some reason. Seven months later, the school was closed for three weeks due to an outbreak of influenza. Morale was just as low as the students' immunity to disease.

The editorial of the December 1915 issue told how very different this term had been from previous years with the 'outside world' being forced on them

> and a sense of responsibility has awakened in us. One day our schoolfellows work beside us in the classroom, and the next they are soldiers in their country's cause. Suddenly we have been made to realize that 'a life spent worthily' should be measured by a nobler line – by deeds, not years.

Novaportan was a lifeline, not only for the boys who were students at the school, but also for those old boys who were away on active service. The old boys in question obviously had their time at the school firmly implanted in their minds as they fought in the trenches because several of them found the time to write to their old headmaster. They relished each copy of the magazine that was forwarded to them and sent many letters back to the school following this plea from the headmaster: 'It is hoped that those Old Boys who are or soon will be taking part in the actual naval and military operation of the war will find time to forward us accounts of their experiences.' They did just this, with the publication printing excerpts from the 'Old Novaportans in khaki's' letters to the headmaster.

In April 1915 the headmaster thanked the 'Old Boys in khaki' for sending such 'interesting' letters and photographs. One such letter with a patriotic tone came from R.G. Pitchford of the ASC (Army Service Corps):

> I am out here in France, and going on well. I was really surprised to come out so soon, but I shall always be able to look back and say that I did my duty. I wish I had learnt more French; it is grand if a chap can speak it well.

A.W. Jenkins also wrote from the trenches of France on 4 July 1915:

> We go to the trenches again tonight – we have been out for a rest. It has been very bad out here and we wish it was over. I have had some very near shaves, and now we are in a very hot shop. The Germans use explosive bullets and it is all up if one of those catches you.

It is sometimes forgotten that the war was also being fought outside Europe and the school continued to receive letters from those fighting further afield too. Corporal G.M. Talbot told of his 'interesting adventures' in Egypt, but on a more melancholy note also wondered how so many of his comrades managed to 'hold on' given the treacherous and dire environment in which they found themselves: 'Had not dysentery and jaundice been so

Adams' Grammar old boy on camel in Egypt. *(AGS)*

prevalent among the troops, a much different tale might have been told.'

It seems it wasn't the want of trying that was hampering the troops but mainly illness and disease. While Corporal Talbot was lamenting the conditions, Private B.R. Morris, writing from France, was tired of the everyday drudgery:

> It is surprising how monotonous the eternal round of trench, reserve, reserve, trench and rest becomes. Both mind and muscle grow sluggish and we long for something to wake us up. 'Fritz' does his best to oblige with his minenwerfers, etc., but, strange to say, we are not at all grateful for his kind attentions.

For another old boy soldier, it wasn't the monotony or disease that irked him most, but the weather:

> It has already exceeded 100 degrees in the shade. Every bally breed of insect generated since the flood seems to congregate here, and they all seem to like the taste of me… Of course, we are all more or less going through it; heat, sickness, and violent 'pantry troubles'.

A. Guilford. Cairo, 12 May 1916.

Whereas some old boys were being put through the mill, it seems that Guilford, at least, was rather enjoying his travels: 'We came from Devonport on a transport… and we had a glorious time: a jolly lot of officers, fine messing arrangements, ripping weather; in fact the best holiday I've ever had. Called in at Gibraltar and Malta… skirted North Africa and the coast of Crete.' He was quite happy apart from the mine-dodging.

W.V. Brunger, Second Lieutenant, 8th Loyal North Lancashires in his letter to the school brought the dangers they faced into sharp relief:

> The thing we dread here is night. We know there is a Hun mine just in front of us ready tamped, and we have been standing to all night every night since we came in, waiting for it to go up. But the enemy is too wily to blow it up yet. He hopes we shall get tired of waiting, and stop standing to at night; then he would catch us napping… I think the strain is beginning to tell on us all.

Another letter came from A.W. Jenkins, 6th Battalion, South Shropshire Regiment, who wrote on 16 May 1915:

> We have been out here for three months, and have been in action nearly two months now. I have seen some exciting times but the worst was when our section had to carry some sand bags from the reserve trenches to the firing line. We were set upon by the enemy

Devastation in France. *(Chris Deaves)*

when they sent up a star shell and they opened fire. Of course we
dropped flat, but luckily only one man was wounded... The towns
are in ruins out here; the people in England can't imagine it.

The images the boys at school who read these letters must have pictured
in their minds about the horror and glory of battle must have made them
both thrilled and fearful, especially the older boys who were nearing the
end of their school life. They would be wondering if the war would still
be raging by the time they were old enough to enlist and what fate might
await them on the battlefield.

Major T.E. Lowe, 6th Battalion, South Staffordshire Regiment wrote
on 11 May 1915:

I was very glad to receive the old *Novaportan* for April as I was not
previously aware that there were Novaportan Old Boys in my
regiment. I immediately made the acquaintance of Grail, S.J. and
Jenkins, A.W. I am surely very sorry to hear that poor Grail was hit
rather badly today. A bullet passed through one of the loop holes,
a very unusual occurrence, and caught him in the thigh – breaking
the bone. I was present as the wound was dressed. It was a very
painful business... but he stood it like a brick. So far I have had
two hours' sleep in the last 42 hours. If I had time I would like to
tell you something of the conditions, horrible conditions, to which
this wretched country has been reduced.

Censorship was also telling in the letters that the old boys sent back to the school. It obviously rankled as this excerpt from one old boy, Major J.R. Pooler, Egypt, shows: 'Wait until after the war and then we will see what can be done in the matter of actual interesting experiences.'

The headmaster, Mr Shuker, who kept a roll of honour for all the old boys who enlisted, wrote of them: 'One and all have shown that they have gained something much more valuable than either book knowledge or skill in games; viz. a sense of duty and patriotism and a spirit of self-sacrifice in their country's cause.'

Some of the old boys who survived, were home on leave or had been injured felt inclined to visit their old school. Perhaps it was the recollection of happier days their old school years had provided them. Dr G.E. Elkington, F.D. Elkington, brothers W.D. and R.G. Budgen, and J.W. Bocking were just a few of them.

The school was not immune to the pressures and financial constraints felt outside its walls either. The boys were more than aware that there were many

S.J. Grail in uniform. *(AGS)*

charities in need of funds. The school sporting events were still to continue but with no prizes as a compromise. Other events, however, were under review because of the war and so many old boys being away at war, notably the annual July Dinner and cricket match.

The mood of the classroom mirrored that of the battlefield as the editorial of April 1917 in the *Novaportan* attests. The editor felt that it was becoming more and more difficult 'to see through the obscuring mists of war-time tension and anxiety, even the remnants of a happy, irresponsible life, the whole-hearted work and play of pre-war days'.

School life was definitely affected by the war and in 1917 it appeared it was the turn of the science

Major J.R. Pooler. *(AGS)*

department to suffer, with the War Office withdrawing all exemptions from service for schoolmasters of the higher medical categories.

By July 1917, with the urgent need to increase food production in Britain, the headmaster sent a letter to the parents informing them of a new scheme to enable the boys to do agricultural work during their school holidays.

In the December 1919 issue of *Novaportan*, the school appeared to be coming to terms with the hard war years and was looking forward to a more peaceful future: 'The lethargy of war conditions is fast becoming a thing of the past, and we are confidently looking forward to the achievement of great things by good honest work.'

However, it hadn't all been negative news for the school during the war and as well as honouring their war dead, they also took great pride in the forty-six former pupils who received decorations for service to their country. Of the decorations received there were 2 OBEs, 11 MCs, 1 DFC, 5 Croix de Guerre, 2 DCMs and 4 MMs. Many also received foreign honours or were mentioned in various despatches. Two older boys of the previous generation who had joined up with their sons gained Territorial decorations: Lieutenant Colonel J. Oldfield, RAMC and Lieutenant Colonel T.E. Lowe.

The war had exacted a toll on the school but one that saw them carry on its traditions with pride, determined not to let their old boys' sacrifices be in vain as they navigated the post-war world; a world that would see them and the town of Newport taking time to recover.

Chapter Ten

Harper Adams Agricultural College

Given the large farming areas in the vicinity, it was only natural that Harper Adams Agricultural College should be sited just out of Newport in Edgmond. Its importance to the war effort was recognized by members of the Shropshire Chamber of Agriculture and local MP Mr Beville Stanier when they visited the college at around the time that news of the war broke.

Mr Stanier spoke of the grave situation in Europe. He was concerned about the likely hike in prices and the fact that ships on the other side of the world were unable to continue providing essential imports. The country was, Mr Stanier felt, at the mercy of agriculturists as they worked hard to increase food production.

Newport and Edgmond were at the forefront of agricultural advancements and their essential contribution to the war effort. The college, officially opened on 26 September 1901, had been built thanks

Beville Stanier MP giving an address in the town. *(NHS)*

to the generosity of its benefactor Thomas Harper Adams who had died in 1892.

The Rt Hon. R.W. Hanbury MP, who was then president of the Board of Agriculture, said Mr Adams had been sure that agriculture was in need of substantial finance and so he willingly gave a large amount of money to fund the college. He would have preferred it as a

Harper Adams Agricultural College, 1900s. *(HAAU)*

private institution rather than with the 'meddling' of the state. Hanbury, however, disagreed and thought it prudent that the state should become more involved in the teaching of agriculture. The intention was to fend off competition from abroad and to retain young people's interest in working the land.

Just before war broke out, the college was facing its own turning-point. Student numbers had expanded and the conflict was about to place further pressure on the already overstretched facilities. No one could

The college's staff and students, 1916–17. *(HAAU)*

STUDENTS'

cation.	NAME.	Address.	Age.	Date of Entry	Course.
	Stones M.J.	Lyndhurst Undredale Rd Stewd	27	May 9	
	Hall. M.S.	3 Granville Av Newport Salop	23	May 11	
	Goswell. N.	15 Maitland Road Saltley	28	May 15	
	Biddle. E.M	120 Woodend Road Erdington	35	May 15	
	Jones. O.E	60 Church St Oldbury	19	May 16	
	Prince. C.A.L.	Ernest Place, Whitchurch Rd Great Barr not Bromwich	32	May 16	
	Moss. H.G.	28 Homes St. Balsall Heath B.Ham	30	May 17	
	Robinson J.M.	The Nock, Main St Stapenhill Burton on Trent	20	May 17	
	Cadie.R.	Cromwell House, Church Road Moseley Birmingham	23	May 18	
	Weaver. E.M.	1 College Court, Shrewsbury	18	May 22	
	Lumley. E.	89 Holly Lane, Erdington	25	May 22	
	Davis. D.	60 Douglass Road Handsworth	26	May 22	
	Fellows. M.	5 Granville Terrace, Anderton St Birmingham	20	May 23	
	Miller L.W	18 Newcastle Rd Trent Vale Stoke on Trent	18	May 23	
			25	May 23	

Original student intake entries. *(HAAU)*

have predicted just how much of a key player the college would be in helping the war effort, least of all the staff and students.

It is testament to the sheer determination of the college that it was able to stay open throughout the war years and other similar institutions were not so fortunate. This was by no means an easy option, as even the Royal Agricultural College had had no choice but to close its doors. The war was to cost Harper Adams Agricultural College dearly.

The Great War would affect the college in many ways. One example came in 1916 and was the result of German Zeppelin air-raids that had occurred elsewhere in the country, a particularly vicious attack taking place on 31 January 1916. The clerk Mr Liddle was asked to look into air-raid damage insurance for the college buildings. There were fears that the raids might reach Newport as they had already crept up on the neighbouring county of Staffordshire. There must have been concerns that the college would be a prime target as its primary intention was to help Britain increase its food production.

Another way in which the college helped the war effort was through its staff and students, many of whom enlisted. Patriotic as this surge of volunteers was, it left the college with a dilemma. Just as the government was calling for an increase in home-grown food production, the men needed to learn the skills to farm the land were engaged abroad on the battlefields and this meant a reduction in student numbers. Even with the college able to retain those under age for military service, it still struggled and the threat of closure was very real. The 1914–15 student intake (for long courses) was just forty-one, with twenty-nine of those leaving to fight in the war.

Because the college had many staff with expertise essential to the war effort – most notably chemists, clerical workers and farm labourers – it soon found itself struggling to obtain the usual high calibre of staff required and many posts were filled temporarily.

The college was in many ways a victim of its own success. It had held very popular and successful poultry trials requiring staff to monitor them and deal with the ever-increasing paperwork. This, along with the reduced levels of staff and demands for increased food production, left the college almost reaching breaking point.

Financially the loss of fees, residencies and boarding at the college in the first year of the war reached into the region of £2,000. This had a knock-on effect for the domestic staff, some of whom found themselves without a job. However, in 1915–16 good news came from the Board of Agriculture and the Treasury which offered the college and other similar institutions a lifeline by way of grants. These were £1,750 in total but did little to help the college when the prices of food, fuel, labour and materials were rising. To help compensate for this and to prevent closure, increasing the fees in 1918 was the only real option. When the college saw an increase in students on long courses to seventy-three in 1917–18, the higher fees began to help ease the financial predicament.

However, this was not the only change that heralded a new era in the history of the college. When the government realized that there were not enough men to farm the land due to their military service requirement, they encouraged women to take on many farming roles but these women would need suitable training. The college, which had hitherto only welcomed male students, saw new short courses being created for this purpose. Great Britain required skilled labour in the fields and on farms and they needed it quickly. When you consider that there were 131 students enrolled for short courses in the 1916–17 period, it is interesting to note that 128 of them were women.

of Application	NAME.	Address.	Age	Date of Entr
	Bolingbroke M. A.	Count Rectory, Shrewsbury		april
	Bayliss E. M.	Woodcote, Himley	20	.
	Byrne J.	16 Bell Lane, Ludlow	17	»
	Carter E. M.	11, Poplar Avenue, Castlefields Shrewsbury.	20	
	Coggins. E.	28. Alexandria Rd. Handsworth Birmingham	20	
	Coombs, L. A.	20. Foregate Street, Worcester	18	
	Drewry, C. C.	Castle Hills, Folkingham. Lincolnshire	26	
	Fishwick D. V.	No1. Croft Cottage, Meole Brace	17	
	Furniss E.	1. St. John's Rd. Selly Park. Birmingham	23	
	Gormall S. E. C. (Mrs.)	Dale Stent, Craven Arms Salop	36	
	Halton E. C.	Broseley Hall, Shropshire	22	
	Haywood A. E.	39. Stirling Rd. Birmingham	30	
	Holdsworth L	Dormer Cottage, Meadow Rd. Cateshill, Bromsgrove	26	
	Hughes E.	36, Banyon Street, Castlefields Shrewsbury	17	
	Mc.Pherson			

Original women's short-course entries. *(HAAU)*

As early as 1915, the college governors had stated that courses for women in term-time could not be accommodated due to the layout of the college in terms of having both male and female students resident on site. A compromise was to hold courses during the Easter holiday. The Earl of Selbourne, President of the Board of Agriculture, asked the college to lay on two short courses for sixty women in basic agricultural skills. Harper Adams was the first college in the country to do this.

The courses not only helped to train women in periods of two weeks' duration, they also helped to relieve the farm labouring crisis and the impending food shortages. Their dedication to this alongside their hard work in the face of a changing and uncertain world and the impact of their input into the war effort cannot be overstated.

Once the women had completed their courses, they registered at the Labour Exchange and their services were soon snapped up. This happened at a time when many had scoffed at the idea of women being able to take on such work, which makes the college's efforts and achievements even more remarkable.

Many committees and forums were set up throughout the war in an attempt to co-ordinate the general effort but things were happening and changing at an incredible pace, resulting in confusion and disorganization.

Women undertaking training at a tractor demonstration, Harper Adams Agricultural College. *(HAAU)*

Things improved with the introduction of the Food Production Department (Women's Section) of the Board of Agriculture in 1917. This led to the formation of the Women's Land Army which gave rise to another of the college's accolades, that of being the first institution to have trained women who became the first so-called Land Girls, ninety-seven of whom trained at the college in 1917–18.

Mr Edward Jones, one of the prominent farmers in the area who we learned about in Chapter 4 and who had the first motorized tractor and a woman to drive it, employed three Land Girls. He said of them:

> Neither the soldiers or the girls could replace experienced labour – man for man – but we were pleased to have them and put up with the fact that their inexperience was costly and it took two to three to do what used to be expected from one previously... The land girls got more experienced during the summer and Miss Fenn tried her hand at riding the tractor plough and soon became expert.
>
> These three girls did good work and were very useful.

Mr Jones also had German prisoners of war working on the farm and when rumours reached him that the Land Girls had been becoming friendly with them they left the farm.

It was not until 1916 that due to increased demand and the college's growing reputation as a centre of expertise, particularly when it came to training women, the governors agreed to admit female students under the same terms as their male counterparts, alterations to the accommodation having been made.

The same year saw the introduction of conscription and yet more pressure was placed on the college. Not only would more staff now be forced to enlist, but the demand for farm labourers also intensified. This saw the introduction of courses in tractor-driving and regular demonstrations at the college showcasing the women's skills.

Not only did the college train women, but in 1915 they also had plans to do their bit to help disabled soldiers and sailors. Unfortunately there are no records to suggest that this happened, despite the Board of Agriculture's best intentions and willingness to see disabled servicemen settle on the land, another of the Earl of Selbourne's initiatives. It had been agreed by the governors, however, to reduce fees for ex-servicemen from Shropshire and Staffordshire. The college also held courses in poultry husbandry at the request of the War Pensions Committee in 1917. Some of the men, due to the nature and severity of their injuries, were unable to take this course, and this brought home the brutality of the conflict to the college.

The war opened up research into many things, one being medicines, and the use of plants with medicinal properties that could be used at the Front was being developed at Harper Adams. The biology department, in the capable hands of Mr Roebuck, collected such plants and dried them. The college was also involved in looking into the reclamation of wasteland for growing extra crops, and in preserving damsons at Springfield's Brewery, Newport.

The ever-increasing demand for timber saw the college branch out into forestry with the planting of conifers. The college's advisory service went from strength to strength as the war progressed and its reputation as one of the leading lights in the world of agricultural research and training was second to none. Their efforts were recognized and acknowledged by Secretary of the Board of Agriculture Sir Daniel Hill in his statement following the end of the war:

> There has been no occasion when the value of colleges has been more thoroughly proved than during the present war. There were many things which came within the purview of farmers, things which might be of considerable assistance when they encountered difficulties, and no institution has done more for the agriculturist than has been undertaken and carried out by Harper Adams College.

A meeting of the Newport Rural District Council in April 1916 saw a discussion on the subject of women working on the land. It was a public meeting with Miss Roddam present as well as a Miss Churton from the Women's National Land Service Corps, Edric Druce, County Agricultural Organizer, and Captain Foster.

The overriding feeling was that all women who were able to help should offer to do so. Some of those present already had women workers on their land. One of these men, Mr Lander, in an attempt to encourage women to come forward, remarked that one of the two women he employed was nearing her 70th birthday!

With courses being made available at the agricultural college, there was some disbelief that more women were not coming forward to take up the places. It was mentioned that some women at the college from Warwickshire and Shropshire were undertaking courses in poultry and dairy management and that a register would be compiled of the names of women wishing to work the land.

Some of the Agricultural College's instructors enlisted in the services, including clerical workers Mr C.S. Merchant, King Edward's Horses; Mr H. Hall, Montgomeryshire Yeomanry; and Second

Lieutenant J.C Urqubert joining the Colours. Also more than a dozen students who had been due to start courses had enlisted instead. This would have a severe knock-on effect on the finances and future of the college as its student numbers fell.

By the end of the war around 200 staff, students and ex-students had served, proving their commitment not only to fighting for king and country in the trenches, but also in raising the profile of agriculture and the importance of home-grown food and their momentous efforts in increasing food production, not only locally but nationally.

Chapter Eleven

'Be Prepared'

Although not involved in active service on the front line, even Baden Powell's Boy Scout movement answered the call to arms. A telegram from the Chief Scout was received by Lord Harlech requesting that they mobilize 1,000 Scouts. There were Scout troops in the Newport, Edgmond, Forton and Sambrook areas.

Scoutmasters up and down the county had informed the police and Post Office authorities of the names of Scouts who were available for duty. Locally, Mr Frank Boughey was prepared to provide accommodation for twenty-four Scouts for a month and farmers were asked to contact the scoutmasters should they need help bringing in the harvest.

Scouts were instructed to carry a notebook and pen at all times to note down any suspicious or unusual activity and to train their memories so that they came to know their communities and environment well. They were to take particular note of the location of water supplies, fire hydrants, fire alarms, doctors, vets, the Post Office and smithies, etc.

The Scouts were soon utilized to guard the telegraph and telephone wires connecting Chester to Hereford. Communication was a vital asset in wartime and it was essential that the channels were kept open; they were potentially at risk of sabotage which would have severely hindered the war effort. The line of poles followed Holyhead Road from Chirk through to Shrewsbury and south by way of Church Stretton, Craven Arms and Ludlow. This was a vital job that the Scouts were undertaking.

Articles in the local newspapers were carried detailing the extension to the Scouts' duties. They would also be helping the fire brigade, Post Office, police, ambulance service and poor relief distribution. Lord Harlech made it known that he had high expectations that every Scout in Shropshire would do his bit for the war effort. They certainly did this and more.

However, it wasn't just the Scouts who were a big help to the war effort; cadets were too. Local lad Cliff Teece was 13 years old and a student at Adams' Grammar School when war broke out and even at this tender age he was keen 'to become a worthy citizen in uniform'.

In his memoirs, he talks about his time in the KSLI Cadets: 'Soon we were all compelled to be trained for the ranks of the KSLI Cadets, and found ourselves kitted out in khaki uniform. There were no exceptions and our parents were obliged to meet the cost.'

Looking back on his time as a cadet, his opinion seems to have changed regarding the war:

Although, perhaps, we may have benefitted from the physical training, stern discipline, etc., the fact remains that in that pseudo-democratic war many boys were totally unsuited for any conflict.

In that period I saw much of the tyrannical, arrogant and dogmatic

trend at school which not only bred fear, distaste and discomfort –
it also created a hatred and loathing so intense that a boy's outlook
and future could be seriously affected.

Perhaps it also had this effect on some of the soldiers on the battlefield.
Here he recalls one of their training days:

> We entrained at Newport for a raid on... no, it wasn't Calais or
> Bordeaux, it was somewhere in a lovely spot near Wellington,
> Shropshire. Our platoon was equipped with Martini Henrys. The

Adams' Grammar School Cadet Corps, 1918. *(NHS)*

Commanding Officer was satisfied with just one Martini. Some of the boys were marching with wooden rifles.

We advanced to the vital position in readiness for the blistering attack on a bunch of Wellington kids who were soundly entrenched about half a mile away in a machine-gun nest. We were forced to make a great detour to the rear of the machine gun, which was a piece of 3" down pipe.

We sneaked up commando-fashion but might have overdone things a bit. We all had a filthy look on our faces. We carefully climbed the ivy-covered wall and peeped through the leaves trying to measure the distance and direction to the wooded area.

Steady now – this was zero hour coming up. The world stood still. Just as well. If anyone had coughed we'd have wet our pants.

We travelled a long way and we decided we must be very close. We moved slowly, crouched very low. Then we were crawling over the ground. We'd lost half the buttons off the tunics and the rest were all 'gobbed' up with grass and cow manure.

We crept quickly round a hedge and found ourselves in a vegetable garden. That was a surprise. We went round another hedge and found ourselves at the rear of a conservatory, and close to some palatial house! We carefully opened the door, moving closely with rifles at the ready.

'Eh! What the hell are you doing in here?'

We just froze. We were lucky indeed that our fingers were not on the triggers, and damned fortunate that we had no bullets either.

'We're trying to capture a machine-gun nest, Sir.'

'Well the battlefield's about a mile away. They've knocked off for lunch, then they're going to bury the dead. Now what are your names, and your school?'

It was all over. We were taken prisoner. Just as well there was no courtyard. We'd have all been shot!

The Scouts' and cadets' help on the home front up and down the country was invaluable, especially in the upkeep of some of the DORA regulations. They took their duties very seriously indeed, and the training they had had would help them should they themselves enlist in the future.

Chapter Twelve

Letters Home and the Role of Newspapers

'The truth, the whole truth and nothing but the truth.'

Headlines

Curiously, the majority of the war news, including the coverage when war broke out, never made the front pages of the provincial newspapers.

Perhaps the local papers at the time thought, quite rightly, that the things that really concerned the people of Newport and the villages around were agriculture, auctions and what was going on in their local rural community. The grumbles across the water had nothing to do with their town and would probably never affect them.

1915 British Expeditionary Force Christmas card.

However, this soon changed as the potential for war escalated. There were soon to be double-page spreads on pages 4, 5 or 6 of the paper, heralding the news of the conflict with headlines such as 'EUROPE ABLAZE' and 'Germans Repulsed by Belgium with Heavy Losses'. The reports even told the people of Newport that the scale of the war was 'monstrous' with 26 million combatants so far.

A Reminder of Home

Apart from receiving old newspapers, letters going to and from the front and other fighting positions were the only communications the soldiers had from home or elsewhere and so were very important to them. Their replies

From Fred
To Gert, wishing you a
very happy Christmas. XXX

P.S. I will write you a
letter later.
Fred

We're well on our way
In the Berlin Express,
The Bulldog – he's going it fine,
You can see by his Stride
And the Name on his hide,
He's a Winner, He'll break the Line.

W. HUNTER, Pte
1/2nd London Regt

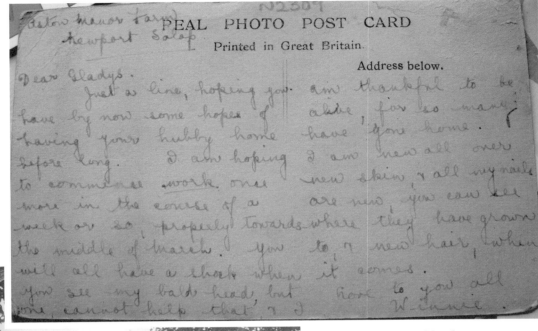

PEAL PHOTO POST CARD

Printed in Great Britain.

Address below.

Dear Gladys.

Just a line, hoping you am thankful to be
have by now some hopes of alive, for so many
having your hubby home have gone home.
before long. I am hoping I am new all over
to commence work once new skin, & all my nails
more in the course of a are new, you can see
week or so properly towards where they have grown
the middle of March. you to & new hair, when
will all have a shock when it comes.
you see my bald head, but love to you all
one cannot help that & I   W-innie.

**Postcard front and back,
'Winnie', Newport area.**
(NHS)

and reassurances that all
was well to their friends and
loved ones waiting at home
for news were equally
welcome.

During the conflict the
Post Office delivered over
2 billion letters and cards
and considering the state of
the battlefields, it's a
miracle that any post went
to and from the front at all.
Yet it did, and due to the
unprecedented demand
the postage charge was
increased from 1d to 1½d.

The newspapers reported the war and the lead-up to it with the attitude that the war had been 'forced upon us' as 'defenders of the weak' and the 'champions of the liberties of Europe'. The *NA* received many war-inspired poems but couldn't publish them due to the increased price and scarcity of paper which meant they had no room to print them.

Each issue also had a 'Letters to the Editor' section in which readers shared their views on the war and its progress. An extract from one such letter shows the writer urging Shropshire to set an example:

> I am absolutely certain that when our young men 'all round the Wrekin' understand that every man is wanted now, that they will come forward as one man to fight for the old flag with courage and confidence, and that the girls will send them off with a smile. Don't let us be second or third, but first in the field for the honour of Shropshire.

As the conflict progressed, the local papers carried blow-by-blow accounts of the various battles as they occurred, including details of wounded and killed soldiers and sailors, although these were not always accurate. One of their other functions, albeit perhaps not intentionally, was to publish items that told of the 'barbaric' actions of the Germans and the bravery, courage and good progress of the British forces and the allies. Local people would have been encouraged and felt some relief that the war seemed to be going in the allies' favour.

Other items included 'With the Shropshires in Wales', detailing what a good job they were doing in guarding Cardiff and Newport (Monmouthshire) dock areas; the 4th Shropshire's headquarters were near Barry Docks, one of the sources of the Royal Navy's coal supply.

The *WJSN* in its issue of 8 August spoke about how the war would affect the newspaper itself, primarily the problem with shipments of newspaper pulp leading to them considering 'curtailing to some extent the general amount of reading matter which it has been the effort of the Journal to supply'.

It seemed there was no area of British life that the war, either directly or indirectly, did not touch. However, the paper was eager to reassure its readers that they could still be trusted to provide the news. The local newspapers were a lifeline to local people and this reassurance would have gone some way towards easing their concerns.

Because the local papers only came out weekly on Saturdays, news about the war was often sketchy, contradictory and misleading or incorrect. The *Advertiser* had a board outside their offices in Newport where news was also posted which drew large crowds, clambering for much-desired information about how the war was progressing and how their loved ones were faring. Every telegram was read intently as soon as they were pinned up. The papers relied on the Press Bureau for its information and letters from soldiers on the front line and other areas of conflict for further updates. However, when censorship became obligatory in 1916, this information could not be relied on. In fact, due to some misconceptions, the following notice appeared: 'In such a time of excitement, all kinds of rumours have been current and some of them have not had the slightest foundation in fact. The Press Bureau will guarantee the items the press are having foisted upon it of so-called "war news" which are either false or misleading.'

The papers printed regularly-updated rolls of honour, giving details of those who had enlisted. As the war raged on, there also appeared quite candid accounts of the various battles that were going on. Alongside these – starting as a trickle but cascading into waterfalls as the war developed – were published details of the number of casualties (nationally), together with the names of local lads who had been wounded, were missing, killed in action or taken as prisoners of war. Such details were often vague and sometimes errors were made. In one edition of the paper there might be reports of a local lad killed, only to find in the next that he was actually a prisoner of war. Similarly, someone originally reported as missing would turn up in a later issue, then in a hospital wounded.

This must have made things extremely difficult for the families and friends left behind, waiting desperately for news of loved ones fighting overseas. However, when the only method of communication was by telegram and considering the huge scale of the war, not only logistically but geographically, it was a wonder that any news got through at all.

Keep Calm and Carry On

The newspapers – the lifeline for rural communities when it came to information about the war – even got in on the act by imploring their readers to enlist. The editor of the *NA* was evidently very keen for his readers to do their duty:

I don't believe at this crisis in giving way to panic and rushing about, making the worst of things, but I don't believe, ostrich-like, in burying one's head in the sand, and so thinking there is no serious danger ahead of us.

... The quicker it is over, the less loss of life and less national suffering will there be in the end. Therefore how imperative it is that all the young single, sound and able-bodied men, between 19 and 30, should join the colours.

The *WJSN* also carried items from the national newspapers which seemed to have the purpose of showing readers that they were not alone in what was happening to them as a town or village and that people's lives and livelihoods were being disrupted up and down the country and that there was some comfort and camaraderie to be had from that knowledge.

At the beginning of the war the headlines had been more buoyant, keen to encourage enlistment, reassure readers and increase patriotism:

'Brilliant Victory'

'Retreating Germans'

'Put the Enemy to Flight'

However, as the war progressed so did the papers' interest, with headlines also appearing to grow in both urgency and alarm:

'War of the Nations'

'Kaiser's All Round Defiance'

'Heroic Defence of Liege by Belgians'

'Heavy German Death Toll'

The newspapers of the time also reported on Germany's lack of food supplies and relished in the rumours that there would soon be rioting in the enemy's homeland; reports designed to show British people that if they thought they were having a hard time, the German citizens were faring no better.

The press was not the only source of information and entertainment. Wright's Picture House held regular showings of various films at the Town Hall including military films of the war as they became available. These included titles such as Britain's Honour or The Great European War.

A Tale of Two Christmases

The *NA* also passed comment on how the town and its people were faring as the war that should have been over by Christmas dragged on. Whereas before the war Christmas and New Year's Eve were celebratory in atmosphere, at the end of 1916 it was a very different story: 'The streets were completely deserted on Friday night and the usual characteristics of New Year's Eve were conspicuous by their absence. No Watch-Night Service was held and the church bells did not ring out their customary peal.'

We Regret to Inform You

More and more names were added to the roll of honour through the pages of the *NA* and letters often appeared, those received by grieving relatives of those who had fallen telling them the awful news. One such letter was about Sniper John Ruscoe, KSLI who was killed at the front on New Year's Day. His father resided at Heathill Lodge, Lilleshall:

> Dear Sir – I very much regret to inform you that your son was shot by a German sniper whilst carrying out his duty as a battalion sniper. He was killed immediately, being shot through the brain, and his body is being removed to Dickebusch for internment. He was a very nice man to work with, and a first class shot, and will be very difficult to replace …

John had enlisted on 14 September 1915, prior to which he worked on the Duke of Sutherland's estate as a gamekeeper.

For the people of Newport and the locality, reading something as blunt as this must have been difficult. From day to day the war for many people was far away but communications like this brought it a whole lot closer.

The papers were the mainstay of local people's lives, giving them important and much-needed information about the war and local life, including the reporting of storms and the threat of German Zeppelin attacks. There had been a close call when such an attack occurred just over the border in Staffordshire, but it wasn't just man-made disasters that they would be worried about. There were a fair few natural disasters too.

Distant Rumbles

One of the most notable of these happened in January 1916. An earthquake was felt across the Midlands including Newport where damage was reported across several areas of the town. The initial shock was felt at around 7.30pm and made the townspeople fear there had been a bomb dropped or that a munitions factory had exploded. The sound that followed resembled that of a Zeppelin, along with another lesser shock that saw bricks and chimney pots knocked into the road.

There was a commotion and panic as people ran out into the streets, fearing for their lives. Eye-witnesses who were situated at the corner of Upper Bar and Avenue Road said they had felt the ground move beneath them and that Mrs Webb's chimney pot had come down. Other reported damage was the falling of many chimney pots in St

Mary's Street, Wellington Road, Upper Bar and in the High Street.

Shirkers

The newspapers and the majority of their readership were fiercely patriotic and the papers often carried letters from disgruntled readers about those 'shirkers' who chose not to volunteer to fight:

> Sir – The papers are full of letters grumbling at a lack of patriotism among farmers who, the correspondents say, ought to enlist. Those people who have already sent husbands, or sons, or brothers to the army of course feel the position keenly, and we cannot wonder at their resentments, particularly in cases of their own locality. But we must not forget that agriculture is being terribly depleted of the active and dependable men. Enthusiastic but incompetent women and wounded soldiers are no substitute!
> Signed, Shropshire farmer.
> *Newport Advertiser*, 11 March 1916.

Defence of the Realm Act

It wasn't long before the Defence of the Realm Act began to affect reporting in the newspapers, particularly advertisements. The *NA* carried a notice about their situation vacant columns stating that they had to comply with section 8(b) of the Act, particularly in the fields of engineering, ship-building, production of arms, ammunition or explosives. These industries could not employ anyone who lived more than 10 miles from the place of work or were already involved in government work.

The paper also, from time to time, published interesting and quite telling statistics. One of these was the 1914 annual report of births, deaths and marriages which showed an increase in the marriage rates but a decrease in the birth rate. Could the increase in marriage rate have been due to the war, either through soldiers getting married before going off to war or in-between stints of battle, or those trying to avoid enlistment?

Just as it had been at the end of 1916, the newspaper reported that on New Year's Eve 1918, things were very quiet again in the town. There was 'nothing to distinguish New Year's Day from an ordinary day'. What with DORA restrictions, rationing and the ongoing bitter fighting overseas, people were not in the mood for a party, apart from carol concerts in aid of the various war charities.

The local newspapers then, as today, even in our world of the internet where information is just the click of a button away, kept their readers up-to-date with the national events that would impact on them. During the war years it was clear to see that they took this role seriously and for many in Newport the war would have been a lot more difficult to cope with without their weekly perusal of the paper.

Chapter Thirteen

Voluntary Aid Detachment

In the early weeks of the war people's thoughts turned to how wounded and sick soldiers would be cared for. A meeting was held in Shrewsbury to discuss how Shropshire may best be able to help the military with this.

The meeting was well supported by Shropshire residents of substance and influence where it was agreed that arrangements were to be made via the Voluntary Aid Detachments across the county, if the nation was to cope with the influx of wounded or sick servicemen.

Major C.R.B. Wingfield, the then mayor of Shrewsbury and officer of the 3rd KSLI was there and he was of the opinion that Shropshire people were only too aware of the gravity of what the world faced, yet they were more than prepared to do their bit for the war effort. Newport was no exception.

Committees, Committees and More Committees
Lord Powys also called a meeting to discuss how such a scheme should be organized, alongside how to deal with the relief of distress. He had the idea of forming a committee comprising himself, the High Sheriff, members of parliament, chairmen of the courts council and quarter sessions, mayors of all the borough, chairmen of the Rural and Urban District Councils, representatives of the Friendly Societies, the Victoria Nursing Association, Voluntary Aid Detachment and others to organize the schemes. Every town and parish would have a subcommittee and they would be responsible for finding out the level of need on their patch so that the relief funds and services could be fairly distributed.

Dr Cureton talked about the association's intentions of having both clearing and stationary hospitals. They were already well versed in improvising the ambulance trains and already had plenty of rest stations. What they needed were more buildings that could be adapted for use as auxiliary hospitals for convalescent men.

Mr Bridgman replied that a small committee met with the intention of forming a committee in the county for the Voluntary Aid Detachment and had found to their delight that there were many people coming forward offering their help. A central committee would be responsible for organizing such offers and where they might best be used.

The Red Cross

In Lilleshall a Red Cross Association was formed with the Duchess of Sutherland as president. Many influential members of the parish had pledged their support at the meeting held at the Institute and donations were already flooding in. Many other offers from people willing to work from home making garments, etc., were also received. Any garments made would be sent to Dunrobin Castle – the seat of the Sutherlands, in the Scottish Highlands overlooking the Moray Firth – which had been offered to the War Office as an auxiliary hospital.

Two of the major organizations involved in the war effort both at home and abroad were the British Red Cross and the Order of St John. They formed the Joint War Committee soon after the conflict began, its main role being to help wounded and sick soldiers and sailors.

The War Committee was responsible for organizing its many volunteers, including professionals, into Voluntary Aid Detachments. These detachments provided many different services throughout the war including the supply of machinery and services across the conflict zones and at home.

One of its major contributions came via fund-raising, making garments for wounded soldiers and sailors, and the people of Newport and the surrounding area threw themselves into this with enthusiasm.

By the end of the war the total amount raised by the War Committee was £21,885,035 with £20,058,355 spent on hospitals, clothing, grants, medicine and the aftercare of the sick and wounded.

All the VADs had basic first-aid training with some of them receiving more in-depth nursing training. Apart from their nursing duties, they also made items for the hospitals including swabs, clothing, bandages and splints. There were central workrooms in various towns up and down the country, usually set up by local prominent and influential townswomen who would also donate money to buy materials, etc., for the volunteer garment-makers to use.

The War Office needed hospitals to house and care for convalescent soldiers and sailors, and local manor houses and stately homes were the obvious choice. Many owners of such houses were only too glad to turn part of their homes into auxiliary hospitals, thereby making a significant contribution to the war effort.

In March 1917 County Director Mr W. Swire of Longden Manor asked the Hon. Mrs Leeke and Mrs Sykes to work towards getting a

Longford Hall VAD hospital. *(Allan Frost)*

VAD hospital for the Newport area. The people of Newport were quick to respond and a portion of the east wing of Longford Hall was given for that purpose, subject to War Office approval.

Mrs Leeke was to become commandant and Miss Burton acted as matron. They had the accommodation and could secure the staff, but they would need to raise money for equipment and supplies not covered by the War Office's allowances.

At a later meeting, due to the fact that there were no houses in Newport that could be adapted for use as a convalescent hospital for wounded soldiers, it was decided that Longford Hall with its 'good, airy rooms' should be inspected by the military authorities and it was deemed acceptable.

There would be a cost of 3s 6d per head with bedding to be provided by the government. Mrs Leeke decided to pay Lady Mabel-Slaney in Hatton as she had run a similar hospital for two years. She agreed with the costs allowed but there would have to be additional funds found for other needs to the tune of £150 to £200 a year. Requests were put out for regular local subscriptions to help cover this expense. The local community was also encouraged to send in vegetables, etc., to assist on the catering side.

Longford Hall with doctors, nurses and convalescent servicemen. *(NHS)*

They didn't let the hospital down. Soon gifts came flooding in. Examples were a gramophone, records, eggs, newspapers, cheese, potatoes, tobacco and cigarettes. A request was even put out for cricket balls. The hospital opened in late May 2017 and within a week was full with twenty-five wounded soldiers in residence.

The valuable contribution made by the owners of such houses to the war effort cannot be underestimated. Without them, the military hospitals and local hospitals would have been inundated and soon overwhelmed. It's possible that many more men would have died had the Red Cross and Order of St John not been so organized. Imagine what it must have been like for these young wounded and sick servicemen, some of whom would have come from more urban environments, to leave the bloody and noisy battlefields and suddenly find themselves in the quiet rural surroundings of Shropshire. Many of them would not even have seen the countryside before, let alone spent any length of time there. They most certainly would not have been used to the grand surroundings of some of the private houses used as auxiliary hospitals where the driveways alone would have seemed like a mile of country lane and the ornate buildings must have been most imposing.

By the end of the war 90,000 Red Cross and Order of St John volunteers had helped tend to wounded servicemen.

The Red Cross was fundamental in helping the war effort in many ways and was certainly very active in Newport and the surrounding area. A Red Cross depot was established at Chetwynd Bank for Newport and Chetwynd where they were allowed to use a room. There were to be articles ready for sewing left there between 2pm to 4pm every Thursday afternoon.

The Newport area was awash with fund-raising initiatives such as sales, whist drives and concerts, too many to mention here, but the *NA* carried a report on the VAD in Shropshire in their 8 April 1915 issue. It heralded the good effort that Shropshire as a whole was making in tending to wounded and sick soldiers and stated that there had been an impressive 1,544 patients through the various auxiliary hospitals with only six recorded deaths. Since November 1915, 7,285 bandages, 22,550 swabs, 959 splints, 310 pressure pads, 50 stretcher cushions, 90 knitted face-washers, 16 pneumonia jackets, 274 pairs of slippers, 31 frostbite boots, 40 carbolized shirts, 3 bed tables and 5 jigsaw puzzles had been sent; a grand total of 31,613 items. The VAD and those in the community helping them meant business.

The local grammar school boys also helped to entertain the wounded soldiers at Longford Hall by inviting them to watch their cricket matches and have tea with them on the field. They also played against each other, and the boys were gracious losers.

The hall was eventually purchased by Adams' Grammar School for use as a boarding-house, being located approximately a mile from the main school buildings. In 2000 part of the grounds was sold off for private housing.

Chapter Fourteen

It's Just Not Cricket

Before the war, Newport was alive with various sports societies and sports fixtures. In football, for instance, the *NA* played Priorslee on 4 January 1913 and Horsehay Albion on 25 January. Even the KSLI had teams that played locally as well.

Hunting was also a treasured sport, although it was reported in the *WJSN* of 4 January 1913 that as the hounds passed nearby Newport, a yearling colt belonging to Mr W. Jones of the Flatt Farm became excited and fell and broke its neck. How many horses from the hunt would be commandeered by the army during the war years for military use? The huntsmen wouldn't have to wait long to find out.

Only a month before war was declared, an advert appeared in the *WJSN* of 4 July 1914 for a boxing match at the Newport Horticultural Show, stating that it was 'open for competitors residing within 12 miles

Newport Football Club, 1914. *(NHS)*

of Newport Parish Church, and scaling ten stone or over'. The first prize was to be £3 and the second prize £1.

Most people in Newport tried to carry on with their lives as normal and it was a case of business as usual with regard to many of aspects of life when war broke out. This was especially so in the field of sport. Many fixtures and games continued, except for a boxing match in Newport that was postponed 'owing to the national crisis'. Otherwise, the sporting life carried on pretty much as usual with fixtures for cricket matches going ahead. One such match was Lilleshall v Cheswardine.

There was, however, pressure from certain quarters to stop these public events. With a war on, some people felt it was disrespectful, frivolous even, for those at home to be having fun and carrying on as though nothing was wrong when there were men dying and suffering on the battlefields, as this extract from the local paper shows: 'We see strong men in our cricket fields and tennis courts...' Local newspapers were angered by certain very able-bodied, fit young men not enlisting, seemingly preferring to stay at home and play sport rather than enlist.

There was much confusion and argument. In Chetwynd Aston the potato show was well attended. In Newport, however, the annual ploughing competition of 1914 was cancelled with an agreement to donate £5 to the Prince of Wales' Relief Fund instead.

Very often the local newspaper would have a dig at some sectors of the townspeople who they felt were not doing as much for the war effort as they ought to be. One example of this came in the editorial of September 1914:

> It is our purpose during the continuance of the war to give only the briefest items of sporting and athletic news. We feel sure our readers will agree with us; in this momentous crisis in the history of our country we should devote our space only to those things that matter, and those ordinarily engaged on the playing fields will be better employed in serving their country.

Some sports teams were forced to abandon their fixtures and training due to the enlistment of several of their members. This was certainly true of Edgmond football club in the 1914 season.

There was even the suggestion that sportsmen could do more to help the war effort at home if they weren't prepared to fight. A reader of the *NA*, F.M. Roberts, in response to Lord Robert's appeal to sportsmen who could not go onto the field to supply field glasses to non-commissioned officers at the front stated that the uptake had been good. The appeal had raised 2,000 such glasses in just three days; an example of how

Newport United, 1900–06. *(NHS)*

sportsmen supported the war effort.

The war was bad enough at home, what with DORA restrictions and rationing, and many saw keeping the old traditions such as sporting fixtures and agricultural shows going as demonstrating their patriotism and keeping the home fires burning for the returning soldiers. A little bit of light relief did the war charities no harm either as the proceeds from these shows and sporting fixtures were often donated to charity.

It wasn't just sport, the cinema and agricultural shows that stirred emotions either. An interesting incident occurred in Newport at the end of November 1918 which, if it hadn't been a known fact that the war was effectively over and it was a British plane – a Sopwith Camel – could have been seen as an attempted attack on the town by enemy aircraft. The plane, piloted by Lieutenant Walter Keight and a colleague, misfired and came down in the grammar school's cricket field, Audley Avenue. He tried to get airborne again but had not enough clearance and consequently hopped over a hedge that bordered the garden of the workhouse. The plane was damaged but luckily neither airman was hurt. A guard was then placed to keep the intrigued townspeople and visitors away.

Chapter Fifteen

Crime, Punishment and Tribunals

Newport had its fair share of crime. Even in wartime, people were being seen in the local police courts. Newport held its own police court, which would see greater usage in the war years following the introduction of conscription.

Not all the local citizens' thoughts were benevolent or patriotic. As reported in the 22 August issue of the *WJSN*, Newport man Samuel Gater was charged with stealing a fowl and was remanded to the petty sessions.

This crime, along with others, was viewed by the majority as a disgrace at a time when the country was fighting for its very survival. This was especially so if the culprit was eligible to fight but had chosen to stay at home and commit crimes. Yet on the other hand, Newport did have a high proportion of poor who may have had little choice but to steal food if they wanted to feed themselves and their families. With the focus of relief shifting from the workhouse and the poor of Newport to the dependants of servicemen who had gone to war, resources and finances were being severely stretched.

One man was even accused of using 'German tactics'. Traveller Henry Crabtree faced a charge of doing 'wilful damage' to The Swan at Newport, as well as attacking the owner. He allegedly hit him with a stick and a broken gas bracket and globe. The traveller worked for a German company based in London but since the start of the war the firm had found itself with no business and so changed its name, presumably thinking that something more anglicized would help it to regain customers. The man was fined £2, including costs and thirty shillings for the assault.

Fighting Germans, Austrians and Drink

With the bleakness of war and financial hardship, it was no wonder that many people turned to drink. The courts were full of men and some women who were charged with being drunk and disorderly, often including violence or damage to property.

In September 1914, local labourer Arthur Worrell was charged with being drunk. On 26 August he had been examined by local physician Dr Elkington who found him lying drunk in the road, claiming to have been run over by a car but apparently uninjured. Worrell was ordered to pay costs of 5 shillings.

Alcohol consumption was becoming a real problem in Britain. In 1914 there were almost 184,000 convictions for drunkenness. This fell to around 84,000 in 1916 and again to 29,000 in 1918. The government and the military were concerned that heavy drinking was adversely affecting the war effort. To counteract this, they reduced both public house opening hours and beer production, making the latter weaker as well.

William Tranter and Samuel Evans of no fixed abode were found drunk in Marsh Road, lying in a manger in a local farmer's shed. They were sentenced to seven days' hard labour for their conduct. Such cases must have infuriated local residents whose sons were away fighting the war while others were rolling around drunk, causing damage and violence at home, especially if they were men of military service age who were able to fight but chose to drink instead. Even if they were unable or too old to fight, the townspeople must have wondered why they were causing a nuisance and finding solace in the bottom of a bottle rather than working towards the war effort on the home front.

Readers of the *NA* were quick to state their disgust at people's drunkenness in the pages of the paper. One reader pointed out that the annual national drink bill in 1915 was £181,959,000 or £3 19s 11d per head in the UK. In a time of austerity when people were being told to reduce waste and undue expenditure, the reader was perplexed by people who still chose to waste money on drink when it could be put to better use by, for example, buying war bonds:

> Whatever we may be able to afford, in the piping times of peace, we cannot afford this waste in times of war. All loyal citizens, loyal to King and Country, are thankful for the curtailment of drinking facilities that has taken place during the war.
>
> … My object in writing this letter is to urge every reader of your paper to abstain himself from drink … and to induce others to do the same.

Edward B. Benson, *NA*, 22 April 1916.

An ex-soldier who had been discharged also found himself in the police court in July 1916, having been found drunk and disorderly on 8 July. The local townspeople and police were sympathetic to Frederick Simpson's plight, he having been wounded; however, he had been warned many times about his drunkenness and offensive behaviour.

Despite the judge's awareness of his troubles, he was still fined 7s 6d including costs.

The Trouble with Tribunals

Soon the courts would be turning their attention to tribunals where applicants could appeal against being called up and attempt to gain some level of exemption. Colonel Leeke attended the tribunals, which must have been difficult as he had lost two sons in the war. Hearing about men trying to avoid enlistment, especially those with no legitimate reason, must have seriously rankled with him.

Tribunals were often disorganized, inconsistent and contradictory, leaving many confused and angry at the outcomes. Unfortunately appeals were no better. Tribunals took place regularly, both in Newport Rural and Newport Urban, and they also met to go over appeals. At one session a father applied for his son's exemption, stating him to be 'indispensable' on the farm. His son had already served two years in the Yeomanry but had been discharged. The tribunal was not sympathetic to the farmer's cause, insisting that he should try to find a replacement for the son. The farmer was incensed as he already had another son in military service and was reluctant to send his remaining son when others around him had managed, somehow, to cling on to theirs. He was allowed a reprieve for three months.

At the same tribunal an elderly man was seeking exemption for his son who helped him out in their smallholding, claiming he could not afford to pay anyone else to take his place. His son was also employed elsewhere, helping on the smallholding whenever he could. This application was refused, whereas two local blacksmiths working at a local colliery tending to the horses' shoes were granted three months exemption.

As the death toll continued to rise sharply, a revised list of reserved occupations was introduced. This would see a flood of appeals and applications, often overwhelming the tribunals. Exemptions were becoming increasingly limited to men of responsibility and experience in firms, such as managers etc., and to married men over the age of 30. All single men who had not already signed up would be called up.

One grocery merchant who applied for the exemption of some of his remaining members of staff pointed out that 20 of them had already enlisted with 8 more leaving shortly; that would be 28 out of a total of 38. A deferment of three months was granted.

Another applicant who ran a pig farm claimed that he would have to kill the pigs if his worker had to enlist. His application was refused. A postman who claimed he had to support his father and his wife (he had married since registration) also had his application for exemption refused.

There was also plenty of room for accusations of foul play. One applicant, a draper applying for the exemption of a manager, had his case postponed for three months. It was noted that the applicant just so happened to be a member of the advisory committee and that the case was heard by the military where the applicant played no part in it. This caused one of the tribunal members to say: 'I enter my protest against that. I did not agree with it, not for a single day.'

Disagreements and controversy were commonplace at these tribunals. One particular protest came from the Shrewsbury Advisory Committee regarding the appointment of paid army officers representing the Chief Recruiting Officer at appeals tribunals. Lord Derby himself replied, stating that the appointment was more economical and efficient, but it wasn't a popular decision.

So concerned was the War Office about the state of some tribunals and how they were managed, especially the conduct of some of the military representatives, that they made the bold statement that they were 'battling with stupidity' because the representatives did not always do as instructed by the War Office.

Can't Do Right For Doing Wrong

Tribunals aside, other cases continued to crop up. In the courts, damaging or stealing food was seen as sacrilege and counter to the war effort, as three young boys found out in the children's court of August 1918. They were charged with stealing eggs and pulling carrots out of the ground. The 9-year-old was sent to an industrial school and his mother would have to pay the costs; the 5-year-old was let off; the 7-year-old was birched and the parents paid costs.

A cattle dealer and butcher also found himself in trouble at the Police Court in the same month. William Hesbrook bought an animal for slaughter but not from a market, and it was thought this could put consumers at risk of eating tuberculosis-infected meat. He was fined £5 including costs.

Another food-related misdemeanour came from a quartet of local lads, William Reece, Harry Jones, Harold and William Carr, who stole apples from a garden in Lilleshall. They were fined 15s each plus costs.

It seems incredible that despite the fact the country was engaged in the worst war in history, it still didn't stop opportunist criminals from operating. What they hadn't bargained for, however, was the patriotism and sense of justice of the local courts. The miscreants were often dealt with severely. After all, there was a war on and anyone who was not toeing the line and doing their duty was looked down upon.

Even on the Western Front crimes were being committed and soldiers were executed for desertion. One Newport man who was reportedly involved in such a case just two months before he died in battle aged 35 was James Lawton, a blacksmith's son. In March 1915 Private Isaac Reid, aged 20, of the Scots Guards was charged with desertion and Lawton's testimony saw him found guilty and shot. Lawton was ostracized by his fellow men for what they saw as his part in Reid's death.

By the end of the war there had been 306 such executions of British and Commonwealth servicemen for the crimes of cowardice or desertion. Nowadays, many of them would be recognized as suffering from shellshock.

Chapter Sixteen

The Role of Religion

Newport was fortunate in being served by a wide range of churches around the time of the Great War. There was St Nicholas's Church in the High Street, a Roman Catholic Church which would come into its own for the Belgian refugees, a Wesleyan Church, a Non-conformist and a Primitive Methodist church. Religion played an important part in the lives of the people of Newport and the surrounding villages, both in a pastoral and charitable sense. Religion was the glue that stuck the community together and gave them guidance in their everyday lives, something they would need to lean on more heavily when the true horrors of war were realized.

Before the war, Newport had a visit from the Diocesan Inspector J.R. Pyle who held his annual examinations of religious knowledge of those children who attended the local Church of England school and his findings were pleasing: 'Work has been carefully ordered and instruction given with the earnest purpose of furnishing the children with useful and practical religious knowledge. The girls show more intelligence and interest than the boys.'

There were also regular organ recitals which would continue through

St Nicholas Church in Church Square, 1900s. *(Allan Frost)*

the war years. A new organ, built by Messrs Nicholson and the Lord of Walsall, was installed in the Newport Congregational Church where they had such a recital, playing All People That on Earth do Dwell on the old organ, followed by a recital on the new organ by Mrs T. Johnson.

At the Primitive Methodist Church an annual treat and prize distribution in connection with the Sunday school took place, at which they had tea and a chapel service with music in the evening.

Father Christmas even made an appearance at Foresters Hall and made 200 children very happy: 'Hearty cheers were given for Miss Roddam and all the ladies present.' Even the elderly were not left out of community activities and the annual Old Folks' Treat was held in the Town Hall where 140 guests were treated to a dinner of roast beef and plum pudding. They sang songs and had a cinematograph exhibition.

The church did much relief work and fund-raising for the poor before and during the war. Evidence of this is to be found in the minutes of the Newport Branch of the Lichfield Diocesan Church Mission subcommittee meeting for Preventative and Rescue Work, which was held in the parish church room. Miss Roddam, who had her finger in many relief work pies, presided at this meeting.

A new nurse was required and Ada Cragg, recommended by Miss Roddam, was appointed after an 'endless' search; she would be lodging at 20 Avenue Road. Foster mothers were also much in demand and this cost Newport dearly, although Miss Roddam described it as a 'very valuable part of our work'.

Conscientious Objectors

The Quakers, of which there were some in the town of Newport, were pacifists who did not agree with war and so campaigned for peace but, in a minority of cases within the Quaker movement, their desire for peace was overridden by a sense of duty and patriotism. This caused immense dispute and conflict. However, as a Quaker wishes to save lives, many of those who answered the call to service took up non-combatant roles such as in the ambulance corps.

The conscience of such people would have been torn between observing their faith and belief in pacifism and reconciling this with society's expectations and their own patriotic wish to do their duty. Yet nationally, 33 per cent of all Quakers of fighting age did enlist.

Conscientious objectors caused much division within their communities. Some people saw them as shirkers who were dodging their responsibilities and the 'white feather campaign' soon made its way onto

War badge. *(Stanley Williams)*

the streets of Newport. If a man of enlistment age was seen wandering the streets, he was often presented with a white feather to show the giver's grievance that they were not away fighting for their country. Some – those who had been invalided out of the army, were on leave, or had some other valid reason for not being at war – were mistaken for dissenters. This led to a 'war badge' being issued to such people to show that they had done or were doing their duty for king and country.

A letter was published in the *NA* in the 15 August issue from the Religious Society of Friends (Quakers), giving readers their take on the war and enlistment:

> To men and women of goodwill in the British Empire.
>
> We recognise that our Government has made most strenuous efforts to preserve peace, and has entered into the war under a grave sense of duty to a smaller state towards which we had moral treaty obligations. While, as a Society, we stand firmly to the belief that the method of force is no solution of any question, we hold that the present moment is not one for criticism, but for devoted service to our nation.

In Newport, as was the case nationally, the overriding feeling and attitude towards the war from religious quarters was one of patriotism and support. They may have advocated peace and disagreed with violence and war, but that didn't prevent them from organizing things on the home front such as giving up church halls and space to fund-raising activities to aid the dependants of soldiers and sailors involved in the conflict. They provided much-needed comfort and support to mothers who lost sons, and to their parishioners the clergy was the glue that kept the community together during this time of great crisis and change.

The war proved to be difficult, ideologically, for all those with religious dispositions and those who opposed fighting and were striving for peace without resorting to war. Some were ridiculed and made out to be cowards for their pacifism, while others from the various churches who did fight were seen as heroic in fighting a just and necessary war that had to be fought in order to rid the world of tyranny and barbarism. They were fighting for the very ideals of Christianity.

Members of the clergy also went to war, albeit in a chaplaincy role, and many of them took up non-combative roles in the fighting zones, for instance serving in the ambulance corps.

The Right Reverend Dr Singleton, Bishop of Shrewsbury, issued a letter to all the clergy in his diocese calling on them to make collections in their churches and chapels in aid of the National Relief Fund. He also addressed a letter to the laity of the diocese asking them to pray for those affected by war and those who had relatives fighting overseas.

The Roman Catholic Church, as with many churches of other denominations in the town, were quick to rally round with their collection plates, seeking and obtaining donations to the various war charities that had sprung up. As well as trying to help the local community as a whole and help ease the financial burden on those left struggling because their sole provider had been lost to the conflict, they also had an important role in spiritually, psychologically and socially supporting their parishioners.

Wartime not only brought about great distress and uneasiness across the town, but it also was a time of great social and economic change. There were harsh winters with more to come and all the hardships those brought with them. Newport had more than its fair share of social and vagrancy issues, including the workhouse. Therefore the church saw that it had a great moral responsibility to help the poor, while still attempting to maintain the churches and other associated buildings, pay for their lighting and heating and other ministrations.

When the war came, another burden landed at the church door; one they could well have done without. Finances and services were being stretched further and further and something had to give as they couldn't afford to cater for all, the need was just too great. So out went all but the most urgent of church building repairs. The donation plates from the Sunday congregations grew lighter as the war went on and began to bite harder in people's pockets. Consequently, there was less to give to the poor. Everyone's prayers for a swift and peaceful end to the conflict would go unanswered for longer than any of the townspeople could possibly have anticipated.

Immediately after it was announced that Great Britain and the Empire were to engage in the war, all denominations of churches in Newport and the surrounding villages were busily organizing financial aid for soldiers, sailors and their dependants who would be left behind. A collection at the Parish Church of St Nicholas in Newport raised £21 7s 9d and the Wesleyan Church raised £1 18s 1d. The following Sunday both the Roman Catholic Church and the Primitive Methodist Church were having collections in aid of the Prince of Wales' Fund, something that would be a regular occurrence but often to the detriment of the churches' own maintenance and upkeep. They couldn't pay for everything.

In May 1917 Newport received a visit from the Bishop of Lichfield, the Right Reverend Dr Kempthorne, as part of the National Mission of Repentance and Hope. In his address he said that the nation was 'passing through the greatest crisis in the history of the country'. It was suggested that the church needed to rethink where they thought they were and where they wanted to be.

It was generally acknowledged that the beautiful surroundings of Newport and district were deceptive in making it harder to visualize and appreciate what was really happening on the battlefields. The question was raised whether Great Britain was 'turning back to God'. This had particular resonance as it was becoming obvious that the war would greatly change life as they knew it and even after the conflict ended there would be obstacles to overcome. The bishop was keen to see the church take action now and not wait for the conclusion of the war.

Locally, the clergy did a great deal for the war effort on the home front. In March 1917, in response to the local War Agricultural Committee's request for help with cultivating local gardens, the Reverend Dan Philipps and some of the Boys' Brigade were keen to help dig the gardens of those servicemen who were away on active duty. They were known locally as 'the Spade Brigade'.

Chapter Seventeen

The End of the War

'Let unity do for peace what unity has done for the war.'

The end of the war couldn't come soon enough for the people of Newport. However, the general relief and joy was tinged with a great sense of loss as many of their lives had been changed irrevocably.

Even before the Armistice was signed, thoughts were turning to what would happen to the soldiers and sailors returning home. It was acknowledged that the country had suffered a severe loss of life, creating a shortfall in labour. However, not all the servicemen would remain in the armed forces and part of the plan was to engage them in farming to help in increasing the production of home-grown food.

Changes that had happened at a national level would have a big impact on Newport in the years following the war. Millions of people worldwide had been affected by the Great War and a conflict of such ferocity and magnitude was bound to leave a legacy. There were still the poor, the sick and the disabled to be cared for. There were also thousands of women and children left without a husband, son or father. Many families did not just suffer the loss of one of their members; often two or more sons had been lost, leaving estates with no heirs to run them. There were also many servicemen still out on the battlefields, yet to be demobilized.

It wasn't just the practicalities and logistics involved that were causing concerns. In 1917, 70 per cent of the British Gross National Product was spent on the war. The total cost of the conflict from start to finish is estimated at $208 billion. It would take some considerable time for the economy to recover and debts to be paid.

Although there was relief that no more lives would be lost on the battlefields, there would be many men returning home who had been wounded or disabled. They would live out the rest of their lives physically and mentally scarred. For some men, in many ways, their personal battle was just beginning.

Changes didn't just affect the men. Women who had bravely and willingly stepped up and taken on many of the jobs the men had left to go to war now found themselves having to take a back seat as the men returned to their posts.

Disabled servicemen who had been medically discharged from the forces found themselves back home without the ability to return to their old jobs and unable to secure new jobs because of their disability. Far from being the war heroes that they were, they seemed to be more of a burden on their local communities and the government. What would the powers that be, which had so urgently and robustly campaigned to get these men to enlist and start fighting, do to help those who had survived but could no longer care for their family or themselves financially or practically?

The end of the war brought about a tumult of emotions and difficult situations. On the one hand, the Armistice was a tremendous relief and blessing. On the other, for all the problems solved by the conflict, its conclusion created fresh ones. The world found itself in an economic crisis, unemployment was high and resources were scarce, resulting in escalating prices. There had been some hard winters during the Great War, with wet springs and summers affecting the harvests. Life would not become any easier for a good few years yet.

Fighting a New Enemy
Just as the end of the war was in sight, a new enemy materialized: the Spanish flu pandemic which infected vast numbers of people and claimed a great many lives. The estimated number of dead in the UK from this virus was 228,000. It was a global catastrophe with a worldwide estimated death toll of at least 50 million, causing more fatalities than the Great War itself.

It was thought that men returning from the trenches of France who had been suffering from symptoms of 'la grippe' brought the virus back from their overcrowded and insanitary living conditions. It was highly contagious and spread like wildfire. Its effects could also be dramatic: someone who seemed fit and well in the morning and displaying no symptoms could be dead by the same evening, so rapid was its progression. Unusually for flu, the Spanish variant most affected those aged 20 to 30, so the young soldiers who had survived the war but were injured stood little chance against it.

Children across the country could be heard singing a new nursery rhyme:

I had a little bird
Its name was Enza
I opened the window
And in-flu-Enza

The already depleted national resources and finances couldn't cope with an epidemic on this scale. The war, lack of good-quality food, rationing, poor health care and a lack of advancement in medicine meant that people's immune systems were not robust and therefore they succumbed all too easily to this dreadful illness.

In an attempt to inhibit the spread of influenza many public buildings were closed for months including churches, halls and picture houses. People were given advice on how to try to prevent themselves from catching it, such as daily washing of the nasal passages, avoidance of wearing mufflers, making themselves sneeze several times a day and walking home from work in the fresh air rather than using crowded public transport.

The epidemic spread throughout Newport in late October 1918 and Adams' Grammar School was closed between 1 and 25 November due to the outbreak. Half the population of school pupils in the area succumbed, with hundreds of cases reported throughout the town and several deaths out in more rural areas.

Positive Thinking

However, things weren't all negative. The war had given rise to new innovations, new ideas from the government and policy-makers that would have a long-standing beneficial effect on the country. New pension laws, for instance, were introduced to help those servicemen who had been injured in the war and those who retired to ease the financial difficulties for them and their families. New farming and agricultural methods and research born during the war stayed with the country and developed exponentially.

Medical advances in the treatment of wounds of servicemen in the trenches had a lasting effect on the health of the nation following the war years. This was especially apparent in innovations in artificial limbs for amputees and plastic surgery for the many men who returned home with facial disfigurements.

Sanctions

Politically, the government was already working with the allies to impose sanctions on the enemy, with treaties being signed in an attempt to ensure lasting peace and that this would be the war to end all wars. The world had taken a battering and no one was keen to see it happen again. Britain was certainly at breaking-point and peace was all-important for her recovery.

As ever, the *NA* kept the locals informed of developments and what was happening in the post-war days, weeks and months. In the 9 November 1918 edition of the *NA* it was reported: 'Austria-Hungary has surrendered. Telephone message from PM in Paris. General Diaz the Italian Commander in Chief signed an armistice on Sunday afternoon which took effect at 3 o'clock on Monday.'

Life Goes On

Life following the war was not easy. Mothers who had lost sons, wives who had lost husbands, children who had lost fathers and sisters who had lost brothers would see ex-servicemen walking the streets of Newport and wonder why they had survived and their family members hadn't. It can't have been easy for the ex-servicemen either as they tried to come to terms with the loss of their own family members, friends and work colleagues and settle back into civilian life.

One of the old boys who survived the war – Harry Brotherhood, son of Mr A.C. Brotherhood of Wellington Road, Newport who had fought in the war with the Grenadier Guards – presented his drum, which had accompanied him throughout his three years' service, to the Prince of Wales at Buckingham Palace. The prince paid £100 for the drum and kept it as a souvenir.

In the *Novaportan* issue of May 1919 the editorial showed the strength of feeling at the school regarding news of the end of the war:

> This is a momentous issue of the school magazine. For the first time for more than four years there is relief from the nightmare of war, and although the final peace has not yet been signed, we are no longer in suspense for those of our Old Boys who are in the forces.

The signing of the Armistice on 11 November 1918 was celebrated throughout the school in the style instructed by the king, marked by three minutes' silence. The boys gathered in the large school room where the headmaster gave an address and prayers were said.

Peace Day

On Saturday, 19 July 1919 the whole country held Peace Day celebrations. Peace Day was a national initiative. It was at first envisaged that this would be a four-day celebration but it was reduced to one day. Not everyone thought the former was appropriate and that the effort and money involved would be of more use in building up resources and facilities to help returning servicemen who had problems with unemployment and injuries, both physical and mental.

Nevertheless, the town of Newport and the pupils and staff of Adams' Grammar School were heartily relieved and joined in the Peace Day celebrations with relish. The schoolboys built ships and aeroplanes for the local parade, a fancy dress carnival and peace pageant.

One of the major institutions to throw itself into the spirit of the day was again Adams' Grammar School. Having lost some of its old boys, there was a determination to spend the day in a spirit of courage and thankfulness in honour of those who had died. Another incentive was the town's authorities giving prizes for the best fancy dress and tableau among other prizes, the tableau being the 'plum' prize they were keen to win. There were reports of 'strenuous ship and aeroplane building' in the school and they were pleased with their tableau entry.

'Nothing was neater or more appropriate for the occasion than the happily conceived "Big Four" from the Grammar school.' The *Novaportan* reported four of the smallest boys, wearing top hats and black coats, being dressed up as the 'Big Four', those men 'who had had the destinies of the world in their hands'. They were drawn around the town seated in a cart drawn by other boys dressed as the allies. There was even a boy dressed as Lloyd George. Other boys were dressed as Red Indians, complete with a wigwam and 'smoking' their peace pipes. Another boy took his fancy dress role very seriously as a policeman. He tried to do his duty in upholding the law in a 'boisterous and threatening manner'. There was also a star-spangled 'Uncle Sam' to add to the affray!

As the weather in the evening was wet after a fine day, they left the other planned events until the Monday. In the grammar school the clock tower was adorned with fairy lamps and fireworks were lit. Later that evening the boys were allowed to attend the town's rockets and flares display over on the cricket ground. 'A pleasant and light-hearted time' was afforded to all; a much-needed letting off of steam and an overwhelming sense of relief that the war was finally over … at least for about twenty years.

The war itself, the repayment of government borrowings and the rebuilding that took place following the end of the conflict took a huge toll on all nations involved. The part played by local communities was tremendous and recovery would not have been so rapid without their help. However, patriotism and doing one's duty did not simply dissipate with the sound of the last guns fired in anger. Now people's thoughts turned to providing more permanent memorials to the war dead.

Chapter Eighteen

War Memorials: A Legacy
'We Will Remember Them.'

Even before the war had ended, there were ceremonies of remembrance including one held in the town's Market Square on 4 August 1918. This was a united service with the Reverend W. Budgen who read out the names of those old boys from the grammar school who had died. He said that the town was

> silently paying tribute to the Empire's sons who have fallen in the fight for freedom ... and mindful also of the loyalty and courage of our sailors, soldiers, airmen, and men everywhere and those working on the munitions of war ... for the preservation of civilisation, unanimously resolve to do all that lies in their power to achieve the ideals on behalf of which so great a sacrifice has already been made.

Remembrance

After the war had ended, the nation's thoughts turned even more to those brave men who failed to return. Questions were asked as to how the world should commemorate and remember those who had made the ultimate sacrifice. Across the entire Western Front and other battle sites there grew a chain of memorials and military cemeteries.

One of the ways in which Britain remembered her war dead lies in Westminster Abbey: the tomb of the Unknown Soldier. In 1920 four soldiers' bodies were removed, one each from the battlefields of the Aisne, the Somme, Arras and Ypres. One was chosen and buried in the abbey on 11 November 1920.

The suffering and grief of the millions of families whose loved ones were killed abroad was magnified by the knowledge that not only would they would never see them again, they would also probably never get to see their grave. In many cases there was no body or no grave at which to mourn. The setting-up of thousands of war memorials across the country gave those who had suffered such horrendous losses a focus, somewhere they could go to grieve and remember. Sadly some names are missing from these memorials because the families at the time did

Newport Cemetery war graves. *(Author)*

not want to accept that their loved ones were gone and it was their responsibility to register their deceased loved one's name. Also some entries differ from official military records as the men had been known locally by another name.

Such memorials were placed in churches, churchyards, by the side of

St Nicholas Church War Memorial today. *(Author)*

Part of the plaque on St Nicholas Church War Memorial. *(Author)*

1914 – 1918	1939 – 1945
OWEN. G. H	AVERY. A
OWEN. P	BEECH. J. R
PEAKE. H	BEVAN. C. J
PHILLIPS. B. W	BIRD. H. B
RABONE. B	BROOKES. J. C
RYLANCE. C	BRITTAIN. J
RYLANCE. T	EDWARDS. J. G
ROBERTS. F	EDWARDS. T
ROBERTS. W	FORRESTER. T
SIMMILL. J	GREEN. T
SIMMILL. W	HUGHES. E
SCOTT. C. E	JONES. A. W. J
SCOTT. R	LIVELY. F
TOMKINSON. W. J	MELLINGS. R
TRUMPER. W	MELLINGS. R. C
WAKELAM. C	NEVILLE. T. E
WARD. C	PLANT. G. W
WARD. E	RATCLIFFE. A. G
WEBB. F	REDFERN. R
WEBB. J. H	SIMMILL. H
WILLIAMS. J. J	STOKES. L. B
WRIGHT. T	WAGG. E
HASELEY. A.	WALSH. C
	WILLIAMS. R. L

The unveiling of the War Memorial in 1920. *(1) (NHS)*

main roads, in the middle of the village green and other such prominent locations, and Newport and the surrounding area has its share of these.

Some cemeteries, such as the one in Newport, have a line of military

The unveiling of the War Memorial in 1920. *(2) (NHS)*

graves from both the First and the Second World War. Some of the churchyards also have such graves.

St Nicholas Church has a Roll of Honour and a war memorial in its grounds. This was built and unveiled in 1920.

The church also has a window and memorial inside dedicated to the Leeke brothers among others. The window and memorial were originally in the family's chapel at Longford Church. Although Longford Church on the Longford estate was deconsecrated in the 1980s, the East Window was commissioned by the Leeke brothers' mother in 1923 and dedicated to their memory.

Also in the church there are six panels of saints painted on the east end wall in 1915. Because an image of St George could not be sourced they used the likeness of one of the sons of a former rector, Lieutenant Budgen, who was killed in the Great War.

Harper Adams Agricultural College, which had done so much work for the war effort in so many ways, decided to honour their war dead in autumn 1921 by making an appeal for funds to build a memorial library which came to

The Adams' Grammar School Memorial in the school's library. *(AGS)*

The Leeke brothers' and others' memorial window and plaque. *(Author)*

IN · LOVE · HONOUR · AND · GRATITUDE
THIS · TABLET · IS · ERECTED · TO · THE · MEMORY · OF · FORMER
PUPILS · OF · THIS · SCHOOL · WHO · LAID · DOWN · THEIR · LIVES · FOR
KING · AND · COUNTRY · IN · THE · GREAT · WAR · 1914–1919

ARTHUR ERIC BAILEY	PERCIVAL E DOUTHWAITE	RAYMOND KETLEY	B. WYNFORD PHILIPPS
RONALD H. BAUGUST	R.C. MACDONALD ELLIOTT	CECIL LANGLEY	W STANLEY PULLEN
JOHN BRUCE BAXLAND	WILLIAM JOHN ENSOR	RICHARD D. LEA	MAURICE WILFRID RAGG
JOHN WEBB BOCKING	JOHN EVANS	GEORGE ADEN MASON	HENRY S. ROBERTS
BERNARD BOCKING	GEORGE F. FROST	THOMAS JOHN MORRIS	ARTHUR P. ROWE
CHARLES W. BRAMPTON	CLIFFORD G. GRAIL	REGINALD H. MORRIS	JOHN NORMAN SELBY
SYDNEY JAMES BOYER	STANLEY JAMES GRAIL	JOHN MULLOCK	REGINALD A. SLANEY
CHARLES BROWNE	VINCENT COLIN HARES	GEORGE H. NEWBOLD	PERCY SMITH
R. GORDON BUDGEN	CHARLES C. HARRIS	NEVILLE L. PARTON	NORMAN P. VINCENT
MAURICE D. CADMAN	WILLIAM M. HARVEY	EWART G. PEARCE	CYRIL SCOTT UNDERHILL
HUBERT CHILTON	WILLIAM HOPE JONES	WILLIAM E. PERKINS	HAROLD ARTHUR WARD

THEIR · NAME · LIVETH · FOR · EVERMORE

The civilian medal. *(NHS)*

fruition by the spring of 1922.

A civilian medal commemorating the end of the war was found by a local metal detectorist in the front garden of Salter's Hall, Newport. It was dug up near the old site of the war memorial of the Catholic Church. It is thought that it was deliberately buried as an act of remembrance but how it got there and whose loved one it commemorates remains unknown.

Even Adams' Grammar School wanted a permanent memorial dedicated to their fallen old boys and this is situated in the library.

'In Flanders Fields'

One of the most striking symbols with which we remember those killed is the Flanders poppy. The idea was first used in the USA and soon swept across the UK. The Royal British Legion took the image forward and artificial poppies are to be seen adorning the chests of many people around the period of Remembrance Day every year. The Legion's annual Poppy Day still raises much-needed funds for war veterans. In fact, wreaths of the flower are laid at war memorials all over the Commonwealth as well as in the well-known ceremony at the Cenotaph in London.

The choice of flower originated from the poem 'In Flanders Fields' written by Canadian physician Lieutenant Colonel John McCrae on 3 May 1915. In this famous poem he makes reference to the red poppies that sprouted up over the graves of fallen soldiers at Flanders.

In 2014 ceramics artist Paul Cummins conceived an installation of 888,246 ceramic poppies as an open-air artwork entitled Blood Swept Lands and Seas of Red at the Tower of London to mark the centenary of the Great War; one poppy for each British or Colonial soldier who had perished in the conflict. Money raised from the poppies when they went on sale helped six different UK-based war charities. Also in 2014, some 45 million of the traditional paper poppies were made and the Royal British Legion Poppy Appeal raised £39 million.

At the eleventh hour of the eleventh day of the eleventh month Remembrance Day is still commemorated each year. An Armed Forces Day was held in

The wreath on the war graves, Newport Cemetery. *(Author)*

Armed Forces Day parade, Newport: Air Cadets. *(Author)*

Armed Forces Day parade, Newport: Royal British Legion. *(Author)*

Newport in 2014 and many of the town's local organizations and dignitaries attended, much as they would have done across the 100 years since the start of the Great War.

Today many of the memorials, if a little worn and battered about the edges, survive and still form a very important and poignant gathering point of remembrance where local people continue to pay their respects to their war dead. Of course, more names have been added from the Second World War and various other conflicts since 'the war to end all wars'.

Armed Forces Day parade, Newport: gun salute.
(Author)

Armed Forces Day, Newport: lowering of the flags.
(Author)

The Great War was a long and bloody battle resulting in hundreds of war dead from Newport and millions from across the world. However, it may well have been a longer and more arduous ordeal had the people on the home front not been so courageous and determined to help the war effort in every possible way. Newport can be proud to say that its ancestors kept the home fires burning, and their continuation of the ceremonies of remembrance shows that the impact of this momentous conflict still lies deep within them.

War Memorial at St Michael's and All Angels Church at Chetwynd, near Newport. *(Author)*

Roadside memorial Longford and Church Aston. *(Author)*

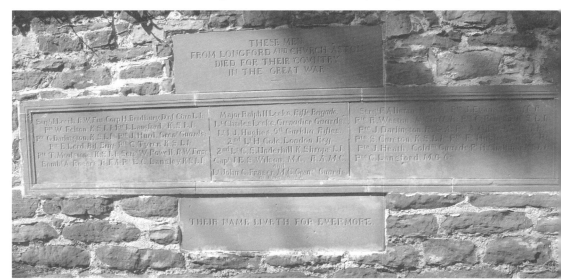

INDEX

es you think you've failed but in the eyes,
m. ~ @rhianna1987 · ...is
ly one. Know you are not...
ndaley · Every Tantrum and scream now
hen they are older! ~ @castlemag · That
ertain person to raise someone that
they're doing. No one. Not even Beyonce.
are to others. ~ @lwsarakrist · We all
~ @carriemorrison · Things will work
en who you are and who you want to be is
ss. ~ @sbentall2910 · When it feels
es lose their leaves every year and they still
~ @angieattar · Look back at all you have
ke of it, not what someone else gives you.
ncyfoster13 · No matter how hard today
~ @imserenalee · You're doing the best

*To my beautiful boy Rudy,
may you always love cooking
and eating as much as I do!*

Natasha Corrett

FAMILY KITCHEN

PHOTOGRAPHY BY LISA LINDER

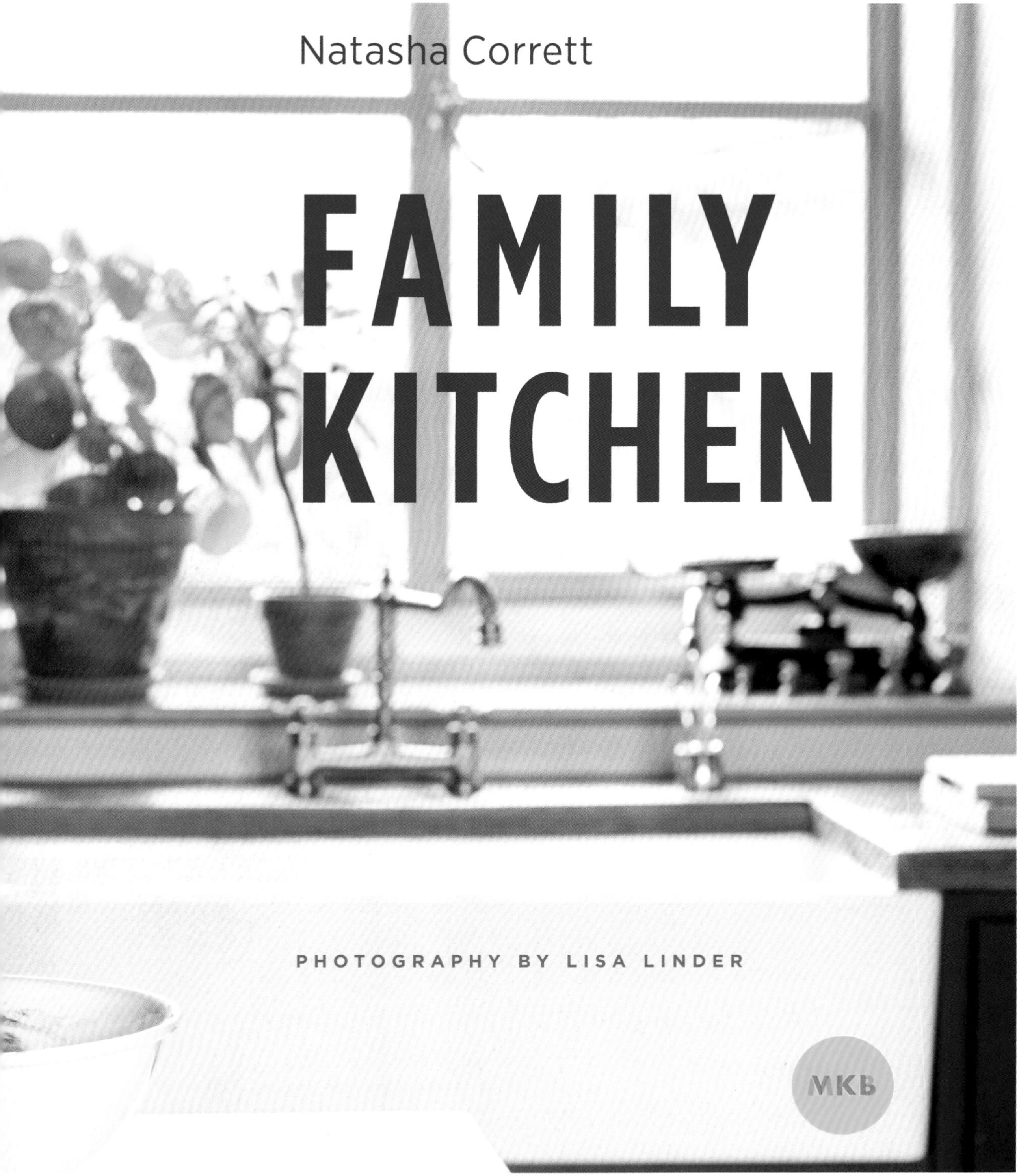

МКЬ

NOTES ON INGREDIENTS

All ingredients are interchangeable, so you can use what works for you and your family, your dietary requirements and, most importantly, what's in your fridge at the time. I am an advocate of eating organic, however it's not always affordable (my husband keeps telling me!) so we eat the Dirty Dozen organic and, when budgets permit, we buy more. However, we always buy organic meat, eggs and dairy. Eat less but better quality is our way of eating more sustainably. For me healthy eating is about moderation and cutting out processed foods, so the more you can cook from scratch, the better for you and your family.

Gluten-free plain and self-raising flours
All the recipes have been created and made using gluten-free flours. I like to use a brand called Doves as it really mimics a normal flour. If you want to swap the gluten-free flour for a normal plain or self-raising flour in a baking recipe, add 20g more as gluten-free flours tend to absorb more moisture.

Tamari
This is a gluten-free version of soy sauce and you can use either.

Butter
If you are dairy free you can swap for a vegan butter or use coconut oil or olive oil, except in baking, where the recipes state what alternatives you can use.

Milk
I have just stated milk in all the recipes as you can use whatever kind you like: cow, cashew, oat, soya, almond or coconut. For baking, I find that cashew or oat works the best if you are dairy free.

Sweeteners
If your child is under one year old you must not use honey. You can use maple syrup instead. This is the case for all the recipes, where you can use either.

Cheese
Most of the time you can use a dairy-free cheese if you wish not to use dairy. There are now so many brands you can get from all the big supermarkets and online.

Eggs
This is a hard one to swap, but for baking cakes and muffins you can try an egg replacer or using chickpea water known as aquafaba. You need to whisk it so it becomes like a foam before mixing it into your bake.
1 egg = 3 tbsp aquafaba
1 egg white = 2 tbsp aquafaba
1 egg yolk = 1 tbsp aquafaba

Bone broth or stock
Making bone broth is a wonderful way of using up the bones from a meat dish (page 170). I personally feel that if you want to eat meat as a family it should be organic and of the highest quality. It's about eating less, but better quality. Once you have made a big batch of bone broth you can freeze it into portion sizes. I would suggest freezing 1 cup (260ml) portions in either large weaning cubes or freezer bags. You can use bone broth in any of the recipes where a stock is made using a vegetable stock powder.

Swapping vegetables
I wholly encourage you to use whatever veg you have in your fridge. Swapping veggies is a great way of not having any leftovers at the end of the week and needing to throw them away. If the recipe calls for a root vegetable, then swap for another root vegetable. Or if it calls for a soft Mediterranean vegetable, then swap for the same kind so that the cooking times are equivalent.

Swapping protein
If you want to swap a vegetarian dish for a meat dish, or vice versa, then just read the intro and method before starting as it will state how to adjust the cooking time and method.

CONTENTS

Suitable for batch cooking

Suitable for freezing

Hidden veg recipe

FROM MY FAMILY TO YOURS
with a sprinkle of choc choc on top ...

Family time is, in my opinion, the most nourishing and exhausting experience you can have. It challenges you and completes you all in the same breath. To allow mealtimes to be enjoyable rather than stressful, I have put together this collection of recipes to make it easier to nourish your whole family.

Each dish is simple to make, with no hard-to-find ingredients, no complicated methods, no time-consuming preparation, just delicious, quick-to-make meals.

These recipes are flexible in every way. Don't want chicken but want fish? Then swap it. Fancy a veggie stew instead of lamb? Then swap it. Don't have broccoli? Swap it. Don't like carrots? Swap them...The recipes are interchangeable and work for the whole family.

Whether you are pregnant with your first child or have a house full of little ones, the recipes are put together so that everyone in your household can enjoy them.

ONE MEAL FEEDS ALL

The recipes are broken down to explain how you can make them weaning friendly, how to hide veg for fussy eaters and how to pimp them up for a simple date night meal. I believe one dish can be adapted for the whole family. Each recipe will explain when to add certain ingredients that are suitable for different age groups, so you only have to cook one dish for each mealtime and don't have to be a restaurant in your own home.

Batch cooking and freezing food has been a saviour for me from day one. Your freezer is just a cold larder! If you have multiple children, work and a hungry partner, stacking a freezer full of purées, stews, risottos and sauces is the easiest way to get dinner on the table in 10 minutes.

WHERE IT ALL BEGAN...

The day I realised I was pregnant I started eating differently. Cravings hit and working out that I had to eat little and often was the main hurdle to overcome to stop me feeling sick, exhausted and overwhelmed. Learning to go with the flow was key. Quick and fuss free was what I needed.

I daydreamed I would be tottering around my kitchen in my apron, perfectly toned with just a big ball of a belly, singing lullabies to my bump in preparation for what was to come ... but the reality was that I was a blubbering whale with a sore back, lying on the sofa, eating not much more than avocado toast, cheese and dry biscuits!

I found myself beyond exhausted, overwhelmed and struggling to rustle up much unless my angel of a husband cooked for us.

Then the second trimester hit and I felt like I could take over the world – I had all the energy I needed. This was the time I now realise I should have stocked my freezer as by the third trimester I was doing very little other than eating chocolate.

So if you are reading this and pregnant, flip through to all the recipes that have the freezer and batch cook symbols and start cooking now! Throw out the bottles of vodka that are stuck to the back of the freezer and the loose peas in the drawers as you need space for all the delicious food you are about to make. I promise you will be thanking me when you are home alone in the early days after birth and need some easy meals to pop in the oven.

PARTNER'S PREP NIGHT AND FAMILY FRIDGE FILL

The greatest gift you can give someone who has just had a baby is filling their fridge. It is something I do for my friends when they come home from having their baby.

There are some recipes I have written specifically with that in mind for this book, which you can cook and drop over to your friends. Or just take a photo and send it to your bestie or partner and ask nicely what they want as a baby gift!

- Fennel and celeriac soup
- Tamari-baked salmon fillets
- Pasta bake
- Ricotta and spinach frittata
- Tomato and mushroom dhal
- Courgette and cheese loaf

- Sweet potato and polenta fish pie
- Pearl barley chicken stew
- Turmeric-roasted chicken
- Tray-baked roasted vegetables
- Gooey brownies
- Apple bircher muesli

Even if you don't have a newborn, these recipes are perfect for batch cooking and popping in the fridge on a Sunday for the week ahead, so weekdays are stress free.

In my last book, *Honestly Healthy in a Hurry*, I spoke a lot about prep night cooking, which I believe is key to making life easy. Roasting up a chicken, some trays of veggies and cooking a few hearty dishes will ease you into Monday feeling like you are winning at life.

WEANING

When the time comes to start the weaning process, it is like an endless pit of information out there. When do you start? What do you start feeding them with? What foods can you offer and what do you have to stay away from? Spoon fed or baby led? There are so many questions parents face. There isn't a one size fits all. Every baby is different and you need to do what you feel is right.

I took the whole weaning process very slowly with tastes and types of foods. Rudy definitely told me when he was ready for something new. This is how I tackled it...

The most important piece of advice I can give you is to do a first-aid course before you start weaning. It is important you know the difference between choking and gagging, especially if you are doing baby led, and what to do in the event your baby is choking. It gives you more confidence in the long run.

FIRST TASTES

I started by introducing individual flavoured purées for 3 days at a time. This showed me if Rudy had any allergies to the foods I was offering. Use either breastmilk or formula to blend the steamed veggies. You can batch cook and then freeze in portion-size pots. After a couple of weeks I started mixing flavours, but I made sure that I still let Rudy taste the individual flavours before mixing so he could get a taste for them, especially the more bitter greens.

Weeks 1–2
Sweet potato / butternut squash / carrot / pumpkin

Week 3
Broccoli / peas / courgette / spinach

Week 4
Apple + butternut / beetroot + avocado / swede + cavolo nero

Week 5
Same as week 4 + add some fruit: papaya + avocado / banana + avocado

Week 6
Blend oats into a flour to make porridge (you don't need to buy baby porridge!), adding a purée to flavour. I made the porridge with coconut water. You can also use breast or formula milk or sterilised water

This week I introduced finger foods: avocado / cucumber / pear

Tip When starting the weaning process babies can get constipated, so you can blend up some cooked pear or apple and prune purée to help. Just a couple of teaspoons normally did the trick for Rudy.

SECOND TASTES

From weeks 6–8 of weaning, Rudy was ready for some new tastes alongside the more simple purées, and to start playing with some finger foods. Here are some of the combinations I tried out on him that he loved.

Purées

- Butter beans, peas, broccoli, parsley + coconut milk
- Blueberry + pear oat porridge
- Mango + cinnamon chia porridge
- Courgette + spinach omelette
- Butternut, split pea lentils + cumin

This is how we continued our journey to food...

Weeks 1–2
Root vegetables

Weeks 3–4
Green vegetables

Week 5
Inclusion of fruit

Week 6
Adding some grains: oats + quinoa

Week 7
Eggs, pulses, spices, herbs, coconut
+ polenta

7 months
Tofu, nut + seed butters, gluten, wheat, all grains

8 months
Fish + bone broth

9 months
Sheep + goat dairy

10 months
White meat

12 months
Cow dairy + red meat

Here is a list of the recipes for the earlier days of weaning once you are past the simple purées stage:

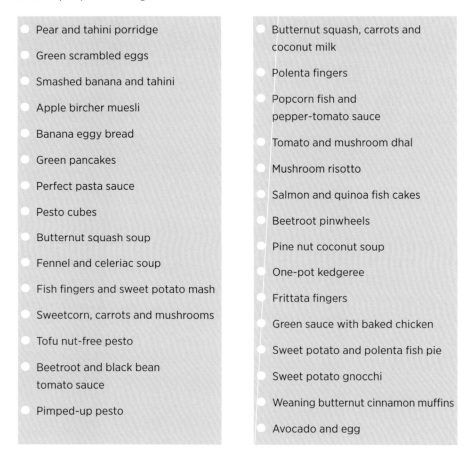

- Pear and tahini porridge
- Green scrambled eggs
- Smashed banana and tahini
- Apple bircher muesli
- Banana eggy bread
- Green pancakes
- Perfect pasta sauce
- Pesto cubes
- Butternut squash soup
- Fennel and celeriac soup
- Fish fingers and sweet potato mash
- Sweetcorn, carrots and mushrooms
- Tofu nut-free pesto
- Beetroot and black bean tomato sauce
- Pimped-up pesto

- Butternut squash, carrots and coconut milk
- Polenta fingers
- Popcorn fish and pepper-tomato sauce
- Tomato and mushroom dhal
- Mushroom risotto
- Salmon and quinoa fish cakes
- Beetroot pinwheels
- Pine nut coconut soup
- One-pot kedgeree
- Frittata fingers
- Green sauce with baked chicken
- Sweet potato and polenta fish pie
- Sweet potato gnocchi
- Weaning butternut cinnamon muffins
- Avocado and egg

When you are cooking for the whole family, make sure you add the salt at the end after you have taken the baby's portion out. Babies can't have salt in the first year.

I am a big believer in cooking smartly to avoid making several different meals for my family. Once you are through the initial exploratory stage of weaning, you can adapt your everyday cooking to make your meals baby-friendly. Use low-sodium stock cubes and don't add sugar or honey to your recipes. You can always season your own food afterwards. Cooking just one meal for everyone will make weaning a lot easier and more enjoyable too!

FROM MY FAMILY TO YOUR FAMILY

Because cooking is my line of work I have been able to streamline recipes and methods to cut out any fussy cooking. Sometimes I have found the lengthy methods in other recipes are just not needed.

In times of haste and to get a delicious meal on the table FAST, you need to sometimes just chuck it all in and put the lid on.

I have found solutions to make mealtimes simple, easy and delicious that the whole family will eat and enjoy. I have learnt so much about being a mother from you. The communities and support on social media are indescribably the 'village' it takes to bring up a family. It's just a modern village that's online!

Every day I am winging it, but every day I learn and understand it more and I love it. Holding a family together is definitely the hardest job in the world, but also the most rewarding.

I really hope that you enjoy these recipes as much as I did creating them and my family did eating them. Thank you from the bottom of my heart for joining me on this journey. I couldn't do it without you.

Natasha x

NUTRITION: FEEDING YOUR FAMILY

BY LAURA BOND

I have known Laura for nearly 10 years. She is an advocate of healthy eating and we became mothers at a similar time. She is an incredible and wise nutritional therapist and I hope she can provide some great insights for you and your family too.

This is the book I wish I had when I started my own family. As a nutritional therapist (DipION) I spent hours researching the best first foods to wean my baby on; but I failed to factor in how to feed us at the same time! A book to nourish the whole family – covering everything from pregnancy and weaning to pescatarian and vegan recipes – is what every busy mum needs. And let's face it, most of us are flat out and mealtimes can end up being either the highlight or lowlight of the day. This book, with its everyday ingredients and simple recipes, aims to bring some harmony back to the dinner table.

PREGNANCY

Pregnancy, in particular, is a time when you want food fast. Waves of nausea coupled with overwhelming tiredness can make mealtimes a drag. But it's also such a vital time to get key nutrients in as it has been found that a women's diet during pregnancy directly affects the nutrients in the womb. In addition, research suggests that a mother's microbiome – that collection of bacteria in our gut – may influence her infant's gut health even before birth. The upshot? Eating healthy wholefoods and taking a probiotic may play a role in a child's future health.

SUPPLEMENTS TO TAKE DAILY

Pregnancy multivitamin with folic acid (400ug) Wild Nutrition's Food-Grown Pregnancy provides folic acid in its natural, folate form. Ideally start taking folic acid before conception.

Fish oil or algae supplement For critical omega-3 fatty acid DHA.

Vitamin D (600 iu) Ask your healthcare practitioner to check your levels, as you may require more or less per day.

Probiotics Choose one that contains several different types of Lactobacillus and Bifidobacterium strains. Lactobacillus rhamnosus HN001 may help reduce the risk of eczema in young children.

GET ENOUGH PROTEIN

Protein provides the building blocks of human tissue. The best sources of protein are 'complete' proteins, which contain all the essential amino acids your body needs:

eggs / fish / chicken / red meat / quinoa / buckwheat / chia seeds / hemp seeds / lentils / nuts / seeds / chickpeas / beans

If you are a vegan mum-to-be, make sure you eat a variety of proteins to get the full mix of amino acids. You might start with a Choc choc spinach smoothie (page 42) in the morning, Aubergine and bean dip (page 156) with oatcakes mid-morning, a Jewelled quinoa salad (page 116) for lunch and Lentil lasagne (page 158) for dinner.

FIRST TRIMESTER

Lentils are a brilliant source of folate, a nutrient that is particularly important in the first trimester to help prevent neural tube defects. One cup of cooked lentils (check out the Tomato and mushroom dhal on page 114) provides 90 percent of your folate needs, while beetroot, spinach and strawberries will add a folate boost to your morning smoothie. If you are suffering from nausea, adding in bananas and avocados will provide B6, which may help. If you are craving carbs, give your body what it needs in the healthiest form – porridge, wholegrain pasta, muffins or a curry with brown rice will provide slow-release energy to sustain you for longer.

SECOND TRIMESTER

With any luck, you will be feeling better and have more energy. Foods rich in calcium, omega-3 and iron are important now. Anaemia is quite common around the 20-week mark when your body's blood volume rises, so getting enough iron-rich foods to boost your haemoglobin is important. Good sources include:

organic meats / spinach / kale / beans / dried apricots / blackstrap molasses

Adequate vitamin C will also help your body absorb iron. Sources include:

strawberries / oranges / broccoli / squeeze of lemon – on your salads or in your water

Calcium is needed for your baby's bone development, however you don't need to overly rely on milk and cheese. Dairy-free sources include:

buckwheat / almonds / tahini / broccoli / sardines

Sardines are also one of the only foods to provide vitamin D and we need this sunshine vitamin to absorb calcium.

Studies suggest 60 percent of pregnant women are vitamin D deficient, so if you live in the northern hemisphere it's a good idea to supplement and to get outside when you can.

Prawns are a rich source of iodine and dietary requirements nearly double during pregnancy! Try the Prawn Thai curry on page 86.

Mackerel and salmon will provide omega-3s, important for a baby's growing brain. I advise pregnant clients to avoid tuna (and swordfish) as they are high in mercury, which may be harmful to the foetus.

THIRD TRIMESTER

Continuing to eat enough healthy fats will support your baby's growth – in the final month of pregnancy your baby will gain around half a pound per week! Good examples of healthy fats are nuts and seeds, avocado, organic meat and eggs. Getting enough choline in the third trimester might also have life-long cognitive benefits for your child, and egg yolks are a good source. If you are feeling sluggish by the third trimester, try including more fibre – roasted veggies (particularly beetroot), chia crackers, Apple bircher muesli (page 34) and even a slice of Saffron sticky toffee cake (page 196) might help to get things moving. If you are feeling exhausted and overwhelmed, have a magnesium bath. This vital mineral helps relax muscles, can relieve leg cramps and is important for building and repairing tissues in both mother and foetus.

FOURTH TRIMESTER

Childbirth is often likened to a marathon, however many mothers find it's nothing compared to the 'fourth trimester.' Those first three months can be brutal in terms of sleep deprivation, relentless crying (you and them...) and feeding. Nourishing yourself when you are doing everything one-handed and running on next to no sleep is tough – especially if you have a child that wants to feed 24/7. B vitamins can really help give your brain and body a boost. If you are struggling, try taking a daily multi B for one month and look for foods rich in B12 (eggs, fish, oysters and organic meat) and B6 (sunflower seeds, chickpeas, salmon and sweet potato).

BREASTFEEDING

If you are breastfeeding you will need an extra 500 calories a day; the hunger is real and many women feel like a 'bottomless pit' for weeks and that's okay. While it's tempting to fill up on empty carbs, opt for quality protein instead. I know one mother who swore by sardines on toast in the morning.

Look to have foods rich in these at each meal:

> protein / fat / plant foods – eating a wide range of vegetables will provide your body with a broad spectrum of vitamins and minerals to support your immune system

Over milk supply and under milk supply are quite normal and you can turn to foods to help increase production.

Oats, fennel and fenugreek are known as glactagogues – foods that can increase milk production. Try having a warm cup of fennel or fenugreek tea in the morning and topping porridge with nuts and seeds for extra protein, vitamins and minerals. Just ¼ cup pumpkin seeds provides 9g of protein (equivalent to one and a half eggs) along with zinc, a mineral many new mums are deficient in.

BABY REFLUX

If diagnosed baby reflux is keeping you awake all night, cutting out dairy and soya from your diet can make a big difference. You might also consider working with a nutritional therapist (or dietician) to identify triggers and support your baby's developing gut through targeted probiotics and soothing remedies. If you had a C-section, I recommend using an infant probiotic to help seed your baby's gut with beneficial flora. You can either add this to their bottle or dust your nipple with probiotics once a day before feeding.

WEANING

So when is your baby ready for solids? The WHO guidelines suggest delaying the introduction of solids until after six months, however research suggests that from four to seven months there is a window when humans are extraordinarily receptive to flavour and that if vegetables are introduced at this age, babies are more open minded.

Organic steamed veg, such as squash, carrot and sweet potato, are a great first choice as their vitamin A is crucial for a developing immune system. After the first two weeks, add greens like courgette, avocado and beans and then, after that, broccoli, cauliflower and spinach. Keep in mind that if you have a reflux baby, broccoli, cauliflower and spinach can cause excess wind issues.

FOODS TO AVOID IN THE FIRST YEAR

- Salt – no salt is advised for the first year. From one to three years old, 2g of salt is the maximum children should be having per day, so it's best to avoid store-bought food and cook from scratch as much as possible.

- Sugar

- Honey

- Mould-ripened soft cheese

- Seafood – high in mercury (tuna, shark and swordfish)

- Foods like whole grapes, cherry tomatoes or whole nuts, which may be a choking hazard

- Any highly processed or deep-fried foods like nuggets and chips

- Dairy milk as a drink

ALLERGIES

Forty-four percent of people in the UK suffer from allergies, including non-food allergies. Rather than postponing the introduction of potential allergens such as eggs and peanuts, the latest clinical trials suggest it's better to offer them to your child earlier on. Breakfast or lunch are the ideal times to introduce a new food, so if there is a reaction it's not happening close to bedtime. You might also consider not serving a new food at rush hour in case you need to make a dash to A&E! If you do notice any reaction, including redness around the mouth, try again after one to three months.

VEGETARIAN OR VEGAN CHILDREN

If you are planning to wean your baby vegetarian or vegan, consider a zinc supplement as plant-based diets tend to be low in zinc, which is vital for immune health. Adding coconut milk and oil to your child's diet will help make up for some healthy fats they'll miss from meat, fish and dairy, while an algae supplement rich in omega-3 fats is good for brain health. Good sources of dairy-free calcium are nuts and seeds (seed spreads for younger children), tahini, buckwheat, carob and blackstrap molasses (also rich in iron).

FUSSY EATERS AND BEHAVIOUR

Most parents will face the torture of fussy eating at one time or another – teething and tiredness are common reasons. The transition from baby to toddlerhood around age two can mark a time of extreme resistance and fussiness, which might have as much to do with 'testing your boundaries' as your child's changing energy requirements (an average infant gains 7kg in weight in the first year, while during the second year of life growth is 2.3kg). Whatever the cause, here are some tips for getting more goodness in:

- Offer vegetables before the meal when they are hungry
- Serve new foods alongside familiar ones (i.e. broccoli and spinach with pesto, see page 66)
- Cut snacks! Do not underestimate the power of putting some space between meals
- Serve dip with vegetables

- Eat with your children, whenever possible. Just make sure you are eating the same healthy food you are serving them
- Consider the texture – if your child hates pumpkin soup, try roasted pumpkin pieces. Young children are extremely sensitive to the 'mouth-feel' of food

WHEN ALL ELSE FAILS...

Foods like toast may sometimes be the only option, but be aware that simple carbohydrates convert to sugar in the body, which can cause a child's energy to spike, then crash. Having a healthy form of fat and protein, such as an egg or nut butter with toast, will keep blood sugar levels stable for longer.

If a child consistently rejects a wide range of foods, it can be a sign to look at their gut health and consider zinc deficiency. Speak to a qualified nutritional therapist or dietitian.

EARLY SCHOOL YEARS

Good nutritious snacks after school are important to keeping children going. Aim to leave at least a two-hour gap before dinner if you want them to eat well at night.

Protein is paramount between the ages of five and ten years old.

It contains the amino acids the body uses to build and repair muscles and tissues, while also providing important vitamins and minerals – like B12 – which are needed to sustain energy and concentration.

Children between five and ten require between 20 to 28g protein per day. Swapping quinoa for brown rice (8g protein per cup vs. 5g in brown rice) or eggs for porridge (2 eggs provides 12g protein) a few days a week are simple ways to up your family's protein intake. Cooking extra chicken for lunch boxes is another.

Exam time creeps up quickly and it's important to feed their brains the best nutrients.

The best ways to optimise their brain health are:

- Balancing blood sugar levels

- Getting adequate essential fats (especially omega-3 DHA)

- Consuming vitamins and minerals (i.e. lots of vegetables!)

- Avoiding anti-nutrients, like sugar, hydrogenated fats and highly processed foods

Foods to calm the brain and boost performance:

- Adding good fats like hemp seeds and almond butter to smoothies for an after school snack

- Topping a piece of salmon with quinoa and broccoli and a handful of walnuts for extra brain-building omega-3 fats and melatonin

- Having natural yoghurt and honey as pudding. The yoghurt is rich in tryptophan, which can aid sleep

- Try introducing herbal teas like chamomile and lemon balm to help calm the nervous system

TEENAGERS

Encouraging children to eat better by helping them understand why food is so important can be hugely motivating. For example:

'Red peppers (rich in vitamin C) can stop you getting colds.'
'Fish helps give you a super brain.'
'Foods rich in zinc help keep pimples at bay.'
'Eating enough protein boosts sports performance'.

Gendered eating can come into play in the teenage years, with boys requesting red meat and girls opting for salads, however this goes against what their bodies require. As Bee Wilson says in *First Bite*, 'Girl food and boy food are dangerous nonsense that prevent us from seeing the real problem of feeding boys and girls.' When girls start to menstruate their iron-needs jump from 8mg to 15mg. The *National Diet and Nutrition Survey* (NDNS, 2014) revealed that 46 percent of 11–18-year-old girls in the UK had a low intake of iron and 7.4 percent had haemoglobin levels lower than the WHO limit compared to 1.8 percent of boys. Red meat is one of the most bioavailable sources of iron, however vegans and vegetarians can optimise their levels by eating dark leafy greens, pulses, blackstrap molasses and spirulina (great additions to porridge and smoothies respectively).

The early teens are when the majority of bone mass is formed, so calcium (see page 16), magnesium (leafy greens, nuts and seeds, raw cacao), vitamin D (shiitake mushrooms, oily fish and eggs) and K2 (a little-known nutrient that tells your body to deposit calcium on your bones, rather than in soft tissues) are important. Hard cheese and egg yolks are good sources of K2, along with fish roe – an easy win if your teens are sushi fans.

Acne can be devastating when insecurity and a desire to fit in are at an all-time high. The first step is to cut down on sugar. Clinical studies reveal a link between the consumption of sugary foods and acne. You can reduce cravings by pre-loading the diet with healthy fats like avocados, nuts, seeds, organic animal protein and coconut oil. There is some research that dairy can contribute towards acne. This might be due to the fact that increased sebum production is associated with increased levels of the insulin-like growth hormone IGF-1, a hormone found in dairy milk (including organic milk and goat milk). If you decide to reduce or remove dairy in your teen's diet, make sure they are regularly eating calcium-rich foods. Zinc has also been hailed as a promising alternative to other acne treatments, so pumpkin seeds, red meat, beans, nuts and wholegrains are top choices.

GUT HEALTH

Looking after the gut is paramount at any age as we now know that the health of our microbiome (that collection of bacteria in our gut) influences not only our digestive health but also our immune system, weight, and even our psychological wellbeing. Did you know the best way to improve your gut health is to eat more fruit and vegetables? The largest study to date on the microbiome found that people with the healthiest gut ate more than 30 different fruit and veg a week. That included nuts, seeds and herbs. Taking a probiotic (including different strains of both Bifidobacterium and Lactobacillus) and including fermented foods like sauerkraut, miso and kefir in your daily diet will also repopulate your gut with good bacteria.

TEN GREAT GUT-FRIENDLY FOODS

- Kefir
- Sauerkraut
- Vegetable or organic chicken stock
- Flax seeds
- Broccoli

- Cauliflowers
- Apples
- Ginger
- Garlic
- Mushrooms

To get more diversity in your diet, think about foods you haven't eaten for a while. If you always cook with onion, consider swapping it for fennel in recipes (try the Fennel and celeriac soup on page 76). If you routinely have broccoli on the side, try your kids with green beans. Frozen peas are an easy vegetable to slip into recipes and they are packed with protein. Peas contain Pisumsaponins, which have anti-inflammatory benefits and are rich in vitamin C.

Set yourself the challenge of eating home-cooked meals five nights a week for two months and you might find everyone in the house feels, and even looks, better.

MORNING
TIME

I remember when morning times used to be relaxing. I'd decorate a tray with flowers and have multiple courses to satisfy all my food desires. I used to enjoy breakfast in bed, sip my tea without spilling it or it going cold, read a book or finish watching a box set.

GONE ARE THOSE DAYS!

The morning is now a juggle of making food as quickly as possible before the hangry monster starts clawing at my leg, shoving it in my mouth while feeding the toddler that keeps throwing it on the floor (although it was their favourite meal yesterday), tripping over the dog, grappling with socks and the shoes they refuse to wear, and getting out of the house without losing my sanity...

Breakfast has to be quick and simple, but filling and nourishing as there is a lot of pressure on this early meal of the day. If children don't fill their tummies up, the rest of the day is potentially a slippery slope in the battle of the wills!

The recipes in this chapter cover everything from 5-minute breakfasts, foods to grab on the go, things to prep the night before to make life a little more streamline, smoothies packed with hidden veg and classics with a veggie twist to one-pan bakes for the weekend and how to use up leftovers and turn them into delicious sweet treats!

PEAR AND TAHINI PORRIDGE

SERVES 1 | **PREP** 5 MINUTES | **COOK** 5 MINUTES

60g rolled oats

¼ tsp ground cinnamon, plus extra to garnish

135ml (½ cup) milk

½ pear, diced

2 tsp tahini

2 tbsp water

ADD-ONS

sliced pear and cinnamon, tahini, berries or chopped banana

In my first 3 months of pregnancy I lived on porridge as it was the only thing that stopped me feeling sick. Adding tahini gives it some protein and helps to keep your blood sugar levels balanced. I continue to make this for Rudy and myself now and he loves it too.

1. Put all the ingredients into a pan and cook over a medium heat for 3–4 minutes until you reach your desired porridge consistency. If you want it thinner, just add a splash more milk or water.

2. Garnish with pear and a sprinkling of cinnamon, tahini, berries or chopped banana.

BREAKFAST COOKIES

MAKES 9 COOKIES | **PREP** 10 MINUTES | **COOK** 15 MINUTES

100g courgette

1 (50g) apple

80g rolled oats

150g gluten-free plain flour
(add 20g more for spelt or plain
wheat flour)

½ tsp bicarbonate of soda

½ tsp salt

1 tsp ground cinnamon

2 tbsp chia or flax seeds

140g dates, chopped (or raisins
or choc chips)

60g butter

2 tbsp honey

1 egg

ADD-ONS

seeds or chopped nuts

The perfect on-the-go treat or snack for everyone in the family. I initially made these when Rudy went through a phase of only wanting to feed himself and it all just got so messy. I found these were a great solution with lots of goodness in them.

1. Preheat the oven to 180°C Fan. Line a baking tray.

2. Grate the courgette and apple and put to one side in a bowl.

3. Weigh out the oats, flour, bicarbonate of soda, salt, cinnamon, chia seeds and dates and put into a blender. Blend until a coarse texture.

4. Melt the butter and add to the mixture with the honey, egg and grated courgette and apple. Pulse again until combined.

5. Portion out heaped tablespoons of the mixture onto the baking tray, evenly spread apart. You can sprinkle with some seeds or chopped nuts of your choice to garnish.

6. Bake in the oven for 13 minutes until golden, then leave to cool. Store in an airtight container for up to 3 days.

BANANA EGGY BREAD

SERVES 1 | **PREP** 10 MINUTES | **COOK** 5 MINUTES

1 egg

½ small banana

1 tbsp milk

2 slices of bread

1 tbsp butter

This is one of our family go-to breakfasts that we have about three times a week. I prepare it while I warm up Rudy's milk in the morning, then leave to soak for about 30 minutes. It then takes only a few minutes to fry in a pan. Of course, my little one puts Marmite on the top, but this is certainly not essential!

1. Beat the egg, mash the banana into it and stir in the milk to make the batter.

2. Dip the bread into the mixture. The longer you leave it to soak, the more it will take in.

3. Warm a pan to a high heat and melt the butter in the bottom.

4. Put the soaked bread into the pan and cook for about 3 minutes each side or until golden and none of the batter oozes out when you pat the back of the piece of bread with a spatula. Serve warm.

CHEESE AND COURGETTE OMELETTE

SERVES 1 | **PREP** 5 MINUTES | **COOK** 5 MINUTES

1 egg

pinch of ground cinnamon

knob of butter

30g Cheddar, grated

10g courgette, grated

This is so soft and silky and if you have a fussy eater, you can peel the green skin off the courgette first so that there is no green in sight! You can swap this up with some grated carrot as well for a change.

1. Beat the egg in a bowl and add the cinnamon.

2. Heat up a good non-stick frying pan and add a knob of butter to melt. Once melted, pour in the egg mixture so it's nice and thin – almost like a crepe.

3. Sprinkle the cheese and courgette evenly over the top of the egg, then slowly start to fold one end so that it rolls up to become a sausage shape.

4. Cook on both sides until a slightly golden brown colour all over, then take off the heat and serve.

KIDDIE FRIENDLY
Put into the fridge to cool a little faster for hungry tummies first thing in the morning and cut into slices for easy-to-hold finger food.

ADULTS PIMP IT UP
This also makes a great lunch box addition. Just add some avocado slices, sliced tomatoes, roasted butternut squash and broccoli!

APPLE BIRCHER MUESLI

SERVES 4 | **PREP** 5 MINUTES PLUS OVERNIGHT SOAKING

2 small apples

100g rolled oats

3 tbsp chia seeds

750ml (3 cups) milk

ADD-ONS

1 tbsp nut or seed butter (almond, cashew, tahini or peanut)

dried fruit (dates, apricots, goji berries, figs or raisins)

nuts and seeds

This is the most perfect thing to have in your fridge as it lasts for 4–5 days. It will also get sweeter and sweeter the longer it stays there. The muesli is good for breakfast of course, but also makes a great midnight feast or afternoon snack.

1. Blend the apples into a purée or grate.

2. Put the oats, chia seeds, milk and apple purée into a large Tupperware and mix together until fully combined.

3. Add in your nut butter, if you wish, and any other extras. If you are adding dried fruit, dice it before putting it in. Leave to soak overnight and enjoy in the morning with some fresh fruit and/or yoghurt.

TOASTS

SMASHED BANANA AND TAHINI

SERVES 1 | **PREP** 5 MINUTES

This was my saviour when I was pregnant. When I woke up in the middle of the night and felt nauseous I would have some on toast and then go back to sleep. Keep in a jam jar or Tupperware in the fridge for up to a day and spread on toast or rice cakes. You can also blend it up so its velvety smooth and freeze to make a delicious ice cream! This is a wonderful weaning pudding for little ones.

1 large banana (or 2 small)

1 tbsp tahini

juice of ¼ lemon

pinch of salt

2 slices of bread, toasted

butter or coconut oil, for spreading

1. Mash the banana with the back of a fork and mix in the tahini, lemon juice and salt.

2. Serve spread on the toasted bread with some butter or coconut oil.

SWEET POTATO MASH AND MELTED CHEESE ON TOAST

SERVES 1 | **PREP** 5 MINUTES | **COOK** 5 MINUTES

In my first trimester I just needed carbs, more carbs and cheese, so I found a healthier way to enjoy them. I always have some roasted sweet potato in the fridge for this very recipe, but if you don't, simply bake a sweet potato in a 180°C Fan oven for 50–60 minutes until soft. We all enjoy this as a lunch with broccoli on the side.

150g roasted sweet potato

1 baby vine tomato, diced

small handful of parsley, finely chopped

1 tsp olive oil

pinch of salt and black pepper

¼ tsp apple cider vinegar

2 slices of bread

small handful of hard goat's cheese or Cheddar

1. Preheat the oven grill and line a baking tray.

2. Mash up the sweet potato in a bowl. Add the tomato and parsley to the sweet potato. Mix in the olive oil, salt, pepper and apple cider vinegar.

3. Partly toast the bread. Take out of the toaster and put onto the baking tray.

4. Scoop the mixture over the top and crumble over the goat's cheese. Leave under the grill until the cheese has melted.

EASY GRANOLA

MAKES 4–6 BOWLS | **PREP** 5 MINUTES | **COOK** 20 MINUTES

150g rolled oats

¼ tsp ground cinnamon

¼ tsp ground ginger

pinch of salt

1 tbsp extra virgin olive oil

3 tbsp honey

3 tbsp chopped hazelnuts

zest of 1 large orange

yoghurt, to serve

COMPOTE (OPTIONAL)

1 tbsp butter

1 tbsp maple syrup

1 nectarine, chopped

handful of blueberries

60ml (¼ cup) water

Store-bought cereal is laden with hidden sugars, so I make up a huge batch of this (I times the recipe by ten) so I always have it on hand for everyone to enjoy. I love it with yoghurt and this compote or just pop in a mini Tupperware and have as a snack.

1. Preheat the oven to 175°C Fan. Line a baking tray.

2. Weigh out the oats and mix in the cinnamon, ground ginger, salt, olive oil, honey, nuts and orange zest until fully combined.

3. Spread out onto the baking tray and put into the oven. Check every 5 minutes and stir so that the oats get a nice even colour on them. This will take 15–20 minutes.

4. Leave to cool and then add in any dried fruit you like. Keep in an airtight container or Kilner jar for up to a month.

5. To make the compote, put the butter in a pan to melt. Add the maple syrup, nectarine and blueberries. Slowly add the water as it starts to dry out – you may need more liquid.

6. Once the fruit is soft, take off the heat and keep in a Tupperware for up to 3 days. Serve with the granola and a spoonful of yoghurt.

SMOOTHIES

PERFECT GREEN SMOOTHIE

MAKES 1 LARGE SMOOTHIE | **PREP** 5 MINUTES

You can use pretty much anything you have in the fridge that you and your family love for this smoothie. If the kids like a slightly sweeter smoothie, try using a banana rather than an avocado. This is perfect for after school – just pop in a water bottle and give it to them on the school run – and if you are weaning, it makes a great breakfast as you can help spoon it into their mouths.

½ cucumber

1 handful of spinach

2 broccoli florets

1 soft pear, cored

1 avocado or banana

small handful of rolled or porridge oats

500–750ml (2–3 cups) milk

ADD-ONS (FOR ADULTS)

protein powder/greens powder

1. Place all the ingredients into a blender, adding more or less milk depending on your preferred thickness. Blend the mixture until you have a smooth smoothie!

BEETROOT AND BERRY SMOOTHIE

MAKES 1 LARGE SMOOTHIE | **PREP** 5 MINUTES

Smoothies are an amazing way of sneaking veg into little ones. Great for weaning and all ages, and a lovely mid-morning or afternoon snack for you. If you only have raw beetroot that is fine – just grate it before blending. You can add any berries you have too.

150g cooked beetroot

40g rolled oats

250ml (1 cup) milk

1 soft pear, cored

60g blackberries

1. Put all the ingredients into a blender and blend until smooth.

CHOCOLATE DRINKS

CHOC CHOC SPINACH SMOOTHIE

MAKES 1 LARGE OR 2 SMALL SMOOTHIES
PREP 5 MINUTES

Rudy calls chocolate 'choc choc' and he is obsessed like me! So I like to try and find ways that indulge him while also getting in some hidden veg. Also great for me when I get a chocolate craving.

80g cucumber

30g spinach

½ pear, cored

30g dates

3 tbsp raw cacao powder

500ml (2 cups) milk

½ banana

ADD-ONS

1 tbsp cashew or almond butter

swap the banana for ½ avocado for extra greens

1. Put all the ingredients into a blender and blend until smooth.

| **KIDDIE FRIENDLY**
| Freeze the smoothie in ice-cream moulds for a healthy twist on a chocolate lolly.

SPICED HOT CHOCOLATE

SERVES 1 | **PREP** 2 MINUTES | **COOK** 3 MINUTES

This is the ultimate comfort in a cup. There's nothing better than curling up on the sofa with a hot chocolate while you have a well-deserved 5-minute break. Swap the honey for maple syrup if you have an under-one year old wanting to join in on this!

500ml (2 cups) milk (if you are using plant milk, use a creamy one like cashew, oat or coconut)

1 cinnamon stick

1 heaped tbsp raw cacao powder

1 tbsp honey

1. Pour the milk into a saucepan with the cinnamon stick, raw cacao and honey and cook on a low heat for 2–4 minutes so the spices infuse into the milk. Once warmed through, pour into a cup and enjoy.

CARROT AND BANANA PORRIDGE

SERVES 1 | **PREP** 5 MINUTES PLUS 30 MINUTES SOAKING | **COOK** 2 MINUTES

SOAKING

40g rolled jumbo oats

90ml (⅓ cup) milk

15g carrots

COOKING

3 tbsp milk

1 tbsp desiccated coconut, plus more to serve

pinch of ground cinnamon

½ banana, mashed

1 tbsp cashew or almond butter, plus more to serve

ADD-ONS

1 tsp raw cacao powder (makes it chocolatey)

1 tbsp chia or flax seeds (seeds make this really filling)

berries and/or sliced banana, for garnish

Making life easy at breakfast needs to be a number one priority. When I wake up I go downstairs, put the kettle on for a cup of tea for me and then start soaking the oats so that when the breakfast rush starts it only takes 2 minutes to heat up. Otherwise, to get a great creamy porridge you need to be standing over it stirring for about 10 minutes, which is hard when you have kids screaming at you and you're trying to get them dressed and out the door for school in a short space of time. You can soak the oats overnight; there won't still be the bite to the oats that I like, but it works just the same if you are short on time.

1. Put the oats and milk in a pan and stir. Very finely grate the carrot and mix it in as well.

2. Leave to soak for at least 30 minutes (if using porridge oats don't soak first), adding the cacao powder or seeds if you're using.

3. When you're ready to cook, add the rest of the milk, the desiccated coconut, cinnamon and mashed banana. Warm up over a high heat, stirring, for about 2 minutes. Take off the heat and add the nut butter.

4. Serve with an extra spoon of nut butter and a sprinkle of coconut or berries and more sliced banana, if you wish.

LEFTOVER PORRIDGE BARS

MAKES 8 BARS | **PREP** 5 MINUTES | **COOK** 15 MINUTES

100g dates

60ml (¼ cup) warm water

150g leftover porridge

60g rolled jumbo oats

2 tbsp desiccated coconut

2 tbsp chia or flax seeds

There is nothing worse than leftover porridge. I hate the waste, but no matter what happens, there is always some! I therefore came up with a little solution of making granola bars, which we all love. You can keep 2–3 days' worth of old porridge in a container in the fridge before making these to ensure you have enough.

1. Preheat the oven to 180°C Fan. Line a 20cm loaf tin with baking paper.

2. Put the dates and warm water into a blender and pulse until they make a coarse purée.

3. Add to the rest of the ingredients and mix together.

4. Spoon into the lined loaf tin and spread so that it is 1cm thick.

5. Bake for 15 minutes, then take out and leave to cool. Cut into squares or bar shapes. The bars can be kept in an airtight Tupperware for 3 days.

HIDDEN VEG BAKED BEANS

SERVES 2 ADULTS AND 2 CHILDREN | **PREP** 10 MINUTES | **COOK** 10 MINUTES

1 small carrot

1 chestnut mushroom

1 garlic clove, grated

1 tbsp olive oil

200ml (generous ¾ cup) passata

240g tinned haricot beans
(drained weight)

1 tsp tamari

1 tbsp maple syrup

ADULT ADD-ONS (OPTIONAL)

salt and black pepper

¼ tsp smoked paprika

thyme leaves

ADD-ONS

toast with eggs, sausages,
mushrooms and/or spinach

baked potato and grated Cheddar

Green waffles (page 50)

Everyone loves baked beans, from tinies to grandparents, so having a good home-made recipe up your sleeves that is freezeable is a winner for a quick supper or breakfast.

1. Finely grate the carrot and mushroom on the fine part of a grater.

2. Heat the garlic and olive oil in a pan and cook for about a minute. Add the carrot and mushroom and stir for another minute.

3. Add the passata and haricot beans with the tamari and maple syrup and cook for 5 minutes on a medium heat, stirring occasionally so that nothing sticks to the bottom of the pan.

4. If you are serving to kids, take their portion out now and then add salt, pepper, a pinch of smoked paprika and fresh thyme.

5. Take off the heat and serve on your choice of toast with eggs, sausages, mushrooms and/or spinach or you can have on a baked potato with cheese. Alternatively, serve with waffles for some extra weekend vibes.

GREEN WAFFLES

MAKES 2 WAFFLES | **PREP** 10 MINUTES | **COOK** 5 MINUTES

35g butter

2 handfuls of spinach

150ml (generous ½ cup) milk

1 egg

160g gluten-free self-raising flour (add 20g more for self-raising wheat flour)

1 tsp baking powder

¼ tsp salt

2 tbsp maple syrup, plus more to serve

ADD-ONS

nut butter, desiccated coconut and sliced banana

fried egg and baked beans

I've always been a fan of waffles, but never had my own waffle iron until now. What was I waiting so long for, I don't know! This is a game changer in the morning to make a really quick brekky. I make the batter the night before and just pour into the waffle iron in the morning. It is also worth knowing this recipe works perfectly without the spinach if you have green-ophobe children!

1. Melt the butter in a saucepan and add the spinach, cooking until wilted. Put into a blender with the milk, egg, flour, baking powder, salt and maple syrup and blend until it has a velvety texture.

2. Heat the waffle iron until it is at the optimum temperature.

3. Pour in the mixture so it covers the whole surface. Close the lid for 4–5 minutes or until the top goes golden.

4. Serve with maple syrup or nut butter, desiccated coconut and sliced bananas or for a savoury fix, eat with a fried egg and baked beans.

KIDDIE FRIENDLY
These are great finger foods for a weaning baby.

ADULTS PIMP IT UP
Cut any leftovers into fingers and dip in hummus along with some sweet potato wedges for a delicious lunch box.

TIP
These taste best fresh, but you can keep them in a Tupperware and then pop them in the toaster and serve with butter and any topping you like. You can also freeze them and then toast from frozen for a super-quick breakfast or snack!

BRUNCH TRAY

SERVES 2 ADULTS AND 1 CHILD | **PREP** 10 MINUTES | **COOKING** 40 MINUTES

3 tbsp olive oil

1 small sweet potato, finely sliced into 2–3mm thick rings

80g mushrooms, thickly sliced

100g baby vine tomatoes

6 chipolatas

100g halloumi, cut into 1cm cubes

100g asparagus, sliced down the centre if thick

4 eggs

ADD-ONS

black pepper

sourdough bread slices

spinach

bacon rashers

Making brunch has never been so simple or straightforward. If you are vegetarian, you can swap the chipolatas for vegetarian sausages or just add in whatever your family's favourite veg are for lunch.

1. Preheat the oven to 200°C Fan.

2. Drizzle 1 tablespoon of the olive oil into the base of a large ovenproof dish, then place the sweet potato rings on top.

3. Place the mushrooms and baby tomatoes over them and drizzle the rest of the olive oil all over.

4. Scatter the chipolatas on top and then put into the oven for 15 minutes.

5. Turn the temperature of the oven down to 180°C Fan and put the halloumi cubes and asparagus over the top. Cook for another 10 minutes.

6. Take the dish out and crack the eggs over the top where you find a little space. Put back into the oven for 12 minutes or until the whites of the eggs are cooked.

7. Serve with cracked pepper, a lovely slice of sourdough to mop up the egg and any of the other extras.

CARROT PORRIDGE MINI 'CAKES'

MAKES 6 SMALL CUPCAKES | **PREP** 10 MINUTES | **COOK** 20 MINUTES

1 small carrot

100g leftover porridge

4 tbsp date syrup

1 tbsp coconut oil or melted butter

¼ tsp baking powder

100g rolled oats

1 egg

Porridge is an issue in our home – there are always leftovers! So I had to find a few different solutions to use them all up. I find these the perfect snack. I like to call them 'cakes' so Rudy thinks they are a great dessert!

1. Preheat the oven to 180°C Fan and line a muffin tray with small cupcake holders.

2. Finely grate the carrot and mix into the leftover porridge. Add in the date syrup, coconut oil, baking powder and oats.

3. Beat the egg and then mix this into the rest of the ingredients as well.

4. Spoon the batter into the cupcake holders and bake in the oven for 20 minutes.

5. Keep in a Tupperware for up to 2 days. Any longer and they start to taste a little sad!

ADULTS PIMP IT UP
Add a pinch of cinnamon and/or a dash of vanilla essence.

TIP
If you don't have carrot try courgette for some extra veg.

GREEN SCRAMBLED EGGS

SERVES 1 | **PREP** 3 MINUTES | **COOK** 3 MINUTES

handful of spinach

1 tbsp butter, plus extra to taste

1 egg

I wish I had thought of this when Rudy was just starting weaning, as it's delicious and he was obsessed with scrambled eggs. Getting kids to eat green foods from an early age so it's not a 'yuck' food is really important and this is a wonderful way of introducing something yummy. The recipe is written for 1 egg, so just double or triple to how many eggs you usually eat.

1. Pour a kettle of boiling water over the spinach in a sieve so it wilts.

2. Pop into a blender with the butter and egg and blend until green and smooth.

3. Add some more butter to the pan and pour in the egg mixture. Stir constantly to scramble the egg until you have the consistency you like.

ADULTS PIMP IT UP
Eat with smoked salmon on toast and some cracked pepper.

0-15
MINUTES

These recipes are for those days when you don't have time, can't be bothered or just need something on the table super quick.

Finding the time to get a meal prepared that isn't time consuming or tricky to make is the key to a happy house in my opinion. The freezer is my larder when it comes to ease in the kitchen. Batch cooking recipes and then freezing them so you don't even have to cook is the best way to stay sane in a busy family. It also means that when you are on the last dregs of the shopping for the week you always have something hearty, filling and warming ready to heat up.

However that's not always life, is it! I have been caught off-guard one too many times with my freezer empty, just 15 minutes before I must feed Rudy and needing to rustle something up really fast. Nine times out of ten Rudy helps me cook these meals as, firstly, I can't be split in half to go play tractors in the other room and, secondly, because it really helps him to get excited about food and cooking. At the dinner table we then talk about how and what we cooked, which is a wonderful way to get children interested in food and how it gets to their plates.

In this chapter you can expect recipes like popcorn fish, dips, loads of sauces that are multi-functional and turn into soups, curries, sauces for pasta and purées for weaning babies, along with veggie pancakes and stir-fries.

EASY GUACAMOLE

SERVES 2 | **PREP** 5 MINUTES

½ chilli, thinly sliced

1cm piece of fresh ginger, grated

1 avocado

juice of 1 lime

1 tsp sesame oil

salt and black pepper

Not much needs to be said about a guacamole... If you are making this for kids, then leave out the chilli and possibly the ginger, and swap the sesame oil for olive oil as these tastes may be too strong for little ones. Try adding crumbled feta and putting it on toast for a very quick and easy meal, possibly with some broccoli and corn on the cob on the side.

1. Put the chilli and ginger into a bowl with the avocado, lime juice, sesame oil and a pinch of salt and pepper. Mash the avocado with the back of a fork and mix into the other ingredients.

2. The guacamole will keep in an airtight container in the fridge for up to 2 days.

SANDWICH FILLINGS

SMOKED FISH

MAKES ENOUGH FOR 2 SANDWICHES
PREP 5 MINUTES

I absolutely love this on toast and you can put it in between two slices of bread for a great energy-giving sandwich. It's healthier and tastier than tuna mayo! Great for on-the-go eating.

100g smoked mackerel

juice of ½ lemon

2 tbsp olive oil

1 heaped tsp tahini

salt and black pepper

1. Take the skin off the mackerel and discard. Put the mackerel into a blender with the lemon juice, olive oil, tahini and a pinch of salt and pepper. Blend to a good pâté consistency with no mackerel lumps.

2. Store in an airtight container for up to 3 days.

AVOCADO AND EGG

MAKES ENOUGH FOR 2 SANDWICHES
PREP 5 MINUTES | **COOK** 7 MINUTES

It is a classic marriage: avo and egg. This is a lovely way to have it on the go if you need to take something with you that is quick and simple to make. You can also serve on toast, oat cakes or crackers.

1 egg

1 ripe avocado

juice of ½ lemon

salt and black pepper

1. Bring a pan of water to the boil, drop the egg in carefully and cook for 7 minutes. Take out and put into a bowl of cold water to stop the cooking process. Peel the egg and dice.

2. In a bowl smash the avocado with the back of a fork and mix in the egg, lemon juice, salt and black pepper.

GREEN PANCAKES

SERVES 2 CHILDREN | **PREP** 10 MINUTES | **COOK** 10 MINUTES

2 tbsp olive oil

⅓ tsp ground cumin

¼ courgette, grated

2 broccoli florets, finely chopped

50g spinach

2 tbsp water

3 level tbsp self-raising flour
(gluten-free or wheat)

1 tsp baking powder

1 tbsp store-brought pesto

1 egg

I love pancakes – they are quick and simple to make even with a toddler hanging from your leg! Introducing greens into a food they already love is also a wonderful way to add more veg to their repertoire, and these are great for the whole family. You can pretty much use any vegetables to make different flavours too. If you batch cook these and freeze, you can just pop them into the toaster while still frozen to heat up.

1. In a frying pan, add 1 tablespoon of the olive oil, the cumin, courgette and broccoli and cook for 2–3 minutes.

2. Add the spinach and water and continue to cook until the vegetables are soft.

3. Take off the heat and put into a blender with the flour, baking powder, pesto and egg and blend until smooth.

4. Using the same frying pan, add the other tablespoon of olive oil to the pan and bring to a medium to high heat. Spoon heaped tablespoons of the mixture into the hot pan and leave to cook for 1–2 minutes until golden on one side, then flip and cook on the other side. Keep warm while you repeat until all the mixture is finished.

ADULTS PIMP IT UP
Add a poached egg and serve with a lovely rocket and chilli salad for a lazy lunch or quick supper.

Make double of the stir-fried greens for your supper and serve with a piece of tamari-roasted salmon from page 88.

Instead of the store-bought pesto, you could use one of the pestos on pages 66–67.

KIDDIE FRIENDLY
Swap up the flavours by using some of the sauces from pages 66–73. Just add 2 tablespoons of the puréed sauce instead of the stir-fried green veg and jump to the blending step.

SAUCES AND PESTOS

The great thing about sauces is that you can hide so many things in them and mix and incorporate them into your family dishes.

- Add more liquid and turn into a soup

- Drain off excess liquid and blend into a chunky purée for weaning

- Use 2 tablespoons of the purée in the pancakes recipe on page 64

- Use for the pinwheels on page 138

- Add to pasta, rice, quinoa or couscous during the weaning phase

- Use as a dipping sauce for burgers, roasted chicken or the fish on page 94

- Use as a dip for a chunky piece of bread or even the Green waffles on page 50

- Add 1 tablespoon to the frittata recipe on page 108

- Use for a pizza sauce

But best of all, these sauces freeze really well and take up very little room in the freezer. Either put into weaning pots or pouches or into reusable freezer bags in portion sizes and freeze. Defrost for 5 minutes in a bowl of boiling water for a very quick and easy meal for the family.

As well as the super-quick sauces in this chapter, make sure you try the delicious Hidden veg and lentil tomato sauce on page 174.

PIMPED-UP PESTO

SERVES 3 CHILDREN | **PREP** 5 MINUTES
COOK 5 MINUTES

Kids often love store-bought pesto, so this little trick is a life-saver if you have a fussy eater as they will know no different. Buy your favourite pesto brand and pimp it up to get some extra greens in their diet.

60g broccoli florets

40g green beans

50g courgette

handful of spinach

4 tbsp store-bought pesto

1. Cut all the vegetables into bite-size pieces, then steam until soft.

2. Put into a blender with the pesto and blend until smooth.

3. You can now freeze this in portion sizes or keep in the fridge.

PESTO CUBES

SERVES 3 (MAKES 12 CUBES) | **PREP** 5 MINUTES

The best way to store pesto long term is in ice-cube trays in the freezer, then when you fancy a simple pesto pasta, you can just pop a few cubes straight into a pan with a splash of water and let them defrost and warm up. If you don't have spare ice-cube trays, you can roll the pesto in parchment paper, wrap in clingfilm and pop in the freezer until it's hard, but soft enough to slice. Slice it into portion amounts about 2–3cm thick and then freeze till you are ready to use.

50g basil

80g feta

4 tbsp olive oil

2 tbsp cashew butter

black pepper

1. Put all the ingredients into a food processor or blender and blend until smooth. Either use straight away or put into ice-cube trays and into the freezer. Once they have frozen, pop them out and put into a freezer bag to save room.

2. To defrost, just put into a pan with a tablespoon of water and heat slowly.

TOFU NUT-FREE PESTO

SERVES 4 CHILDREN | **PREP** 10 MINUTES
COOK 5 MINUTES

I was asked if I could create a nut- and cheese-free pesto for a children's club. It was hard to create that taste without two main ingredients, but I nailed it and the best bit is that there is extra veg in it. This doesn't freeze well, as the basil and tofu are quite watery.

2½ tbsp olive oil

1 garlic clove, diced very small

1 mushroom, diced

35g courgette, diced into ¼cm cubes

1 tsp water

35g basil, thick stalks removed

40g tofu, diced

1½ tsp lemon juice

1 tsp vegetable stock powder

1. Add 1 teaspoon of the oil to a frying pan with the garlic, mushroom, courgette and the water to loosen it. Cook for 2 minutes, stirring constantly, then take off the heat. Don't overcook it; you want to keep the texture – this is very important.

2. Put all the remaining ingredients along with the cooked mushrooms and courgette into a food processor and pulse until you have a pesto texture. Don't overblend as you want texture.

3. Store in the fridge.

SAUCES

CAULIFLOWER, BEAN AND FETA WHITE SAUCE

SERVES 2 | **PREP** 10 MINUTES | **COOK** 5 MINUTES

A simple white sauce pimped up. I like to roast the cauliflower sometimes to give extra flavour. If your baby is under one, use Cheddar not feta.

80g cauliflower florets

¼ courgette

35g feta or Cheddar

60g tinned cannellini beans (drained weight)

60ml (¼ cup) milk

knob of butter (optional)

1. Steam the cauliflower until soft. Peel the green off the courgette and then grate.

2. Put both into the blender with the cheese, beans and milk and blend until velvety smooth.

3. When ready to use, heat in a pan and the feta will melt and become creamy. You can add a knob of butter for extra creaminess.

PIMP IT UP
This is excellent as a mac and cheese. Make a roux first by putting 1 tbsp butter into a pan with 2 tbsp flour and whisking in 250ml (1 cup) milk until all lumps have disappeared. Stir in the cauliflower sauce, mix through macaroni and sprinkle over grated cheese before baking.

PERFECT PASTA SAUCE

SERVES 2 | **PREP** 10 MINUTES | **COOK** 10 MINUTES

Since becoming pregnant and now with a little person to feed, my cooking has become quick and fuss free, so most of my recipes are very much of the chuck-it-all-in-the-pan variety! Nothing beats a simple tomato pasta for dinner and this sauce is delicious and simple, and you can freeze batches of it. It's also great for when you start weaning. My little boy Rudy loves it.

½ red onion, diced

1 garlic clove, diced

1 tsp olive oil

200g baby vine tomatoes, halved

2 large chestnut mushrooms, diced

3 tbsp boiling water mixed with ¼ tsp vegetable stock powder

1. Put the red onion and garlic into a saucepan with the olive oil and cook for 1–2 minutes. Add the tomatoes and mushrooms to the pan with the water and vegetable stock powder.

2. Cook for 5 minutes over a medium heat until the tomatoes have broken down and created a thick sauce. The longer you cook the sauce, the thicker it will become as the broth reduces.

3. Serve with pasta, rice, grains or spooned over a baked potato!

SAUCES

BEETROOT AND BLACK BEAN TOMATO SAUCE

SERVES 4 CHILDREN | **PREP** 5 MINUTES
COOK 5 MINUTES

You can use this sauce as a filling for a Mexican night if you want to mix it up a bit by adding some sweet potato wedges, Easy guacamole from page 60, rice and, of course, some cheese melted over the top! It's a wonderful dish for everyone to enjoy. Alternatively, spoon over a baked potato or, my favourite, use as a hidden veg pizza topping. Brilliant for freezing in ice-cube portions too.

130g cooked beetroot

1 red pepper

100g baby vine tomatoes

160g tinned black beans (drained weight)

4 tbsp olive oil

1. Put all the ingredients into a blender and blend until smooth.

2. If you are using for a sauce, put into a pan and heat for 2–3 minutes to cook the raw vegetables. If you are using this as a pizza tomato sauce, it will cook when in the oven.

BUTTERNUT SQUASH, CARROTS AND COCONUT MILK

SERVES 4 CHILDREN | **PREP** 10 MINUTES
COOK 10 MINUTES

This also works so well as a soup. We make it in the winter and have with a great hunk of sourdough bread. I often add chilli flakes for some extra kick.

1 tbsp olive oil

¼ tsp ground coriander

½ red onion, diced

1 carrot, diced

3 mushrooms, diced

200g butternut squash, peeled and diced into 1cm cubes

200ml (generous ¾ cup) coconut milk

1. Add the olive oil to a pan and cook the ground coriander for 1 minute. Add in the red onion and cook until it softens a little.

2. Add in the rest of the ingredients and put the lid on. Cook over a medium heat for about 8 minutes until the butternut is nice and soft.

3. Put the mixture into a blender and blend until velvety smooth.

4. Serve as a sauce for pasta or add 250ml (1 cup) water and use as a soup!

SWEETCORN, CARROTS AND MUSHROOMS

SERVES 4 CHILDREN | **PREP** 5 MINUTES | **COOK** 10 MINUTES

½ sweetcorn

1 tbsp olive oil

1 garlic clove, diced

70g baby vine tomatoes

¼ courgette, diced

3 chestnut mushrooms, diced

2 small carrots, diced

300ml (1¼ cups) boiling water mixed with 1 tsp vegetable stock powder

This makes a beautiful soup. I cooked it for my grandmother when she came for lunch and used the leftovers for a pasta for Rudy. Add some crumbled feta over the top and cracked pepper.

1. Cut the sweetcorn off the kernel

2. Add the olive oil and garlic to a pan and sauté for 1 minute.

3. Add the rest of the ingredients and leave to cook on a medium to high heat for approximately 7 minutes or until the carrots are soft enough to blend.

4. Blend until smooth and reheat the soup to serve.

KIDDIE FRIENDLY

If you are weaning and would like to use this as a thick purée, just drain off any excess liquid before blending.

If you want to make this into a soup for the whole family, just add another 250ml (1 cup) water before blending and quadruple the recipe to serve 2 adults and 2 children.

SOUPS

BUTTERNUT SQUASH SOUP

SERVES 2 | **PREP** 5 MINUTES | **COOK** 5 MINUTES (IF RAW BUTTERNUT, 1 HOUR TO ROAST)

I find butternut really comforting. Its velvety texture is wonderfully soothing. The easiest way to cook a butternut is to pop it into a 180°C Fan oven whole with the skin on for 50–60 minutes. Then it's easy to peel and you can slice, mash or blend the flesh. This is a perfect purée for weaning or a pasta sauce for older ones.

750g butternut squash (340g roasted with the skin off)

400ml tin coconut milk

1 tsp vegetable stock powder

juice of ½ lemon

1 tbsp tahini

salt and black pepper

1. Roast the butternut squash (see above).

2. Put 340g of the roasted flesh into a blender with the coconut milk, vegetable stock powder, lemon and tahini. Blend until smooth and season with salt and black pepper. Heat up the soup in a small pan.

3. Either freeze in portion-size bags or put into a Tupperware – it will keep in the fridge for up to 4 days.

FENNEL AND CELERIAC SOUP

SERVES 2 | **PREP** 10 MINUTES | **COOK** 15 MINUTES

Wonderfully velvety and brilliant to have as a quick lunch with a big wedge of bread and butter. It is a lovely sweet soup, so little people like it too.

1 tsp cumin seeds

1 tbsp olive oil

2 garlic cloves, sliced

1 fennel bulb, peeled and cut into 1cm cubes

200g celeriac, peeled and cut into 1cm cubes

250ml (1 cup) boiling water mixed with 1 tsp vegetable stock powder

200ml (scant 1 cup) coconut milk

salt and black pepper

1. In a deep pan, fry the cumin seeds in the olive oil with the garlic. Add the fennel and celeriac with the stock and stir. After 2–3 minutes when the stock starts to evaporate, add the coconut milk and cook over a medium heat for 10 minutes or until the celeriac is soft.

2. Season with salt and black pepper and blend. If you want it a little thinner, just add a touch of hot water. Reheat the soup.

3. This soup is perfect to freeze. Just leave to cool, then pop each serving into a freezer bag.

RAMEN BOWL

SERVES 2 | **PREP** 5 MINUTES | **COOK** 15 MINUTES

1 tsp sesame oil

2–3cm piece of fresh ginger, grated

2 spring onions, sliced

60ml (¼ cup) good-quality beef stock or bone broth

2 tbsp brown rice miso paste

185ml (¾ cup) water

1 tsp tamari

50g shiitake mushrooms, sliced

3 baby vine tomatoes

½ red chilli

1 egg

100g soba noodles

3 broccoli florets

squeeze of lime juice

30g spinach

I love broth soups. They are so quick to make and really packed full of flavour. You can pretty much add any vegetables to this dish that you have in the fridge. If you want to add some more protein to the dish, prawns would taste great too.

1. Put the sesame oil into a pan with the ginger and spring onions. Cook over a medium heat for 1 minute. Add the beef stock and the miso paste and leave to infuse for a couple of minutes. Add the water, tamari, mushrooms, baby tomatoes and red chilli. I like to put the chilli in whole as it infuses the broth beautifully, but you don't have to eat the chilli. Cook for 5 minutes.

2. While this is cooking, bring a pan of water to the boil and add your egg. Cook for 7 minutes, then put into cold water straight away (this is so it doesn't continue cooking), then peel and halve.

3. Put the soba noodles into the ramen broth with the broccoli and cook for 2–3 minutes until soft. Add a squeeze of lime and the spinach and leave on the heat until wilted. Pour into bowls and place an egg half on top of each one.

4. Serve and eat straight away.

KIDDIE FRIENDLY
To make a kiddie-friendly portion, use the same veg and noodles as for you, but strain off the broth and mix through a simple pesto or a tomato sauce so that you are not cooking twice.

CHEESY POLENTA AND GREENS

SERVES 2 | **PREP** 10 MINUTES | **COOK** 15 MINUTES

1 garlic clove, diced

1 tbsp olive oil

½ tsp ground turmeric

½ tsp ground cumin

380ml (1½ cups) milk

1 tsp vegetable stock powder

70g thick coarse polenta

WHIPPED FETA

60g feta

1 tsp olive oil

½ red chilli (optional)

GREENS

1 tbsp olive oil

juice of ½ lemon

100g sugar snap peas, sliced

½ fennel bulb, sliced

3 tbsp water

50g kale, chopped

100g spinach, chopped

salt and black pepper

ADD-ONS (OPTIONAL)

chilli slices and pan-roasted chickpeas with smoked paprika

cubes of chicken or salmon

I absolutely love polenta. It's so comforting and I find it a perfect food for when the house is struck down with colds – it's thick and creamy and really filling. It takes no time at all to make as well, so you don't have to be standing on your feet for too long. Have it with the greens or add your own choice of protein. If you have any leftovers, grate in some veg and set into Polenta fingers (page 92).

1. Whip the feta by putting it into a blender with the olive oil and chilli. Blend until it has a soft cream texture.

2. To make the greens, put the olive oil and lemon juice into a frying pan, add the sugar snaps and fennel and cook for 3 minutes. Add the water and the rest of the vegetables and cook until soft. Add slices of chilli if you want to make it spicy, and season.

3. Put the garlic into a pan with the olive oil, turmeric and cumin and cook for 2 minutes, then add the milk and vegetable stock powder. Bring to a simmering boil and add the polenta. Turn the heat down to a low simmer (if it is too high the polenta will bubble and spit everywhere). Whisk constantly so no lumps appear, cooking for 5–10 minutes until it is soft and creamy. Add more milk if you need to loosen it up.

4. Serve the polenta with the whipped feta, greens and chickpeas or cooked chicken or salmon, if using.

KIDDIE FRIENDLY
Serve the polenta with some grated cheese and flaked salmon over the top and broccoli and peas on the side.

MACKEREL PATTIES

SERVES 2 (6 PATTIES) | **PREP** 10 MINUTES | **COOK** 10 MINUTES

200g smoked mackerel

juice of 2 limes

large handful of coriander

2 tbsp olive oil, plus 2 tsp for frying

2 eggs

2 tbsp plain flour (gluten-free, spelt or wheat)

2 tbsp sweet chilli sauce (optional)

salt and black pepper

These are delicious and perfect as a snack or main meal. You can eat with a salad or have some roasted veg with a grain to make it a more substantial meal. This recipe also makes a delicious dip to have with crudités or on toast – just leave out the egg and flour. These freeze really well!

1. Remove the skin from the mackerel and put the flesh into the blender with the juice of the limes, coriander, olive oil and eggs and blend until a thick, chunky texture forms. Mix in the flour and season with salt and pepper to taste.

2. In a non-stick frying pan, drizzle in 1 teaspoon olive oil and bring to a high heat.

3. Put 1 heaped tablespoon of the mixture into the pan and flatten so it's about ½cm thick. Cook for 2–3 minutes on each side. Repeat until the mixture is used up. It should make six.

4. Eat straight away and leave any extra patties to cool, then put into a freezer bag with a layer of baking paper between each one and freeze.To reheat, just put the frozen patties onto a baking paper-lined baking tray in a 180°C Fan oven for 15 minutes or until warmed through. Serve with the sweet chilli sauce, if using.

SPICED GINGER PRAWN STIR-FRY

SERVES 2 | **PREP** 10 MINUTES | **COOK** 15 MINUTES

1 tsp coconut or olive oil

2–3cm piece of fresh ginger, diced

1 garlic clove, diced

2 red peppers, sliced

100g sugar snap peas

200g raw prawns

3 tbsp water

50g frozen peas

50g baby vine tomatoes, halved

100g spinach

small handful of coriander

SALSA

small handful of coriander

2 tbsp olive oil

juice of 2 limes

½ red chilli

pinch of salt

I really love this dish as it's super quick and tasty. If you don't like prawns, you can use tofu or chicken. Serve alone or with some noodles or rice.

1. Make the salsa by putting all the ingredients into a blender and blending until smooth.

2. To a large frying pan, add the coconut oil, ginger and garlic and half of the salsa and cook over a medium heat. Add the peppers, sugar snap peas and prawns. Stir continuously and cook until the prawns start to go pink.

3. Add the water to loosen up the mixture, the peas, tomatoes and spinach. Continue to cook until the peppers soften. Add the coriander.

4. At the very end add the rest of the salsa and stir through over the heat.

PRAWN THAI CURRY

SERVES 2 | **PREP** 10 MINUTES | **COOK** 10 MINUTES

1 tsp sesame oil

½ red onion, diced

2 heaped tbsp Thai green curry paste

400ml tin coconut milk

150g raw king prawns

100g mushrooms, sliced

50g baby sweetcorn

1 red pepper, sliced

100g spinach

Curries are particularly warming and nurturing. For this dish you can use chicken or tofu instead of prawns if you prefer. If you are making this for kids, hold back half of the curry paste to make it a little milder.

1. Heat the sesame oil in a suacepan, add the red onion and cook for 1–2 minutes. Add the curry paste and cook for a further 2 minutes.

2. Add the coconut milk and stir into the paste. Once combined, add the prawns, mushrooms, baby sweetcorn and peppers and cook for 5 minutes until the vegetables are soft.

3. Add the spinach to wilt at the end and serve straight away.

4. This curry will keep in a Tupperware in the fridge for up to 2 days or you can freeze straight away. To freeze, leave to cool, then put into a freezer bag in portion sizes. When you're ready to eat, you can just put it into a pan and heat from frozen.

TAMARI-BAKED SALMON FILLETS

SERVES 2 | **PREP** 2 MINUTES | **COOK** 15 MINUTES

2 salmon fillets

1 tbsp olive oil

2 tbsp tamari

5 tbsp water

black pepper

This is a quick and simple dish to have on hand in the fridge for a lunch or supper. It can be served with pasta, grains or veg and works for the whole family. Lovely served with the quinoa salad on page 126.

1. Preheat the oven to 180°C Fan.

2. Put the salmon fillets, skin down, into an ovenproof dish with sides and lined with baking paper. Pour the olive oil, tamari and water over the top and season with pepper (you won't need salt as tamari is naturally salty).

3. Bake in the oven for 15 minutes, then take out and serve straight away or leave to cool.

4. This can be stored in a Tupperware container in the fridge for up to 2 days.

FISH FINGERS AND SWEET POTATO MASH

SERVES 2 | **PREP** 10 MINUTES | **COOK** 20 MINUTES

2 sweet potatoes, peeled and cut into 1cm cubes

1 tbsp tahini

pinch of paprika

1 tsp olive oil, plus more for frying

2 white fish fillets, skinned

coarse polenta or ground almonds, for rolling

100g peas

1 tsp butter

5g mint leaves, chopped (optional)

salt and black pepper

BATTER

1 egg

2 tbsp plain flour (gluten-free, spelt or wheat)

zest of ½ lemon

salt and black pepper

I love fish fingers! This version is really simple to make from scratch and the whole family can enjoy it. If you have little ones, I've found that ground almonds work better as they're less crispy for their gums, but I love the polenta and it tastes more like a traditional fish finger. This batter also works for making delicious chicken nuggets.

1. Steam or boil the sweet potato until soft. Mash with the back of a fork and mix in the tahini, paprika and olive oil and season with salt and black pepper. Put to one side.

2. Meanwhile, make the batter by mixing together the egg, flour, lemon zest and seasoning. Whisk until combined and there are no lumps.

3. Cut the fish into 1cm-wide and 7–8cm-long fingers. Dip into the batter and coat well, then roll in the polenta and put to one side on a plate or on some baking paper. If you are making ahead, you can now pop onto a baking tray to freeze. Once frozen, pop into a freezer bag to save space, then cook from frozen in a medium oven.

4. Heat a frying pan with oil and bring to a medium heat. Put the fish fingers into the pan and cook until golden on each side.

5. Boil a kettle and pour the water over the frozen peas to heat them up. Drain and mix through the butter and mint. Season and serve with the mash and fish fingers.

POLENTA FINGERS

SERVES 2 CHILDREN | **PREP** 5 MINUTES | **COOK** 5 MINUTES PLUS 1 HOUR SETTING

40g coarse polenta

185ml (¾ cup) milk

¼ tsp vegetable stock powder

¼ courgette, grated

½ tsp pesto

I made these for Rudy when he was weaning and refusing to be spoon fed. They are a brilliant baby-led weaning recipe as they can pick them up easily in their little hands, are super filling and you can hide veg in them too. They also melt in the mouth, so they are great for the no-teeth stage.

1. Put all the ingredients into a pan and bring to the boil, making sure you whisk so you don't get any lumps. Once boiling, take the temperature down to a simmer and stir constantly for 5 minutes.

2. Pour into a small Tupperware no bigger than 10cm square and put into the fridge for about an hour to set.

3. If you want to have the polenta warm, add another 125ml (½ cup) milk while cooking.

ADULTS PIMP IT UP
Times the recipe by four and add a handful of feta. Serve the polenta warm with a piece of salmon, chicken or pan-roasted chickpeas and smoked paprika.

POPCORN FISH AND PEPPER-TOMATO SAUCE

SERVES 2 CHILDREN | **PREP** 10 MINUTES | **COOK** 10 MINUTES

POPCORN

100g hake

2 tbsp olive oil

1 tbsp self-raising flour (gluten-free or wheat)

SAUCE

1 red pepper

75g tomatoes

2 tbsp olive oil

SERVE WITH

brown rice, quinoa or pasta

This was an absolute favourite for Rudy when he was weaning. The fish is so delicious and you can make it into mini burgers as well as popcorn. I chose to use hake as it's the least fishy-tasting fish, but you can use pretty much any other white fish or salmon. You can freeze the batter before you cook it as well if you want to batch cook this. Just defrost for a couple hours before making the popcorn.

1. Put the hake, 1 tablespoon of the olive oil and the flour into a food processor or blender and blend until it becomes a paste.

2. Heat a pan with the remaining 1 tablespoon olive oil and and drop in ½ teaspoons of the fish paste in the shape of little balls. Flip the fish balls over after about 2–3 minutes and cook until they are golden all over and then put into a bowl.

3. To make the sauce, put all the ingredients into a blender and blend until a smooth liquid. Transfer to a pan and cook for 4–5 minutes over a medium heat.

4. Serve the popcorn with the sauce and rice, quinoa or pasta.

ADULTS PIMP IT UP
If you buy an extra couple of fillets of hake, pan-fry them with a little butter or olive oil, double the recipe for the sauce and serve with the fish and whichever grain you are cooking for the little ones.

FRIDGE-RAID STIR-FRY

SERVES 2 ADULTS AND 1 CHILD | **PREP** 10 MINUTES | **COOK** 15 MINUTES

1 tbsp olive oil

1 garlic clove

150g protein (fish, chicken, tofu or beef), cut into small chunks

300g vegetables (I use courgette, baby corn and mangetout), cut into 2cm pieces

150g mushrooms (exotic ones taste fab if you can get them), cut into 2cm pieces

185ml (¾ cup) water

150g greens (pak choi, cabbage, tat soi), cut into 2cm pieces

1 tbsp tamari

½ chilli, thinly sliced (optional)

TERIYAKI SAUCE

125ml (½ cup) water

80ml (⅓ cup) tamari

3 tbsp honey or maple syrup

1 tbsp rice vinegar

1 tbsp grated garlic

1 tbsp grated fresh ginger

1 tbsp cornflour mixed with 2 tbsp water

You really can use anything you have in your fridge and then either follow the recipe to make your own teriyaki sauce or use store-bought. This is also a great recipe for making the cooked veg to use for the Green pancakes on page 64. Remember you can swap the tamari for soy sauce if you prefer.

1. To make the teriyaki sauce, heat the water, tamari, honey, rice vinegar, garlic and ginger in a pan over a medium high heat, stirring until smoothly combined. Bring to a boil.

2. Add the cornflour paste and whisk constantly for about 1–2 minutes until the sauce is thickened, then take off the heat and put to one side.

3. Add the olive oil to a pan with the garlic. If you are using chicken or beef, add now too and make sure it is browned off before going to the next step.

4. Add the vegetables and mushrooms and most of the water and cook for about 3–4 minutes over a medium heat.

5. If you are eating fish or tofu, add this now with the greens and tamari. Add the remaining water and cook until your protein is cooked and any excess water has been absorbed.

6. Take off the heat, add the teriyaki sauce and serve the stir-fry by itself or with grains or noodles, sprinkled with chilli, if using.

ADULTS PIMP IT UP
If you want a nice flavour change, source some sweet miso and stir in 2 tablespoons when you add the greens instead of the teriyaki sauce.

KIDDIE FRIENDLY
You can omit the teriyaki sauce and make a veg version for adding as a side to your kids' dinner or maybe mix through some pesto for a simple dish with pasta.

SALADS

I have always had a theory with salad ... it has to be substantial enough to feel like a meal. So I will show you the blueprint of how to put it together. It's pretty simple and you can use whatever you have in the fridge at home.

Grain
You can buy precooked packets to make this super quick or cook from scratch at home.

Quinoa / brown rice / white rice / pearl barley / millet / couscous

Protein
You can add any protein you like here, whether you are a vegetarian, flexitarian or meat eater. I didn't put nuts and seeds here as I like to add them as a topping for a great add-on.

Chicken / salmon / tuna / lentils / feta / white beans / chickpeas

Veg
Roast, steam or have raw ... if you make extras you can always turn them into a simple soup by blending them up with some hot water and vegetable stock powder.

Sweet potato / carrots / beetroot / asparagus / green beans / courgette / white potato / tomato / peas / baby corn

Leafy
Add in a crunch or soft leaf to fill it out and give you that lovely vibrance.

Rocket / spinach / lettuce leaves

Toppings
Chopped nuts / seeds / blended flax seeds / chopped fresh herbs / chilli flakes / cracked pepper

Dressings

- Tamari, balsamic, olive oil

- Olive oil, lemon juice, apple cider vinegar, honey

- Teriyaki sauce (page 96)

- Tahini, water, lemon, salt

- Yoghurt, lemon juice, vinegar

- Mustard, olive oil, honey, lemon juice

ONE-POT SUN-DRIED TOMATO PENNE

SERVES 4 | **PREP** 5 MINUTES | **COOK** 15 MINUTES

1 garlic clove

1 tbsp olive oil

1 tsp ground cumin

250g baby vine tomatoes

120g cooked beetroot, grated

60g shiitake mushrooms, sliced

30g sun-dried tomatoes, diced

500ml (2 cups) water mixed with
1 tsp vegetable stock powder

175g penne pasta

60g feta

400g tinned cannellini beans
(230g drained weight)

spinach or herbs (optional)

grated Parmesan, to serve

For the fussiest of eaters this goes down a storm. You can add some chicken or salmon to the pot while cooking for extra protein if you wish, with perhaps some spinach or herbs thrown in at the end.
I love it with chilli flakes and a turn of cracked pepper.

1. Grate the garlic into a heavy-bottomed saucepan with the olive oil and cumin and cook on a medium heat for 2 minutes.

2. Add the tomatoes, beetroot, mushrooms, sun-dried tomatoes and half the vegetable stock. Bring to the boil.

3. Once boiling, add the rest of the stock and the pasta, stir and put the lid on. Stir frequently so it doesn't stick to the bottom of the pan.

4. After 5 minutes, add the feta and cannellini beans, put the lid on, turn down to a low heat and leave to cook until the pasta is soft. Make sure you stir frequently so that it doesn't burn or stick to the bottom.

5. If you are adding spinach or fresh herbs, just add them at the very end and let wilt in the heat. Serve the pasta with grated Parmesan.

KIDDIE FRIENDLY

For a toddler lunch box, this is perfect cold the next day. Add some bread to let them mop up the juices and a corn on the cob.

It is also brilliant for second-stage weaning. Just chop up small – great for young gums!

ONE-POT CREAMY SPAGHETTI

SERVES 4 | **PREP** 5 MINUTES | **COOK** 10 MINUTES

2 garlic cloves

2 tbsp olive oil

160g aubergine

1 courgette

2 x 400ml tins coconut milk

1 tbsp vegetable stock powder

180g spaghetti (I use spelt)

400g baby vine tomatoes

grated Parmesan, to serve

I can promise you that when I say this dish is insanely delicious, I mean it. Rudy loves it and so do Simon and I. You can add prawns and a sprinkle of chilli flakes to make it adult friendly for a perfect supper!

1. Grate the garlic into a large heavy pan with the olive oil.

2. Dice the aubergine into 1cm cubes and ribbon the courgette with a potato peeler (or you can just dice if you prefer).

3. Place the pan onto a medium heat and cook the garlic for 1 minute. Add the aubergine, coconut milk and stock powder and stir.

4. Add in the spaghetti and slowly push it down so it doesn't break in half.

5. Add the baby tomatoes once the spaghetti is covered in the liquid and then the courgette ribbons.

6. Stir frequently until the spaghetti is cooked – this takes about 8–10 minutes, depending on the type you use. Serve with grated Parmesan.

ADULTS PIMP IT UP
Add prawns and chilli flakes or simply more veg, if you wish, such as mushrooms, green beans and a handful of spinach at the end.

KIDDIE FRIENDLY
You can use penne pasta instead of spaghetti, if you wish, as it's easier for little hands to pick up!

15–30
MINUTES

I have never felt such a huge sense of excitement or fear as when it comes to feeding my family! I have spoken to so many mothers and we are all in the same boat. You slave away in the kitchen making nutritious food and it gets thrown on the floor or given to the dog while your back is turned.

Children go through fussy stages and this is not a reflection on you or your cooking. Please try to remember that when nothing seems good enough for your biggest critics, it is all a phase. Something I say to myself daily is, 'This too will pass,' just like the last few hours of the day till you can sit down with a nice glass of wine and eat your dinner in peace.

Navigating mealtimes can be tricky and the last thing you want to feel is that you are running a restaurant with everyone requesting different meals. That is the reason that most of these recipes can be adapted for all ages and meal requirements. It really is a 'one dish feeds all' approach. You will see that I make suggestions for everything from adapting a recipe for weaning or creating a more adult-friendly dish to saving leftovers from dinner to make a quick lunch for a toddler or snacks for a lunch box.

I got caught in that trap of cooking several meals a day in the early days, but having worked out a way to make life easier with this one-dish philosophy, I hope it will help ease the strain off your kitchen like it did mine and make mealtimes enjoyable again!

PASTA BAKE

SERVES 4 | **PREP** 10 MINUTES | **COOK** 20 MINUTES

300g fusilli or penne pasta

1 red onion, diced

2 tbsp olive oil

2 x 400g tins tomatoes

2 sprigs of rosemary

2 small sweet potatoes, peeled and cut into 1cm cubes

2 courgettes, diced

2 carrots, grated

200g hard goat's cheese, grated

Pasta is a winner in our family. If you want to eat this later, follow all the steps and stop at putting it in the oven. When ready to eat, preheat the oven to 180°C Fan and bake until heated through.

1. Preheat the oven to 180°C Fan. Cook the pasta just until al dente.

2. If you have an ovenproof pan, use that as then you can cook it on the hob and bake it in the oven and not have to create more cleaning up! Add the onion and olive oil to the pan and sauté over a medium heat for 1–2 minutes. Add the tinned tomatoes, rosemary and sweet potato and cook on a high heat for 5 minutes. Add the courgette and grated carrot and continue to cook until the sweet potato is just soft.

3. Once the pasta is cooked, drain and mix through the tomato sauce. Add half of the goat's cheese and mix in. Put the rest of the cheese on top and bake in the oven for 10 minutes.

4. Serve warm or cold. The bake will last for 2–3 days in an airtight container in the fridge.

RICOTTA AND SPINACH FRITTATA

SERVES 2 | **PREP** 5 MINUTES | **COOK** 20 MINUTES

80g sweet potato

1 tbsp olive oil

1 garlic clove, grated

¼ tsp nigella seeds

3–4 tbsp water

50g spinach

6 eggs

60g ricotta cheese, goat's cheese or feta

salt and black pepper

I cook a frittata pretty much once a week as they are quick to make, last 4 days in the fridge and are packed with so much protein for energy. You can add any vegetables to it as well.

1. Preheat the oven to 180°C Fan.

2. Thinly slice the sweet potato, or use a mandolin to get it really thin.

3. To an ovenproof non-stick pan, add the olive oil, garlic, nigella seeds and sweet potato and cook over a medium heat for 2–3 minutes until the sweet potato starts to soften. Add the water and spinach and cook until the water has been absorbed and the spinach wilted. Take off the heat.

4. Beat the eggs in a bowl and season. Pour over the mixture in the pan. Add the ricotta cheese in lumps and evenly spread. Put back onto a medium heat for 2 minutes until the edges just start to cook.

5. Put the whole pan into the oven for 15 minutes or until the egg is fully cooked/hardened.

6. Take out of the oven and leave to cool. Store in an airtight container in the fridge.

APRICOT TAGINE

SERVES 3-4 | **PREP** 10 MINUTES | **COOK** 25 MINUTES

2 tbsp olive oil

2 small red onions, diced

2 garlic cloves, diced

2 tsp ground cumin

1 cinnamon stick

125ml (½ cup) boiling water mixed with 1 tbsp vegetable stock powder

600g butternut squash, peeled and cut into 1cm cubes

2 x 400g tins chopped tomatoes

120g unsulphured apricots, roughly chopped

2 courgettes, cut into 1cm slices

2 x 400g tins chickpeas

20g parsley, roughly chopped

salt and black pepper

I love tagines and this is so easy to make and perfect to pop into the freezer in portion sizes for when you don't want to cook. I often eat half the night I cook the tagine and freeze the rest for another day. If you want to add meat to this dish, lamb or chicken would both work well instead of chickpeas. Add the diced meat just after cooking the spices, stir until brown, and then add the stock.

1. In a pan put the olive oil, red onion, garlic, ground cumin and cinnamon stick and sauté over a medium heat for 2 minutes. Add the stock and stir.

2. Add the butternut and mix through the spices. Add the tins of tomatoes, apricots and courgette. Bring to the boil with the lid on, then take the lid off and cook over a high heat for 15 minutes. Add the chickpeas and parsley and stir through for a further 2–3 minutes until warmed through. Season to taste.

3. Serve the tagine by itself or with couscous, quinoa or rice.

EASY AUBERGINE CURRY

SERVES 4 | **PREP** 10 MINUTES | **COOK** 20 MINUTES

1 tbsp olive oil

1 small white onion, diced

2 garlic cloves, chopped

2 tbsp garam masala spice

2 tsp ground turmeric

1 aubergine, cut into chunky cubes

300g baby vine tomatoes, halved

1 tbsp vegetable stock powder

1 red pepper, diced

140g mushrooms, thickly sliced

400ml tin coconut milk

1 head broccoli (200g), cut into florets

handful of coriander

This is a perfect batch-cook recipe to freeze. It is a simple veg curry, however you can add different proteins to it, such as diced chicken, at the beginning when you fry off the spices or some tinned chickpeas or lentils when you add the broccoli at the end. Serve the curry on a bed of rice or quinoa or just by itself.

1. In a deep-bottomed pan, add the olive oil, onion, garlic, garam masala and turmeric and fry off over a medium to high heat for 2 minutes. Add the aubergine, tomatoes and stock powder. Bring the temperature down to a medium to low heat and cook for 10 minutes.

2. Add the pepper, mushrooms and the coconut milk. Cook for another 5–7 minutes, then add the broccoli and cook for 3 minutes until it is soft. Chop the coriander and stir through just before serving.

TOMATO AND MUSHROOM DHAL

SERVES 2–3 | **PREP** 5 MINUTES | **COOK** 30 MINUTES

1 red onion, diced

1 garlic clove, chopped

1 tbsp garam masala spice

1 tsp ground turmeric

1 tbsp olive oil or coconut oil

400g tin tomatoes

150g red split lentils

500ml (2 cups) boiling water mixed with 1½ tbsp vegetable stock powder

150g mushrooms, sliced

100g baby vine tomatoes

I love dhal – for me it's such a warming food and it's packed with protein from the lentils. We live off it at home. Serve with some brown rice.

1. In a pan sauté the onion, garlic, garam masala and turmeric in the oil for 2–3 minutes. You want to make sure the spices get cooked well without burning.

2. Add the tin of tomatoes and lentils and stir until combined.

3. Add the stock, mushrooms and whole baby tomatoes and cook for 20–30 minutes over a medium to low heat until the lentils are not recognisable any more.

4. Serve the dhal by itself, or I like to add some yoghurt.

5. The dhal freezes really well and will keep in the fridge for up to 4 days.

JEWELLED QUINOA

SERVES 2 | **PREP** 10 MINUTES | **COOK** 20 MINUTES

100g quinoa

1 red pepper, diced

1 carrot, grated

handful of coriander,
roughly chopped

50g frozen sweetcorn or tinned

100g frozen peas or broad beans

DRESSING

2 tbsp olive oil

1 tbsp tamari

juice of 1 lime

salt and black pepper

This is so perfect for tired parents. Have the quinoa cooked and veg mixed through and store in the fridge, then all you have to do is chuck it into a pan and heat up or even eat raw! It will last for up to 4 days in the fridge like this. For kids, swap the dressing for some pesto, warm through and serve with a protein of your choice. Perfect with roast chicken or the Tamari-baked salmon on page 88.

1. Cook the quinoa and drain under cold water immediately – this means it will last longer in the fridge.

2. Put the pepper, carrot and coriander into a bowl with the cooled quinoa and mix together. Add the sweetcorn and peas and combine.

3. Make the dressing by combining the olive oil, tamari and lime juice and season.

4. When ready to eat, put the dressing into a frying pan, add the quinoa vegetable mixture and cook for 3–5 minutes until warmed and cooked through.

ADULTS PIMP IT UP
Scatter with some sticky seeds: add a handful of mixed seeds, 1 teaspoon maple syrup and 1 tablespoon tamari to a frying pan and fry until lovely and sticky.

MUSHROOM RISOTTO

SERVES 4 | **PREP** 10 MINUTES | **COOK** 25 MINUTES

2 tbsp olive oil or butter

2 red onions, thinly sliced

2 garlic cloves, diced

400g risotto rice

360ml (1½ cups) hot water

300g mushrooms, sliced

2 sprigs of lemon thyme, leaves stripped

500ml (2 cups) boiling water mixed with 2 tbsp vegetable stock powder

squeeze of lemon juice

2 heaped tbsp cream cheese

grated Parmesan and lemon zest, to serve (optional)

This is perfect for freezing and batch cooking. Just freeze in portion bags so it's easier to defrost. However, do remember to undercook the risotto by 5 minutes so as not to overcook when cooking from frozen. And try changing the mushrooms to asparagus when in season and add a handful of prawns too for a change.

1. In a deep, heavy-based pan, put the olive oil with the onion and garlic and sauté over a medium heat for 2 minutes. Add the risotto rice and hot water and cook for 2 minutes, stirring continuously so the rice doesn't stick to the bottom of the pan.

2. Add half the mushrooms, the thyme leaves and two ladles of the hot stock. Stir intermittently, adding more stock as the rice absorbs it, until all the stock is finished. After 10 minutes, add the rest of the mushrooms and the lemon juice and continue to stir. This will take a total of 15–20 minutes depending on whether you prefer al dente or softer. If you are freezing the risotto, take it off the heat after 15 minutes so that it doesn't overcook when you heat it up again.

3. Stir through the cream cheese and serve with a sprinkling of Parmesan and lemon zest, if using.

4. To reheat, take out of the freezer and leave to defrost fully, then put into a pan with 120ml (½ cup) of stock and cook for 5 minutes or until it is the desired texture.

FENNEL RISOTTO

SERVES 2–3 | **PREP** 5 MINUTES | **COOK** 25 MINUTES

1 fennel bulb, diced

½ white onion, diced

1 garlic clove, chopped

1 tbsp oil

200g risotto rice

750ml (3 cups) boiling water mixed with 1 tbsp vegetable stock powder

260ml (1 cup) milk

60g feta

3 tbsp pesto

salt and black pepper

If you don't like fennel (sometimes I find people don't like the aniseed taste) you can swap it for any other vegetable and use fennel seeds when frying off the onions. If you are breastfeeding, fennel is known to be great for increasing milk supply.

1. Sauté the fennel, white onion and garlic for 2–3 minutes in the oil. Add the risotto rice and 60ml (¼ cup) of the stock and cook for a further 2 minutes.

2. Slowly add stock with a ladle as the rice starts to absorb the stock. This will take about 15 minutes for al dente and 20 minutes for the rice to be very soft.

3. After you have finished adding the stock, add the milk and feta and stir until creamy. Just before serving, spoon over the pesto and season to taste.

KIDDIE FRIENDLY
Kids love this with butternut squash instead of fennel as it's so soft and creamy. This also makes a brilliant weaning recipe. You could use the Pimped-up pesto recipe on page 66 for extra greens.

PUFF PASTRY PIZZA

SERVES 1–2 | **PREP** 5 MINUTES | **COOK** 20 MINUTES

1 roll of shop-bought puff pastry

30g coriander

4 tbsp olive oil

½ small red onion, thinly sliced

20g hard goat's cheese

10g feta

4 figs, halved

1 tsp balsamic vinegar

If you crave a pizza, but don't want to take the time to make your own base, this is such a clever cheat's option – we do it all the time in our house. You can add whatever toppings you like to make it seasonal and if you don't have the time to make the green sauce, use store-bought pesto instead. I often make the Beetroot and black bean tomato sauce recipe (page 72) for Rudy and sprinkle over grated cheese. This topping is more adult friendly, but you can make the two side by side to suit everyone's preferences.

1. Preheat the oven to 180°C Fan. Line a baking tray with baking paper cut large enough for the pastry to lie completely flat.

2. Take the puff pastry out of the packaging and put onto the baking paper. With a knife score 1cm around the edge so that when it goes into the oven it creates a little crust.

3. Put the coriander and olive oil into the blender and blend until a pesto-like texture. Spread onto the puff pastry, leaving the 1cm scored 'crust' area free.

4. Spread the red onion over the pesto. Grate the hard goat's cheese and crumble the feta over the pizza. Place the figs on the top and drizzle with the balsamic vinegar.

5. Put into the oven for 20 minutes until the crust is golden and the toppings perfectly cooked.

KIDDIE FRIENDLY
Use the hidden veg sauce on page 150 with mozzarella or grated Cheddar sprinkled over for a really simple kids' option.

EGG-FRIED RICE

SERVES 2 | **PREP** 10 MINUTES | **COOK** 20 MINUTES

100g rice (brown basmati)

1 tbsp olive oil, plus extra for the eggs

1 red pepper, diced

1 carrot, grated

1 courgette, diced

1 tbsp tamari

2 eggs

salt and black pepper

ADD-ONS (OPTIONAL)

dried seaweed

spring onions

peas

coriander

Quick and easy – seriously quick if you buy precooked rice! And this is a great one to take to work with you the next day. If you want to add more veg and some chicken, prawns or tofu, they would all work well. If you are adding raw meat or prawns, add them before you cook the vegetables so that they have long enough to cook through properly.

1. Cook the rice according to the packet instructions.

2. Put the olive oil into a large frying pan and heat up. Add the red pepper, carrot, courgette and tamari and cook over a medium to high heat for 3 minutes or until the veg starts to soften.

3. Add the cooked rice and mix through. Push the mixture to one side of the pan, creating a space to crack in the eggs. Add a little drizzle of olive oil to the bottom of the pan and crack in the two eggs. Leave to cook until the whites are almost 'white', then start to fold and scramble them. Don't stir quickly as it will break them up too much: I love the egg still being recognisable in an egg-fried rice. Once scrambled, fold through the rice and veg mixture.

4. Season, sprinkle over any of the add-ons, if using, and enjoy!

QUINOA TAMARI-ROASTED SALMON SALAD

SERVES 2 | **PREP** 10 MINUTES | **COOK** 20 MINUTES

60g quinoa (or 100g precooked)

2 salmon fillets

2 tbsp olive oil

2 tbsp tamari

5 tbsp water

1 carrot, grated

100g spinach, thinly sliced

1 tbsp tahini

juice and zest of 1 lemon

1 tbsp apple cider vinegar

1 red chilli, thinly sliced (optional)

salt and black pepper

This is such a simple recipe to make and you can swap the salmon for any other protein you like. Having a quick, nutritious dish like this to come home to after a long day is key to keeping your energy up.

1. Preheat the oven to 180°C Fan.

2. Cook the quinoa, if not using precooked, for 20 minutes according to the packet instructions. Once cooked, drain under cold water straight away. Leave to drain so it's not sodden.

3. Meanwhile, put the salmon fillets, skin down, into an ovenproof dish with sides. Add 1 tablespoon of the olive oil, the tamari, some pepper and the water to the dish. Put into the oven for 15 minutes.

4. Add the carrot and spinach to the cooked quinoa. Add the remaining olive oil, tahini, lemon juice and zest, apple cider vinegar and salt, along with the chilli, if using, and mix together to combine all the flavours.

5. Once the salmon is ready to come out of the oven, gently flake it over the mixed quinoa and serve.

KIDDIE FRIENDLY
For kids, serve the salmon with plain quinoa and some carrot sticks and hummus.

SALMON AND SWEET POTATO TRAYBAKE

SERVES 2 | **PREP** 10 MINUTES | **COOK** 20 MINUTES

½ red onion

1 small sweet potato

2 salmon fillets

150g baby vine tomatoes, halved

1 tbsp olive oil

¼ tsp ground coriander

¼ tsp ground ginger

1 tbsp tamari

½ tsp nigella seeds

60ml (¼ cup) water

salt and black pepper

'One-pot wonders' are my absolute favourite since having a baby. Chuck everything in and wait for the goods. Minimal effort, maximum gains! You can use this recipe for chicken as well, just adjust the timings. Serve with a salad, quinoa or rice.

1. Preheat the oven to 180°C Fan.

2. Very thinly slice the onion and sweet potato. If you have a mandolin, use this or you can use a peeler.

3. Get a large ovenproof dish and spread the sweet potato slices over the bottom. Place the salmon on the top.

4. Spread the tomatoes and onion around the salmon and over the potato. Pour the olive oil over the salmon and then sprinkle the ground coriander and ginger over the top.

5. Drizzle the tamari and sprinkle the nigella seeds and some seasoning over the salmon and potatoes, then pour the water into the bottom of the dish.

6. Put into the oven and bake for 20 minutes until the salmon is cooked through.

SALMON AND QUINOA FISH CAKES

SERVES 4–5 (16 MINI PATTIES) | **PREP** 10 MINUTES | **COOK** 30 MINUTES

200g quinoa

2 salmon fillets (about 160g each), skinned and cut into small chunks

100g feta

2 tbsp olive oil, plus extra for frying

zest of 2 lemons

juice of 1 lemon

salt and black pepper

These fish cakes are very quick to make, so are great to cook from scratch or to freeze and have as a quick lunch or dinner. They are so zesty and delicious – both my husband and I love them. Serve with a salad, roasted veg or noodles.

1. Cook the quinoa for 20 minutes according to the packet instructions. Once cooked, drain under cold water straight away. Leave to drain so it's not sodden.

2. Put the salmon into the blender with the feta, olive oil, lemon zest and juice and blend to a thick paste.

3. Mix with the quinoa in a bowl and season well.

4. Make into 16 small patties and flatten in the palm of your hand. Get a frying pan, drizzle in a tablespoon of olive oil and bring up to a medium to high heat. Put half the patties into the pan and cook for 2–3 minutes each side or until cooked through. Repeat with the remaining patties.

5. Leave to sit for about 5 minutes before eating as they will firm up a little. If you are freezing the extra patties, let them cool, stack with baking paper between each one and put into the freezer wrapped in foil.

6. To reheat, just put the frozen patties on to a baking paper-lined baking tray in a 180°C Fan oven and bake for 15 minutes or until warmed through.

PARCEL-BAKED COD AND FRIDGE-RAID VEG

SERVES 2 | **PREP** 10 MINUTES | **COOK** 20–30 MINUTES

100g kale or spinach

2 cod loin fillets

1 tbsp olive oil

2–3cm piece of fresh ginger, grated

1 garlic clove, grated

1 courgette, chopped

30g cherry tomatoes, quartered

50g mushrooms, sliced

¼ tsp ground coriander

1 chilli, diced

juice and zest of ½ lemon

60ml (¼ cup) boiling water mixed with ½ tsp vegetable stock powder

This is called 'fridge raid' as you can use any veg that are in your fridge. However, make sure you use 'soft' veg. If you use 'harder' vegetables like root vegetables, make sure you dice them small or ribbon them so they cook through. You can use pretty much any flaky fish for this too.

1. Preheat the oven to 180°C Fan.

2. Get a large ovenproof dish and lay a piece of baking paper double the width of the base of the dish on the bottom (leave the excess draping over the sides for now: this will wrap around the fish to create a parcel).

3. Layer the bottom with the kale and then place the two cod fillets, skin down, over the top. Drizzle the fish with olive oil, then rub the ginger and garlic into the flesh. Place the rest of the vegetables over the top of the cod and sprinkle with the ground coriander. Add the diced chilli (as much as your taste buds can handle).

4. Add the lemon juice and zest over the top. Pour the stock into the bottom of the dish. Wrap the excess baking paper over the top of the fish and the vegetables and tuck it in to create a parcel.

5. Put the fish in the oven and bake for 20–30 minutes until your fish is done. You will know it is ready as the flesh will flake away easily when touched.

COURGETTE AND CHEESE LOAF

MAKES 8–10 SLICES | **PREP** 10 MINUTES | **COOK** 25–30 MINUTES

120g butter

150g gluten-free plain flour (add 20g more for spelt or wheat flour)

1 tsp xanthan gum

1 tsp baking powder

¼ tsp salt

1 sprig of rosemary, finely diced, or 1 tbsp dried rosemary

2 eggs

65g soft cheese

1 tbsp tahini

180g courgette, grated

I am always trying to hide extra vegetables in my recipes because why not! This is a beautiful loaf that packs a punch as it is really filling.

1. Preheat the oven to 180°C Fan. Line a loaf tin.

2. Melt the butter in a pan, then set aside to cool.

3. Weigh out the flour, xanthan gum, baking powder, salt and rosemary and put into a bowl.

4. Put the eggs into a food processor with the soft cheese, cooled melted butter and tahini and blend. You can also do this by hand if you like, but it's easier and quicker with a blender!

5. Add in the flour mixture and blend again. Stir in the courgette by hand.

6. Pour into the loaf tin and if you want to decorate it, put an extra sprig of rosemary on the top. Bake in the oven for 25–30 minutes (I find 27 the perfect number!) Leave to cool.

ADULTS PIMP IT UP
This is great to add to a lunch box, have with hummus as a snack or use to soak up the delicious juices of a stew like on page 166.

MEXICAN NIGHT

SERVES 2 ADULTS AND 2 KIDS | **PREP** 10 MINUTES | **COOK** 15–20 MINUTES

1 fat garlic clove, grated

2 tbsp olive oil

½ tsp ground cumin

400g tin black beans, drained

1 red pepper, diced

8 chestnut mushrooms, diced

160g courgette, grated

170ml (⅔ cup) water

salt and black pepper

¼ tsp smoked paprika

handful of chopped coriander

wraps, tacos or pita pockets, to serve

ADD-ONS (OPTIONAL)

basmati rice

avocado slices

lime

grated Cheddar

soft cheese

steamed corn on the cob

steamed green beans

fresh chilli

I love a good Mexican night, especially when the nights get cold and you need some warming comfort food. This is a very versatile dish as you can use whichever sides you want that you and your family love to eat. It is also a great way to get fussy eaters trying some new tastes.

1. If you are serving with rice, put the rice on to cook now and follow the packet instructions.

2. Cook the garlic in a non-stick frying pan with the olive oil and cumin. Add the black beans, red pepper, mushrooms, courgette and water to the pan and bring up to a simmer over a high heat, then put the lid on and cook over a medium to high heat for 5–7 minutes.

3. While that is cooking, warm the wraps, tacos or pita pockets and steam the beans and corn on the cob, if using.

4. Once the red pepper is soft, take the lid off, turn up to a high heat and cook off the excess water. This will only take about a minute.

5. If you are serving to kids, take their portion out now and then add salt, pepper, a pinch of smoked paprika and fresh coriander.

6. Serve with any or all of the optional add-ons!

TIPS

My favourite version of this is using a taco and layering the beans, avocado, fresh chilli, grated cheese and a squeeze of lime. Rudy's favourite is a pita pocket with cream cheese, avocado, beans and grated cheese and corn on the cob on the side. Simon's favourite is a wrap with rice, beans, avocado and cheese, served like a burrito – so everyone can choose their fave!

Of course, the beans can also be turned into pinwheels (page 138) and mixed through pasta for little toddlers and weaning babies.

BEETROOT PINWHEELS

MAKES 10 PINWHEELS (APPROX. 2–3 PER WEANING CHILD) | **PREP** 10 MINUTES | **COOK** 30 MINUTES

100g beetroot (raw or cooked), grated

100g cooked puy lentils

60g feta (use grated Cheddar instead if under one)

1 tbsp olive oil

1 roll of shop-bought puff pastry

1 egg, beaten

Pinwheels are a winning formula for kids of all ages, especially for baby-led weaning stages as they are so easy to pick up. You can add whatever filling you like once you know how to make them.

1. Preheat the oven to 180°C Fan. Line a baking tray with baking paper.

2. If you don't have precooked beetroot, put the grated raw beetroot in 125ml (½ cup) water in a pan and boil for 5 minutes until soft. Strain and squeeze out any excess water.

3. Put the beetroot, cooked lentils, feta and olive oil into a blender and blend until a chunky purée. Leave to cool before putting the filling into the pastry. If you're using Cheddar, don't add the cheese to the blender, just layer it over the purée when it's spread out before rolling.

4. Lay the puff pastry out on a floured surface. Leaving an inch around all the edges, spread the beetroot mixture evenly across the sheet of pastry.

5. Brush the egg around the edges. To roll up the pastry, start by tightly folding the long side over to create your first 'roll', then continue rolling the pastry, making sure it is as tight as possible. Fold the ends over so it is secure.

6. Slice the roll into 2cm thick slices to create your pinwheels. Place each pinwheel flat-side down on the baking paper with about 3cm between each one, as they puff up.

7. Bake in the oven for 25 minutes. Take out and leave to cool. If you want to freeze them, only put them into the oven for 20 minutes and when ready to eat, bake in the oven from frozen for 15 minutes until warm through.

TIP
You can really use any purée in pinwheels. Try one of the sauces on pages 66–73.

POTATO AND LENTIL PASTIES

MAKES 5 PASTIES | **PREP** 25 MINUTES | **COOK** 20 MINUTES

250g new potatoes, cut into ½cm cubes

250ml (1 cup) water

1 tbsp olive oil

½ tsp ground cumin

40g spinach, diced

250g cooked puy lentils

80g Cheddar, grated

2 rolls of shop-bought puff pastry

1 egg, beaten

This is a very versatile recipe – there are so many variations you can do with this one for everyone to enjoy. I tend to use just one roll of pastry and make the rest of the filling into a supper for me and Simon by adding an extra handful of spinach, some baby tomatoes and prawns and heating through. If you want to make pasties only, either buy two rolls of pastry to make ten pasties and freeze some or halve the lentil mixture. These can also be plant-based if you leave the cheese out and use some grated courgette instead and vegan pastry.

1. Preheat the oven to 180°C Fan and line a tray with baking paper.

2. Put the potatoes into a pan and cover with the water to come 1cm above the potatoes. Cook on a high heat until all the water is absorbed and the potatoes are soft. If they are not soft before the water is absorbed, just add a touch more.

3. Once the water is absorbed, add the oil, cumin, spinach and lentils. Stir until the spinach wilts, then add the cheese and take off the heat.

4. Roll out the pastry, if it isn't already rolled out, to about 3–4mm. Fold one corner over so that it forms a triangle, then cut around. Repeat this until you have five folded-over triangle pieces.

5. Put 1 tablespoon of mixture into the centre of half a triangle, brush the inside edges with egg and fold the other side over the top. Push down the edges with a fork and pop the prongs of the fork into the top of the middle of the pasty so there is air going into it.

6. Repeat this process with the other triangles. Egg wash over the top of the pasties, put onto the tray and into the oven for 20 minutes. You can also freeze these. Once you have made the pasties and brushed the egg on, put into freezer bags and cook from frozen for 25 minutes.

PIMP IT UP
Mix the lentil filling through a sauce like the ones on pages 66–73 and serve the filling with pasta or rice for a change.

PINE NUT COCONUT SAUCE/CURRY/SOUP

SERVES SAUCE 4/CURRY 2 ADULTS | PREP 10 MINUTES | COOK SAUCE 10 MINUTES/CURRY 25 MINUTES

SAUCE

100g tomatoes, roughly chopped

1 red pepper, sliced

1 large carrot, finely diced

1 tbsp olive oil

1 tsp vegetable stock powder

400ml tin coconut milk

70g pine nuts

TO TURN INTO A THAI CURRY

1 tbsp olive oil

1 garlic clove, diced

1 tsp ground cumin

1 tsp ground coriander

10 curry leaves (5 if fresh)

250ml (1 cup) water

¼ aubergine, diced

140g potatoes, diced

1 courgette, diced

1 red chilli

½ lime

handful of coriander and spinach

TO TURN INTO AN INDIAN CURRY

Remove the curry leaves and add
2 tbsp garam masala instead of
the cumin and coriander

One recipe fits all! This can just be a simple sauce for pasta, or you can add some cooked chicken or salmon, serve as a warming soup or turn into a spicy Thai or Indian curry.

1. Put all the sauce ingredients apart from the pine nuts into a pan and bring to a boil. Put the lid on and reduce to a medium heat for 7 minutes or until the carrot is soft. Add the pine nuts and cook for a further 3 minutes. Take off the heat and blend until velvety smooth.

2. To turn into a Thai curry, put the olive oil into a pan with the garlic, spices and curry leaves and cook them off for 1 minute. Add half of the sauce (approx. 180g) to the pan with the water to serve two, or add all of the sauce to serve four.

3. Add the aubergine, potato, courgette and whole chilli, bring to the boil, then put the lid on for 10 minutes on a medium to low heat or until the vegetables are soft.

4. Add a squeeze of lime, the coriander and spinach and cook until the spinach wilts. Serve with rice.

TIP
If serving as a soup, garnish with some crumbled feta and cracked pepper or a few pine nuts and a drizzle of olive oil.

ONE-POT KEDGEREE

SERVES 2 ADULTS AND 2 CHILDREN | **PREP** 10 MINUTES | **COOK** 20 MINUTES

1 large carrot

½ red onion

1 small courgette

1 tbsp olive oil

1 garlic clove

1 tsp mild curry powder

200g white basmati rice

1 tsp vegetable stock powder

4 eggs

100g baby vine tomatoes

2 salmon fillets, cut into 3cm chunks

80g frozen peas

handful of coriander leaves

20g butter

This is a great dish to change up depending on your family's tastes. It's also a lovely way to introduce a milky curry flavour to weaning babies, but you can leave the curry powder out and swap with cumin if you prefer. If you want it as just a veggie rice dish, you can add any vegetables you like and leave the salmon out. And if you are feeling super lazy and don't want to wash up another pot for the eggs, you can crack them on top 5 minutes before the end of the cooking time and put the lid on to steam cook.

1. Dice the carrot, onion and courgette into small pieces (the smaller they are, the softer they will be, so great for little ones).

2. Put the olive oil, onion, garlic and curry powder into a pan and cook for 2 minutes. Add the rice and cover with water so it's 1cm above the rice level.

3. Add the stock powder, carrot and courgette and stir through. Put the lid on and leave to cook over a medium heat for 10 minutes, stirring regularly.

4. While it is cooking, bring another pan to the boil, put the eggs into the boiling water and cook for 6 minutes. Take out of the water and put into a bowl of cold water before peeling.

5. Take the lid off the rice dish. If you need to add a little more water, do that at this stage, but just a touch, then add the tomatoes, salmon and peas. Put the lid back on and cook for a further 6–8 minutes or until the rice is cooked.

6. Stir through the coriander and butter. Peel and cut the eggs in half. Serve the rice with the eggs.

PAD THAI

SERVES 2 ADULTS AND 1 CHILD | **PREP** 10 MINUTES | **COOK** 20 MINUTES

200g flat rice noodles

3 tbsp fish sauce

2 tbsp tamari

2 tbsp rice vinegar

1 tbsp sriracha (leave out if for kids and add to your portion)

3 tbsp smooth peanut butter

2 tbsp sesame oil

2 garlic cloves, finely grated

2–3cm piece of fresh ginger, finely grated

100g mixed vegetables, roughly chopped (I use a stir-fry pack with beansprouts, carrots, peppers, spring onions, cabbage and spinach)

2 pak choi, roughly chopped

60ml (¼ cup) water

2 eggs, beaten

juice of 1 lime

70g chopped peanuts

large handful of coriander leaves

Living out in the country we don't have any Thai restaurants and I miss a good pad Thai. I thought it would be difficult to make, but it's the opposite! If you have a fussy eater at home, you can always scoop out some veg and noodles before adding the sauce and either add a simple teriyaki sauce or a tomato pasta sauce like on page 70.

1. Cook the rice noodles in a pan of water while you make the sauce and chop your veg. This saves time and washing up! Once cooked, drain and reuse the same pan.

2. Make the sauce by adding the fish sauce, 1 tablespoon of the tamari, the rice vinegar, sriracha, peanut butter and 1 tablespoon of sesame oil to a bowl and mixing well.

3. To the pan add the remaining sesame oil with the garlic and ginger.

4. Add all your vegetables and the remaining tamari to the pan with the water. Once they are soft, push all the ingredients to one side of the pan.

5. Add the eggs to the space in the pan and leave to cook like an omelette. Once it starts to harden, gently fold the mixture so that it breaks up but doesn't scramble. You want the eggs to be nice and formed rather than a sloppy scramble. Break them up and mix into the vegetables.

6. Pour in the cooked noodles, sauce and lime juice and mix together. Serve with the coriander and peanuts mixed through.

FRITTATA FINGERS

SERVES 2 ADULTS AND 1 CHILD | **PREP** 10 MINUTES | **COOK** 30 MINUTES

100g carrots

80g broccoli florets

1 tsp olive oil

60ml (¼ cup) water

6 eggs

1 heaped tbsp plain flour (gluten-free, spelt or wheat)

100g feta

Eggs can be a funny texture for your little one during the fussy stage, so when I saw in a recipe to add a little flour to the mix, it changed everything. Rudy started eating them again – it turns them from being eggy to a more cakey texture. You can add any veg or cheese in here – this is just our favourite as a family.

1. Preheat the oven to 180°C Fan and line a 20cm loaf tin with baking paper.

2. Finely grate the carrot, very finely dice the broccoli and put them into a frying pan with the olive oil and water. Cook until the broccoli is soft.

3. In a bowl, beat the eggs with a whisk, then add the flour and beat again until completely combined. Crumble in the feta and add the vegetable mix.

4. Pour the mixture into the tin and bake in the oven for 25 minutes. Cut into fingers to serve.

KIDDIE FRIENDLY

Try adding diced mushrooms, peas or Cheddar cheese if your little one is under one and can't have feta. Add in a pinch of cumin too or some garlic when winter colds are on the up.

HIDDEN VEG GLUTEN-FREE PIZZA

MAKES 1 MINI KIDS' PIZZA (DOUBLE FOR AN ADULT ONE) | **PREP** 10 MINUTES | **COOK** 20 MINUTES

HIDDEN VEG SAUCE

½ red pepper

20g cooked beetroot

2 tbsp passata tomato sauce

PIZZA BASE

35g gluten-free plain flour
(or spelt or wheat), plus extra
for dusting

pinch of salt

¼ tsp baking powder

½ tbsp olive oil

35g yoghurt

TOPPING

small handful of grated courgette

handful of Cheddar or mozzarella
cheese (I find mozzarella is too
tough to chew with gums for
teething ones, so grated Cheddar
works better for us)

There are great recipes for normal wheat and spelt pizza out there, so I felt the need to create one for the gluten-free gang. Everyone loves a pizza, so this is a great time to hide some extra veg in the sauce. The sauce can be used for a simple pasta sauce too. You can also batch cook these and freeze, then cook from frozen to save time.

1. Preheat the oven to 180°C Fan.

2. To make the sauce, put all ingredients into a blender and blend together until smooth.

3. To make the pizza base, combine the flour, salt and baking powder in a bowl. Add the olive oil and yoghurt and knead with your hands for a couple of minutes to make sure they're all combined well. It should be a very soft, squidgy dough. Roll into a ball between your hands.

4. Sprinkle a piece of baking paper with flour. Get a little more flour, cover the ball of dough with it and flatten with the palm of your hand. Gently roll the dough out on the parchment paper with a rolling pin, or flatten with your hands if you don't have one, until it is about 2mm thick.

5. Add about 3 tablespoons of the sauce and spread evenly. Mix the grated courgette and cheese together and sprinkle over the top. At this point you can place the pizza in the freezer with a sheet of baking paper over the top of it. Once frozen, transfer to a freezer bag and then you can bake from frozen to save time! Just add on about 3 minutes to the baking time.

6. Bake in the oven for 18–20 minutes. Take out before the edges change colour.

GREEN SAUCE WITH BAKED CHICKEN

SERVES 2 | **PREP** 10 MINUTES | **COOK** 20–25 MINUTES

½ head of broccoli (approx. 60g), cut into florets

40g kale or spinach

150g penne pasta

120ml (½ cup) milk

salt and black pepper

FOR THE CHICKEN (OPTIONAL)

2 chicken breasts

1 tbsp tamari

1 tbsp olive oil

½ lemon

FOR THE ROUX

1 tbsp olive oil or butter

1 tbsp plain flour (gluten-free, spelt or wheat)

260ml (1 cup) milk

Once you nail this simple recipe you can add the sauce to anything to make it taste delicious and freeze it. This was one of the first recipes that I put through pasta for Rudy and he demolished it. You can also have it as a dipping sauce for little ones. You can use fish instead of chicken if you wish.

1. If you are adding chicken to your recipe, preheat the oven first to 180°C Fan.

2. Put the chicken breast into an ovenproof dish and drizzle with the tamari, olive oil and a squeeze of lemon. Bake in the oven for 20–25 minutes until cooked through, then shred.

3. Meanwhile, bring a pan of generously salted water to the boil, drop the broccoli into the water and blanch for 3 minutes. Add the kale just at the end for about 30 seconds. Drain really well and then use the same water to cook the pasta. Alternatively, you can use a steamer.

4. Put the vegetables into a blender with some salt and pepper. Add the milk and blend until smooth.

5. To make the roux, add the olive oil or butter to a saucepan and melt over a medium heat. Pour in the flour and whisk until it comes together in a thick paste. Add the milk in slowly and never stop whisking, otherwise it will be lumpy! Once you have added all the milk and it is a thick, creamy consistency, add the broccoli mixture and keep stirring over a low to medium heat until you have a thick sauce.

6. Once cooked, drain the pasta and mix through the green sauce and shredded chicken, if using.

30–60
MINUTES

'All good things come to those who wait,' someone once said a long time ago!

Don't be put off by the cooking times on these recipes. The prep will take no time at all, then you can pop the dish in the oven or leave on the stove to simmer away while you can get on with other things in the house. In actual fact, these recipes are less time consuming then some of the quicker ones.

The recipes in this section are all hearty family meals, which you could cook double the amount of and freeze the rest for a day you might have less time on your hands. If you have friends coming over for lunch on the weekend or dinner, these are also excellent to warm up in the oven again the next day for the rest of your family.

I have created the recipes to be flexible. The ingredients are interchangeable, so if you don't have a specific vegetable or meat don't worry, just swap it for something else you do have in the fridge. Same with allergens. If you have someone that is gluten-free, you can just swap the flour, and same for milk. If you want to make a chicken curry, but it's a veggie curry recipe, you can just add the meat where it suggests you do in the recipe. I suppose you could call them flexi-recipes!

AUBERGINE AND BEAN DIP

SERVES 2–3 | **PREP** 5 MINUTES | **COOK** 45–50 MINUTES

1 aubergine

400g tin cannellini beans
(or chickpeas)

juice of 1 lemon

4 tbsp yoghurt

2 tbsp olive oil

handful of parsley, chopped

salt and black pepper

This is a delicious, protein-rich snack or a side for a main dish with lots of veg. It's simple to make once you have the aubergine cooked. If you don't have an aubergine, butternut squash, carrot or beetroot work well too. Eat as a dip with crudités, oat cakes, toast or rice cakes. You can even have with roasted veg and a salad.

1. Preheat the oven grill.

2. Stab the aubergine a couple of times with a knife so it doesn't explode in the oven. Put into the oven whole for 45–50 minutes, turning occasionally, or until really soft on the inside and burnt on the outside. Leave to cool so you can scrape off the burnt skin.

3. Drain and pour the tin of beans into a blender. Add the aubergine flesh, lemon juice, yoghurt, salt and pepper. Blend until smooth.

4. Make a parsley oil by mixing together the olive oil and chopped parsley. Swirl over the dip.

5. The dip can be stored in an airtight container in the fridge for up to 3 days.

LENTIL LASAGNE

SERVES 2 ADULTS AND 2 KIDS | **PREP** 15 MINUTES | **COOK** 1 HOUR

2 tbsp olive oil

2 garlic cloves, diced

2 small white onions, diced

2 tbsp ground cumin

4 medium carrots, diced

300g red split lentils

2 x 400g tins tomatoes

200g mushrooms, diced

1 litre (4 cups) boiling water mixed with 1 tbsp vegetable stock powder

8–10 lasagne sheets (you can get spelt, which is what I use)

WHITE SAUCE

2 heaped tbsp butter or olive oil

4 heaped tbsp plain flour (gluten-free, spelt or wheat)

500ml (2 cups) milk (if you are using plant milk, use a creamy one like cashew, soya, oat or coconut)

100g hard goat's cheese or Cheddar

I love a good hearty lasagne – it reminds me of home. This is perfect for freezing. You just need to layer it in an ovenproof storage container (you can get Pyrex glass ones or use the foil ones you get from takeaways) and this way you can take it out of the freezer and pop it straight into the oven. If you are freezing it, layer as normal but don't cook it in the oven – pop straight into the freezer.

1. To a medium pan, add the olive oil, garlic, onion and cumin and sauté for 2 minutes over a medium heat. Add the carrots and cook for a further 2–3 minutes.

2. Mix in the lentils, tinned tomatoes and chopped mushrooms and combine over a medium heat. Add half the stock and leave to simmer away for 15–20 minutes, stirring occasionally so the lentils don't stick to the bottom. Add the remaining stock in intervals as the liquid is absorbed, so the lentils can cook slowly.

3. While the sauce is cooking, make the white sauce. In a small pan add the butter and melt over a medium heat. Once it starts to bubble (don't let it burn), add the flour and whisk fast. Once it is a paste, turn the heat down a little and slowly add the milk while whisking continuously so that no lumps appear. Once it's at a nice, thick sauce stage, add the cheese to melt. Leave a little cheese behind to add to the top of the lasagne.

4. Preheat the oven to 180°C Fan.

5. Get a 30cm ovenproof dish and add a layer of lentil sauce to the bottom, then add a thin layer of white sauce followed by a sheet of raw lasagne. Add another layer of lentils, then another thin layer of white sauce. Repeat until you get to the top of the dish, with the last layer being the white sauce over the top of the lasagne sheets. Sprinkle with a little cheese and put into the oven for 30–40 minutes or until the top is golden and bubbling away.

6. To reheat, put the frozen lasagne into a preheated 180°C Fan oven for 45–55 minutes or until warm and cooked through.

INDIAN FENUGREEK CURRY

SERVES 2–3 | **PREP** 5 MINUTES | **COOK** 45 MINUTES

2 garlic cloves, diced

½ red onion, diced

1 tbsp olive oil

½ tbsp ground cumin

½ tbsp ground coriander

½ tsp ground ginger

¼ tsp mustard seeds

(or 2 tbsp garam masala instead of all the above spices)

1 tsp ground turmeric

1 tsp fenugreek seeds

3 tbsp water

400g tin tomatoes

1 mango stone

150ml (generous ½ cup) boiling water mixed with 1 tbsp vegetable stock powder

40g baby vine tomatoes, cubed

½ aubergine, cubed

1 red pepper, sliced into 'fingers'

½ red chilli

½ courgette, diced

100g spinach

handful of coriander

cucumber, to serve

dairy-free yoghurt, to serve

I asked my friend to teach me how to make a traditional curry when he came to stay with us and, my goodness, he really did. The big trick is all to do with using a mango stone. Yup, I know it sounds odd, but if you ever eat a mango, freeze the stone so that when you want to make an Indian curry you have one to hand. The second tip is to cook it slowly. The longer you let it simmer away, the more amazing the flavour will be. A great family meal – children like curry too!

1. Put the garlic, red onion, olive oil and all the spices into a pan and fry on a medium heat for 2 minutes. Add the 3 tablespoons water and, with the back of a wooden spoon, bash the spices while stirring for 1 more minute.

2. Add the tinned tomatoes, mango stone, stock, fresh tomatoes, aubergine, pepper and chilli. I like to put the chilli in whole so that it infuses the flavour, but you can take it out before serving.

3. Cook on a low heat for 30 minutes, stirring occasionally, then add the courgette and cook for another 10 minutes on a low heat.

4. Add the spinach and fresh coriander and stir through until it wilts.

5. Dice the cucumber, mix through some yoghurt and serve alongside the curry with some rice, naan, poppadoms and mango chutney.

CAULIFLOWER AND BROCCOLI CHEESE

SERVES 2–3 | **PREP** 20 MINUTES | **COOK** 45 MINUTES

½ cauliflower, cut into florets

½ broccoli, cut into florets

1 tbsp butter or oil

1 tbsp plain flour (gluten-free, spelt or wheat)

250ml (1 cup) milk

80g cheese

salt and black pepper

Sneaking some greens into this well-loved, comforting favourite is a perfect disguise! Of course you can make it as just a cauliflower dish or just a broccoli one – the choice is yours!

1. Preheat the oven to 180°C Fan.

2. Bring a pan of generously salted water to the boil and put the cauliflower and broccoli in to blanch for 3–4 minutes until just soft (don't overcook otherwise they will be too mushy after baking in the oven). Alternatively, use a steamer. Drain well and put into an ovenproof dish.

3. To make the sauce, get a small saucepan and heat the butter or oil over a medium heat. Once melted and hot (not burning or boiling), add the flour and whisk fast and continuously. Once a paste has formed, add the milk gradually and continue to whisk fast so that no lumps occur. Keep on the heat until a nice thick sauce has been created. Add 65g of the cheese to the sauce and season.

4. Pour the sauce over the broccoli and cauliflower and sprinkle the extra cheese over the top. Bake for 30 minutes until golden.

SWEET POTATO AND POLENTA FISH PIE

SERVES 4–5 | **PREP** 15 MINUTES | **COOK** 45 MINUTES

2 garlic cloves, diced

4 spring onions, sliced

2 tbsp olive oil

2 tsp ground coriander

1 tsp fennel seeds

560ml (2¼ cups) fish stock or any other stock

2 tbsp plain flour (gluten-free, spelt or wheat)

240ml (1 cup) milk (if you are using plant milk use a creamy one like cashew, soya, oat or coconut)

500g salmon fillet, cut into 2cm chunks

400g smoked haddock, cut into 2cm chunks

handful of dill, chopped

40g peas

½ fennel bulb, diced

salt and black pepper

TOPPINGS

4 sweet potatoes (640g), peeled and chopped

220ml (generous ¾ cup) milk

200g polenta

knob of butter

handful of Cheddar (optional)

I love adding polenta to mash as it makes it a bit more hearty and filling. You could mix it up a bit and swap the sweet potato for other root vegetables like white potato, celeriac, carrot or even beetroot – just swap the amounts of the sweet potato like for like.

1. Preheat the oven to 180°C Fan. Get one ovenproof dish approximately 30cm in size ready.

2. In a pan, add the garlic and spring onions with the oil, coriander and fennel seeds and cook for 1–2 minutes. Add 120ml (½ cup) of the stock and cook for a couple of minutes. Add the flour and whisk in until a paste. Add the milk and carry on whisking over a medium to low heat.

3. Put the fish into the milk mixture with the dill, peas and fennel and leave to cook on a low heat for about 4 minutes. Season with salt and pepper. Pour the mixture into the ovenproof dish.

4. To make the sweet potato topping, boil the sweet potato for 7–8 minutes until soft. Drain and put into a blender.

5. In a separate pan, add the rest of the stock and milk and bring to a simmering boil. Add the polenta and whisk. Do not turn the heat up too high as the polenta will boil and spit. Continue to cook for 10 minutes until the polenta is thick and smooth. Stir in the butter.

6. Put the polenta into the blender with the sweet potato and blend until smooth. Spread the topping over the top of the fish mixture in the baking dish. Sprinkle with cheese and bake in the oven for 30 minutes until golden. If you are freezing it, pop it into the freezer before cooking.

7. To reheat, just put the fish pie into the oven direct from frozen and cook for 40–45 minutes until piping hot through.

PEARL BARLEY CHICKEN STEW

MAKES ENOUGH FOR 2–3 PLUS THE SAME TO FREEZE | **PREP** 10 MINUTES | **COOK** 30 MINUTES

2 tbsp olive oil

1 red onion, diced into 1cm cubes

2 garlic cloves, crushed

2 tbsp ground coriander

2 tsp ground cinnamon

300g chicken thigh fillets, diced into 2cm cubes

1.5 litres (6 cups) water

3 tbsp brown rice miso paste (or 2 tbsp tamari or soy sauce)

200g pearl barley

1 aubergine, diced into 1cm cubes

80g mushrooms, sliced

juice of 1 lemon

1 courgette, cut into ½cm-thick half-moon chunks

100g green beans

salt and black pepper

ADD-ONS (OPTIONAL)

spinach

parsley

This is a brilliant, warming and filling meal. If you don't want to use chicken you can substitute with chickpeas instead. I think using chicken thighs is best as they are cheaper and tastier than chicken breast, but if you prefer breast, you can use that too. This is perfect family-friendly food – if you have little ones, just chop the veg nice and small so it's bite-size and when you serve, cut up or shred the chicken.

1. Put the olive oil, red onion, garlic, coriander and cinnamon into a frying pan and sauté over a medium to high heat for 2 minutes. Add the chicken, coat with the spices and cook until the edges of the meat turn white in colour.

2. Add 1 litre (4 cups) of the water, the brown miso, tamari or soy, pearl barley, aubergine and mushrooms and cook on a high heat for 10 minutes.

3. Add the remaining water, lemon juice, courgette and green beans, turn down the heat to a low temperature and put the lid on. Cook for a further 10 minutes, stirring occasionally so it doesn't stick to the bottom or burn.

4. Once the pearl barley is soft, season and take off the heat. Add a handful of spinach and parsley at the end if you wish.

TURMERIC-ROASTED CHICKEN

MAKES 1 ROAST CHICKEN | **PREP** 5 MINUTES | **COOK** 1 HOUR

1.3kg whole organic chicken

2 tbsp olive oil

1 tsp ground turmeric

1 tsp ground cumin

1 red onion, quartered (you can leave the skin on)

½ lemon

4 carrots, cut into large 2–3cm chunks

3 garlic cloves, halved

625ml (2½ cups) boiling water mixed with 1 tsp vegetable stock powder

salt and black pepper

Having a Tupperware of perfectly roasted chicken in the fridge when you are a busy family is perfect for picking at, adding to salads, putting on toast for a snack, tearing through pasta or using as a topping for a pizza (why not try on the recipe for Puff pastry pizza on page 122).

As soon as you have roasted the chicken, allow to cool and strip it of all the meat, leaving just the bones. Then follow the recipe for Bone broth on the following pages. Bone broth is great for using as a stock in everyday cooking or drinking for immunity and good gut health.

1. Preheat the oven to 190°C Fan.

2. Put your chicken in a large enough oven dish or baking tray, with at least 5cm sides, for it to fit with plenty of space around it for the veg.

3. Drizzle the chicken with the olive oil, then sprinkle the ground turmeric and cumin over the top and generously season with salt and pepper.

4. Put a quarter of the onion inside the chicken with the lemon half. Drop the carrot, the rest of the onion chunks and the garlic around the outside of the chicken. Pour the stock into the base of the dish.

5. Bake in the oven for approximately 1 hour. Every half an hour, pour 4–5 tablespoons of the gravy over the top of the chicken to keep it moist.

6. I find that turning the oven off at the end of the cooking time and leaving the chicken in there for 20–30 minutes to carry on cooking and resting the meat makes it really tender and the meat comes off the bones easier.

7. Once cool, strip the chicken from the bones, but do save the bones for the bone broth on page 170! The chicken can be stored in the fridge for up to 3–4 days.

HOW TO MAKE BONE BROTH

YOU WILL NEED

chicken bones

water

2 tbsp apple cider vinegar

18 hours or more!

There are two main reasons I make bone broth. The first is to use every part of the piece of meat I am cooking, and the second is because of the benefits of bone broth for your immune system and gut health. Once you try it, you will see how easy it is and always want to make it after cooking a roast. You don't have to use it straight away, you can freeze in ice-cube trays and use as stock when a recipe calls for it.

1. Put the chicken bones into a very large, deep pan. Cover with water until it's about 5cm above the bones. Add the apple cider vinegar and bring to the boil. Once boiling, bring down to a very, very low simmer. I have an induction hob (numbers 1–14) and put it on number 3. Leave this now for as long as you can. I make sure it's a minimum of 12 hours, but usually do 18 hours. If you go to bed or go out, you can turn it off and back on when you return. Just bring to the boil again, then take the temperature back down to a low simmer.

2. When ready, strain the bones and you can freeze the broth. I have found that my 60ml Food Cube Tray from NUK is the perfect size for freezing bone broth into cubes. You can buy it on Amazon (type in 'weaning freezer trays' and the product from NUK should come up – it's green with nine cubes and has a lid. If you don't get this one, make sure you get a silicone one as it's easier to pop out the cubes and store in a freezer bag).

TRAY-BAKED ROASTED VEGETABLES

MAKES ENOUGH FOR 2-4 MEALS | **PREP** 10 MINUTES | **COOK** 40-50 MINUTES

1 aubergine

1 butternut squash

4 carrots

2 sweet potatoes

1 cauliflower

1 tbsp olive oil

½ tsp ground cumin

salt

OTHER VEG YOU CAN THROW IN

peppers

courgettes

portobello mushrooms

fennel bulb

celeriac

Having a Tupperware of roasted vegetables in the fridge is great for adding to salads, precooked grains or having on toast. It's quick, easy and so simple to pull together something to eat once you have them. The recipe below is just a guide as it uses the veg that was in my fridge, but you can roast pretty much anything. Just remember hard root vegetables take longer to cook than softer vegetables. Generally, soft veg take 20-30 minutes and root veg take 40-50 minutes.

1. Preheat the oven to 180°C Fan.

2. Line a baking tray and place your vegetables onto the tray. You can slice them if you like, but I tend to put them all in whole and then you can slice or dice them as you wish for each dish you create.

3. If you are baking an aubergine, either slice it in half or if you are keeping it whole to perhaps make a dip with, just stab it with a knife a couple of times to make sure it doesn't explode in your oven!

4. For the butternut squash, put into the oven whole as this is the easiest way to roast it. It will take 50-60 minutes. Then you can make the Butternut squash soup on page 76.

5. Drizzle the vegetables with olive oil and sprinkle with some ground cumin and salt. Bake for 40-50 minutes until soft. The cauliflower will only take 20 minutes, so take this out before the others.

HIDDEN VEG AND LENTIL TOMATO SAUCE

SERVES 4–5 | **PREP** 10 MINUTES | **COOK** 1 HOUR

1 tbsp olive oil

1 garlic clove, diced

½ red onion, diced

1 tsp ground coriander

75g butternut squash, peeled and diced into ½cm cubes

30g carrots, diced into ½cm cubes

50g red pepper, diced into ½cm cubes

40g courgette, peeled and diced into ½cm cubes

50g aubergine, peeled and diced into ½cm cubes

30g mushrooms, diced into ½cm cubes

½ x 400g tin chopped tomatoes

200ml (¾ cup) water

50g red split lentils

2 tsp tomato purée

2 tsp tamari

2 tsp vegetable stock powder

1 bay leaf

This is my absolute go-to sauce for Rudy, packed with veg and lentils. I use it as a bolognese, lasagne and everything in between. We ALL love this as a family and often bring it out when friends come to visit on the weekend.

1. Add the olive oil to a non-stick pan over a medium heat and sauté the garlic and onion for 1–2 minutes, then add the ground coriander.

2. Add all the chopped vegetables with the tinned tomatoes, water and lentils. Reduce the heat to a low temperature and stir.

3. Add the tomato purée, tamari, vegetable stock powder and bay leaf and stir. Leave on a low heat and stir intermittently so the bottom doesn't burn. Cook for 40–50 minutes, depending on when the lentils are soft.

4. Blend until you have a very smooth, velvety 'tomato' sauce. Freeze or refrigerate.

TIP
Use this sauce as a pizza topping to get in loads of goodness for the whole family.

CHICKEN AND LENTIL TRAYBAKE

SERVES 2 | **PREP** 10 MINUTES | **COOK** 40 MINUTES

500ml passata

400g tin puy lentils

1 tbsp dried oregano

1 tbsp ground cumin

1 tbsp tamari

1 carrot, diced into ½cm cubes
(the smaller they are, the softer
they will be)

1 courgette, diced

60g mushrooms, diced

1 red onion, diced

2 garlic cloves, diced

2 chicken breasts or 4 thigh fillets
(add 1 more breast if serving
children as well)

When you just need to throw everything into a dish and leave to do something else, this is the recipe for you. Add whatever veggies you have in the fridge at home and swap the lentils for white beans or chickpeas to mix it up a bit. Serve with rice, pasta, quinoa or couscous.

1. Preheat the oven to 180°C Fan.

2. Pour the passata, lentils, oregano, cumin, tamari and all the diced vegetables into an ovenproof dish and mix together.

3. Add in the chicken breasts and cover with the mixture.

4. Put into the oven for 40 minutes until the veg and chicken are cooked through.

KIDDIE FRIENDLY
Blend up the sauce to make a protein- and veg-laden pizza base sauce and just add grated cheese over the top.
Or use as a pasta sauce and finely dice the chicken over the top for toddlers and weaning ones.

FILO RICOTTA AND BUTTERNUT PIE

SERVES 2 ADULTS AND 2 CHILDREN | **PREP** 10 MINUTES | **COOK** 40 MINUTES

knob of butter

1 tsp olive oil

1 tsp cumin seeds (or ground)

1 tsp thyme

1 garlic clove, grated

210g butternut squash, peeled and diced into ½cm cubes

½ leek, finely diced

2 large mushrooms, finely diced

60ml (¼ cup) water

large handful of spinach, finely diced

6 sheets of filo pastry

2 eggs

250g ricotta cheese

salt and black pepper

This is a real show stopper for a dinner party, but also brilliant for kids' tea. You can make this into mini parcels too, which is what I did for Rudy when he was weaning and only wanted to feed himself. You can add any filling you want – try sweet potato instead of butternut, and peas, sweetcorn or tomatoes instead of leek and mushrooms.

1. Preheat the oven to 180°C Fan and get a low-sided 18cm cake tin.

2. Melt the butter so you can use it to brush each of the layers of pastry later.

3. To a pan add the olive oil with the cumin seeds, thyme and garlic. Cook off the garlic for 1 minute, then add the butternut, leek and mushrooms and cook for 2–3 minutes on a high heat. Season well. Add the water and bring to a medium heat, stirring at intervals. Cook for about 10 minutes until the butternut is soft enough to cut. Add the spinach to just wilt and salt to taste.

4. Meanwhile, brush a little butter in the base of the tin, then place two sheets of pastry on the base. Brush with the butter, then place another two sheets across at an angle. Brush with butter, and then place the last two sheets across in the opposite direction, again making sure you have plenty of overhang of the pastry.

5. Beat the eggs and ricotta together and pour into the tin on top of the filo. Pour the veg mixture onto the ricotta and make sure it's mixed into it. Be careful not to cut the pastry at the bottom.

6. Fold the pastry that is overhanging the sides over the top, one sheet at a time. Brush the top with the rest of the butter and bake for 25 minutes. This tart is best served cooled as it cuts better.

KIDDIE FRIENDLY
Use a muffin tin and place half a filo sheet in the base of each muffin hole, then add the filling and close over the top. Bake for 20 minutes for little handheld versions – great for lunch boxes.

TOAD-IN-THE-HOLE WITH ONION GRAVY

SERVES 2 ADULTS AND 1 CHILD (MAKES 8 MINI TOAD-IN-THE-HOLES) | PREP 15 MINUTES | COOK 40 MINUTES

olive oil

250ml (1 cup) milk

100g plain flour (gluten-free, spelt or wheat)

3 eggs

1 sprig rosemary

8 organic chipolatas or veggie sausages, halved

ONION GRAVY

1 white onion, sliced

40g butter

4 garlic cloves, crushed

2 shiitake mushrooms

750ml (3 cups) chicken stock (use veg if vegetarian)

2 tbsp balsamic vinegar

This can also be used as a Yorkshire pudding recipe – just take the sausages out or make into a veggie toad-in-the-hole. You can use either gluten-free or normal wheat flour as it works with both. Serve with mashed potato and greens on the side as a simple, but super tasty supper. The key to this recipe is timing – if you get this right then it's really easy to make and will all come out on time!

1. Preheat the oven to 220°C Fan. Pour a teaspoon of olive oil into the base of eight muffin holes in a tin and put into the oven for 10 minutes to heat up.

2. Mix the milk, flour and eggs together to make the batter, then chop the rosemary up into small pieces, mix into the batter and pop into the fridge until you are ready to use it.

3. Put two halves of the sausages into each of the eight muffin holes and pop back into the oven for 20 minutes.

4. Make the onion gravy by frying the onion in the butter with the garlic until translucent. Add the mushrooms, stock and vinegar and bring to the boil. Drop the heat down to medium for 15 minutes and simmer until the toad-in-the-holes are ready to come out of the oven. Strain the onions off before serving.

5. After the 20 minutes is up cooking the sausages, carefully take out of the oven, as the oil might spit. Ladle the batter from the fridge into each muffin hole, filling it about a centimetre below each rim.

6. Put back into the oven for 20 minutes. Don't open the oven door as they can be temperamental to rise!

7. Take out, serve with the gravy and enjoy your masterpiece!

SPICED LAMB, ROAST VEG AND COUSCOUS

SERVES 4–5 | **PREP** 10 MINUTES | **COOK** 1 HOUR

1.2kg half leg of lamb, bone in

6 garlic cloves

100g butter, at room temperature

1 tsp ground cumin

1 tsp ground coriander

½ tsp smoked paprika

½ tsp ground cinnamon

420g potatoes, cut into 2–3cm chunks

6 small carrots

100g mushrooms, diced

100g green beans

80g couscous

handful of parsley (optional)

black pepper

This a showstopper of a dish. Everyone I have made it for says it's melt-in-the-mouth delicious. The spices are not too strong for kids, but add incredible flavour and a twist to normal lamb. It's also fuss-free as it's a one-pot dish that takes hardly any prep. To turn this into a proper Sunday roast, don't add the couscous at the end, swap the potatoes for celeriac and serve with roasted potatoes. You can even prepare it the night before and pop in the oven when you're ready.

1. Preheat the oven to 200°C Fan.

2. With a small sharp knife, cut about 12 slices into the flesh of the lamb – around one every 1cm on the top and then the rest in the side. Put the lamb into a large ovenproof dish. Slice four of the garlic cloves in half and slot them into some of the holes you created in the lamb.

3. Put the butter into a bowl and add the cumin, coriander, paprika and cinnamon. Grate the remaining two cloves of garlic into it and mix together with a spoon until combined. Push the mixture into any of the holes in the lamb not filled with garlic, then spread the butter all over the top and as much as you can on the sides. Put the potatoes, carrots and mushrooms around the lamb and put into the oven.

4. For medium lamb, which I think is perfect, cook for 13 minutes for every 450g of meat, plus add 20 minutes on to the end. For a 1.2kg leg of lamb a perfect cooking time is about 1 hour. Always leave to rest for 10 minutes when finished cooking. (If you want well done, cook for 20 minutes for every 450g, plus 20 minutes at the end.)

5. After about 10 minutes of the lamb being in the oven, just spoon the juices over the vegetables and the lamb and put back into the oven. After 45 minutes, put the green beans into the dish and coat with the juices. Spoon over the meat at the same time.

6. After the cooking time, take the meat out of the dish to rest for 10 minutes. Make sure there is 1cm of liquid in the bottom of the dish, adding stock or water if needed, then mix the couscous through the veg and cover with some foil. Once the lamb is rested, serve sliced with the vegetables, black pepper and fresh parsley, if you wish.

SWEET POTATO GNOCCHI

SERVES 2 CHILDREN | **PREP** 10 MINUTES | **COOK** 30 MINUTES–1 HOUR

195g sweet potato

35g self-raising flour
(gluten-free or wheat), plus extra
for dusting

1 heaped tsp cornflour

olive oil

This was a winner with Rudy during the weaning process – just make them a little longer so children can pick each one up like a fish finger. Simon and I love this, too, with a delicious chilli tomato sauce and a fresh rocket and Parmesan salad.

1. Preheat the oven to 180°C Fan.

2. Bake the potato whole for 50 minutes, then leave to cool. You can then just peel the skin off and chop the potato. Alternatively, steam the sweet potato by heating 5cm of water in a saucepan. Chop the sweet potato, place in a sieve and add to the pan, without touching the water, and place a lid on top. Steam for 20–25 minutes until soft (do not allow the water to boil as the potato will get too wet and the gnocchi won't work).

3. Mash the cooked sweet potato with the back of a spoon in a bowl. Add the flour and cornflour to the bowl and mix well.

4. Cover a work surface with flour and, with two small teaspoons, shape the mixture into small balls and drop onto the floured surface (you don't have to be neat). It is a wet mixture, not like a normal gnocchi that you roll, so sprinkle with a little more flour and gently rock backwards and forwards (as if you were rolling) just so the flour sits on the surface of the sweet potato. Press the back of a fork gently onto each one: this will help the tomato sauce to stick to the gnocchi.

5. Boil a very large pan of water, drop each gnocchi into the pan and cook them for 3 minutes. Take out of the water and add into a bowl with some olive oil. Serve with any sauce or pesto.

TIP
To freeze after rolling out the gnocchi, place on a lined baking tray and line them up so they are not touching. Freeze like this, then transfer into a freezer bag once frozen so they don't stick together. Cook from frozen by putting into boiling water for 3–4 minutes.

TREATS AND SNACKS

We are huge fans of sweet stuff in our household! I didn't want to give Rudy refined sugar till he was two, so I came up with lots of delicious alternatives that use fruit to sweeten bakes and that taste just as fantastic.

Remember, if you have a child under one year old you mustn't give them honey. So if a recipe calls for honey, you can swap it, like for like, for maple syrup or another syrup of your choice.

A snackfest can attack at any time, so having a stash of bakes in a Tupperware is essential to staying human throughout the day. I don't know about you, but a cup of tea and a muffin sounds heavenly to me right now. However, unless the children are asleep, out or glued to the TV, it's more likely to be sipping cold tea and shoving a slice in where you have a second between washing up, playing hide-and-seek and resolving whose turn it is to wear the superman costume.

The beauty of baking, though, is that it's so inclusive and everyone can get involved from such an early age. It's a wonderful thing to do as it helps to practise maths, reading and the all-time hardest thing in the world ... patience! Waiting for the 'beep beep' on the oven alarm is the longest wait. And for us parents, the life lesson is ... letting go of control. Yup, not easy! The joy and engagement outweighs the mess, and the best bit is the enjoyment of making a delicious bake. Go on, get your apron on and have a go!

GINGER AND ALMOND COOKIES

MAKES 12 COOKIES | **PREP** 15 MINUTES | **COOK** 15 MINUTES

130g gluten-free plain flour
(add 20g more for spelt or plain
wheat flour)

¼ tsp bicarbonate of soda

½ tsp baking powder

¼ tsp salt

3 tbsp melted butter (cow, goat's
or coconut oil)

80g almond butter

70g honey

15g piece of fresh ginger, plus
12 slices to garnish

People say that ginger is great for morning sickness and nausea and I found that munching on these all day helped me. They take 10 minutes to make so you are not on your feet for a long time, and they will keep in an airtight container for about a week (if they last that long in your house!). If you fancy mixing up the flavour, swap the ginger for ½ teaspoon cinnamon.

1. Preheat the oven to 175°C Fan and line a baking tray.

2. Weigh out the flour, bicarbonate of soda, baking powder and salt into a bowl.

3. Melt the butter in a pan over a low heat – be careful not to burn it.

4. Mix the almond butter and honey into the butter. Finely grate the ginger so it is almost like a pulp and mix into the butter mixture.

5. Combine the dry and wet ingredients until completely incorporated.

6. Pinch off pieces of dough about the size of a ping-pong ball and roll them between your hands. Flatten them until they are 1cm thick and then put onto the baking tray – repeat until the mixture is finished.

7. Garnish the cookies with a slice of fresh ginger and bake in the oven for 10 minutes or until golden brown. Remove from the oven and transfer to a wire rack to cool.

GOOEY BROWNIES

MAKES 9 BROWNIES | **PREP** 10 MINUTES | **COOK** 1 HOUR 20 MINUTES

320g sweet potato

160g butter

360g honey or maple syrup

2 eggs

200g gluten-free plain flour
(add 20g more for spelt or plain
wheat flour)

2 tsp bicarbonate of soda

1 tsp salt

140g cacao powder

ADD-ON (OPTIONAL)

100g choc chips

I first wrote a sweet potato brownie recipe 8 years ago for my first book. Since then everyone has created a version, so I thought it was about time to update my old one! We bake this at home all the time as we are all chocoholics!

1. Preheat the oven to 180°C Fan and line a 23cm baking tray.

2. To cook the sweet potato, you can either put the whole potato in the oven and bake for 50–60 minutes until soft the whole way through or peel, chop into small chunks and steam until soft.

3. Put the cooked sweet potato into a blender with the butter, honey and eggs. Blend until smooth.

4. Put the flour, bicarbonate of soda, salt and cacao powder into a bowl and mix together so there are no lumps.

5. Add your blended wet mix to the dry and mix thoroughly until completely combined.

6. Put into the baking tray and bake in the oven for 20 minutes. Take out, sprinkle with the choc chips if using, and leave to cool on a wire rack before cutting.

BARS

GRANOLA BARS

MAKES 12 BARS
PREP 10 MINUTES PLUS 1 HOUR SETTING

Make these and keep them in the freezer for everyone when they need a little energy kick. If milk supply is on the low side for you while breastfeeding, these are also excellent to help boost production – just add brewer's yeast to the ingredients.

80g rolled oats

30g flaked almonds

2 tbsp coconut oil

1 tbsp almond butter

1 tbsp ground cinnamon

1 tbsp honey

100g dates

ADD-ON (OPTIONAL)
2 tbsp brewer's yeast

1. Put all the ingredients into a food processor and blend until it becomes a sticky texture (when you squeeze it between your hands it should stick together).

2. Push into a lined tin or Tupperware and put into the fridge to set for at least an hour. Cut into squares and either freeze or put into the fridge and store for up to 7 days (make sure you keep in the fridge).

ENERGY BARS

MAKES 8-10 BARS
PREP 10 MINUTES PLUS 30 MINUTES FREEZING

These quite literally taste like white chocolate and I'm not sure why!

100g coconut oil

20g seeds or nuts (sunflower, pumpkin, cashew and hemp)

70g almond butter

30g honey

⅛ tsp vanilla essence

pinch of salt

70g flaked almonds

100g rolled oats

1. Melt the coconut oil in a pan over a very low heat (you don't want it to boil). Put the seeds or nuts into a food processor and blend until coarse (or you can chop by hand).

2. Mix together the melted coconut oil, almond butter, honey, vanilla essence and salt in a bowl until combined. Stir in the chopped seeds or nuts, almonds and oats until fully mixed.

3. Line a baking tray and spread out the mixture until it's about ½cm thick, pushing down so it's very compact. Pop in the freezer for 30 minutes or until set. Cut into bars and keep in the fridge until you are ready to eat.

CARROT CAKE

SERVES 6–8 | **PREP** 10 MINUTES | **COOK** 35–40 MINUTES

150g gluten-free plain flour
(if you want to use plain wheat or
spelt flour, the recipe works the
same. Just omit the xanthan gum
and use 20g more of the plain
wheat flour)

1 teaspoon xanthan gum

1 tsp ground cinnamon, plus extra
to sprinkle

1 tsp baking powder

1 tsp bicarbonate of soda

¼ tsp salt

100g dates

2 eggs

180g butter or coconut oil

1 apple, grated

180g carrots (about 3), grated

FROSTING

100g cream cheese

1 tsp honey

There's nothing more homely than a carrot cake. You can swap half the carrot for courgette if you want to add some more greens into your life! And leave off the cream cheese for a simple loaf rather than a cake.

1. Preheat the oven to 180°C Fan and line a 20cm loaf tin.

2. Weigh out your flour and put into a bowl. Add the xanthan gum, cinnamon, baking powder, bicarbonate of soda and salt to the flour and mix so that it's completely incorporated.

3. In a food processor, blend the dates with the eggs. If you don't have a food processor, finely chop the dates and mix into the whisked eggs.

4. Melt the butter or coconut oil, add the apple and carrot and stir. Mix the apple and carrot into the date and egg mixture.

5. Add in the flour mixture and stir until combined.

6. Pour into the loaf tin and pop into the oven for 35–40 minutes.

7. Leave to cool, then combine the cream cheese and honey and spread over the top. Sprinkle a little cinnamon over the top.

SAFFRON STICKY TOFFEE CAKE

MAKES 8 SLICES | **PREP** 30 MINUTES | **COOK** 40 MINUTES

100g butter or olive oil

medium pinch of saffron
(8–10 strands)

130g gluten-free self-raising flour
(add 20g more for self-raising
wheat flour)

50g cornflour

1½ tsp baking powder

¼ tsp salt

70g coconut palm sugar or
brown muscovado

2 eggs

100g maple syrup or honey

100ml (scant ½ cup) water

200g dates

CUSTARD

500ml (2 cups) milk

2 tbsp vanilla extract

2 tbsp maple syrup

2 eggs

2 tbsp cornflour

DATE SAUCE

100ml (scant ½ cup) date syrup

100g butter

This cake was inspired by a trip to Marrakesh. My husband and I went for dinner and had a kind of sticky toffee pudding infused with saffron. I've always wanted to re-create it, and now I have, I am never having sticky toffee again without saffron – it's amazing and not so strong that children won't like it. I've added a quick custard recipe, but you can also have it with ice cream or cream. Don't miss out on the date syrup though as it's essential! Use leftovers for lunch boxes.

1. Preheat the oven to 180°C Fan. Line a 20cm round baking tin with baking paper.

2. Put the butter or olive oil into a small pan and add the saffron. Cook for a couple of minutes over a very low heat until the butter starts to bubble, but don't let it burn. Take off the heat and leave for 30 minutes (or more if you have the time) to infuse.

3. Weigh out the flour, cornflour, baking powder, salt and sugar into a bowl and mix well. To a blender add the eggs, maple syrup, water and dates and blend until the dates are still recognisable, but not in chunks. Once the butter is infused, add into the wet mixture.

4. Mix the wet mixture into the dry ingredients and combine so there are no lumps. Pour into the baking tin and bake for 30-35 minutes. The cake is ready when a skewer inserted in comes out a little wet.

5. Meanwhile, make the custard and the date sauce. Heat the milk in a saucepan with the vanilla extract and maple syrup over a medium heat. Bring to almost boiling, then remove from the heat. Make sure it's not too hot when you do the next part or the eggs will scramble.

6. Beat the eggs and cornflour in another bowl until combined. Pour the hot milk over the eggy mix and whisk in well. Pour back into the pan and cook over a gentle heat for 10 minutes, stirring until it thickens and coats the back of the spoon. If you're making ahead of time, cover the surface with clingfilm to avoid a skin forming.

7. To make the date sauce, heat the syrup and butter in a pan over a medium heat. Pour over the cake and serve with custard on the side.

CHOC CHOC PEANUT BUTTER BALLS

MAKES 10 ENERGY BALLS | **PREP** 5 MINUTES PLUS 1 HOUR SETTING

2 tbsp coconut oil

100g rolled oats

2 tbsp cacao powder

2 tbsp peanut butter

100g dates

GARNISH (OPTIONAL)

cacao powder or desiccated coconut, to coat

A great energy snack for everyone in the family. Rudy loves chocolate, which he calls 'choc choc', so we make these a lot! You can swap peanut butter for almond or cashew butter.

1. You don't need to melt the coconut oil fully, just until it is soft like spreadable butter. Put the oats, cacao powder, peanut butter, dates and coconut oil into a blender and blend until it forms a coarse texture and sticks together when you squeeze the mixture.

2. Roll into balls about 4cm in diameter and roll in the cacao or coconut, if using. Put into the fridge to set for 1 hour. Keep the energy balls in the fridge until you're ready to enjoy.

FETA, TOMATO AND SPINACH MUFFINS

MAKES 8 MUFFINS | **PREP** 20 MINUTES | **COOK** 45 MINUTES

150g baby vine tomatoes, halved

1 tsp olive oil

1 tsp balsamic vinegar

150g gluten-free plain flour
(if you want to use plain wheat or spelt flour, the recipe works the same. Just omit the xanthan gum and use 20g more of the plain wheat flour)

40g ground almonds

1½ tsp baking powder

1 tsp bicarbonate of soda

1 tsp xanthan gum

1 sprig of rosemary, chopped

100g butter

2 eggs

110g yoghurt

50ml (¼ cup) cold water

100g feta

50g spinach

salt and black pepper

These taste like a pizza and are insanely good. They are packed with protein, so are great for energy levels for the early stages of labour, for your partner or afterwards with a cup of tea. They also freeze well, so you can make them in advance and keep them in the freezer. They will only take 10 minutes to defrost in an oven.

1. Preheat the oven to 180°C Fan. Line eight holes of a muffin tray with cases.

2. Put the tomatoes onto a baking tray with the olive oil, balsamic vinegar and a pinch of salt. Roast for 20 minutes, then leave to cool.

3. Put the flour, ground almonds, baking powder, bicarbonate of soda, xanthan gum, ½ teaspoon salt and a big pinch of pepper into a bowl. Mix together and add the chopped rosemary.

4. Melt the butter, but don't burn or take to a high heat. Allow to cool and then mix together with the eggs, yoghurt and water. Crumble the feta into small chunks and mix through.

5. In the empty pan you melted the butter in, quickly wilt the spinach with 1 teaspoon of water.

6. Mix the wet ingredients into the dry ingredients, add the tomatoes and stir, being careful not to break the tomatoes up too much. Stir through the spinach.

7. Put the mixture into the muffin cases and bake in the oven for 20 minutes until golden. Take out and leave to cool.

CHOCOLATE AND RAISIN COOKIES

MAKES 10 COOKIES | **PREP** 10 MINUTES | **COOK** 15 MINUTES

100g gluten-free plain flour
(add 20g more for spelt or plain
wheat flour)

150g rolled oats

½ tsp ground cinnamon

½ tsp ground ginger

½ tsp bicarbonate of soda

80g coconut palm sugar or
brown muscovado

80g raisins

60g butter or coconut oil

60g dark chocolate

1 egg

These are really good. They lasted about 1 day in my house, so hide them if you don't want them demolished in seconds. They have lots of oats in them, which are also great for milk production if you are breastfeeding. Good excuse, hey?!

1. Preheat the oven to 180°C Fan. Line a baking tray.

2. Weigh out the flour, oats, cinnamon, ginger, bicarbonate of soda, sugar and raisins in a bowl.

3. In a small pan melt the butter or coconut oil and leave to cool.

4. Grate or very finely slice the chocolate and add to the other dry ingredients.

5. Beat the egg into the cooled butter. (Be sure to let it cool first as you don't want scrambled egg!)

6. Add the wet mixture into the dry ingredients and stir until well combined.

7. Wash your hands so they are slightly wet/cool. Take a palm-sized piece of the mixture and roll into a ball, then squash in the palm of your hand to create a cookie shape and place on the lined baking tray. Repeat this ten times to finish the mixture. If the mixture starts to stick to your hands, just wash them again as this helps the mixture to not stick.

8. Bake in the oven for 10–15 minutes. Take out and leave to cool before enjoying with a cup of tea. Store in an airtight container for up to 4–5 days.

BLUEBERRY MUFFINS

MAKES 8 MUFFINS | **PREP** 10 MINUTES | **COOK** 20 MINUTES

150g ground almonds

80g rolled or porridge oats

1½ tsp baking powder

1 tsp bicarbonate of soda

½ tsp salt

60g coconut palm sugar or brown muscovado

75g butter

230g banana flesh

1 egg

50g yoghurt

80g blueberries

ADD-ON (OPTIONAL)

2 tbsp brewer's yeast

You will find a few muffin recipes in this book as I think they are the perfect solution for on-the-go snacks, lunch boxes, breakfast, weaning and everything I haven't mentioned! If you are breastfeeding and need an extra boost for your milk, add 2 tablespoons brewer's yeast to the ingredients.

1. Preheat the oven to 180°C Fan. Line eight holes of a muffin tin with cases.

2. Weigh out the ground almonds, oats, baking powder, bicarbonate of soda, salt, coconut palm sugar and brewer's yeast (if using) into a bowl and mix together.

3. Melt the butter on a low heat and put into a blender with the banana, egg and yoghurt. Blend until there are no lumps.

4. Mix the wet ingredients into the dry and fold in the blueberries.

5. Scoop the mixture into the muffin cases and bake in the oven for 18–20 minutes.

6. Leave to cool and then keep in an airtight Tupperware container for up to 5–6 days.

WEANING BUTTERNUT CINNAMON MUFFINS

MAKES 8 MUFFINS | **PREP** 10 MINUTES | **COOK** 40–45 MINUTES

220g butternut squash or 1 small sweet potato, chopped

60ml (¼ cup) melted coconut oil or butter

2 eggs

100g gluten-free plain flour (add 20g more for spelt or plain wheat flour)

1 tsp ground cinnamon

These are not sweet muffins, they are a savoury snack for weaning, though you can add 1 teaspoon baking powder to give these more rise. When Rudy was weaning I decided that the consistency without it was softer and easier to eat with no teeth. However, for adults they are much nicer with the baking powder as it's more like a muffin texture!

1. Preheat the oven to 180°C Fan.

2. Steam the butternut or sweet potato by heating 5cm of water in a saucepan. Place the butternut or sweet potato in a sieve and add to the pan, without touching the water, and place a lid on top. Steam for 20–25 minutes until soft, then cool slightly.

3. Put the butternut or sweet potato, coconut oil, eggs, flour and cinnamon into a blender or food processor and blend until smooth.

4. Pour into eight holes of a lined muffin tin and bake in the oven for 20 minutes.

5. Leave to cool, then let the little ones feed themselves.

CHOCOLATE PROTEIN POTS

SERVES 5–6 | **PREP** 10 MINUTES PLUS 30 MINUTES CHILLING

3 tbsp coconut oil

145g Medjool dates (roughly 8)

260g cannellini beans, drained

40g cacao powder

45g almond butter

pinch of salt

1 tbsp milk

berries, for garnish

We are all obsessed with chocolate in our house and these are such a great healthy alternative packed with beans as protein and just sweetened with dates. Great for a dinner party or a kids party too! Everyone will love them.

1. Melt the coconut oil.

2. Take the pits out of the dates and put them into a food processor with the oil, drained cannellini beans, cacao powder, almond butter and salt.

3. Blend until smooth, then add the milk at the end for one last blitz.

4. Divide evenly into ramekins or small glasses and pop in the fridge for 30 minutes or until you are ready to serve.

5. Garnish with fresh berries.

SEEDY OAT COOKIES

MAKES 6 COOKIES | **PREP** 10 MINUTES | **COOK** 10 MINUTES

150g rolled oats

100g dates

3 tbsp pumpkin seeds

3 tbsp chia or flax seeds

50g butter or coconut oil

1 egg

1 tbsp maple syrup

½ tsp bicarbonate of soda

There is nothing that beats a cup of tea and one of these cookies. You can add any seeds or nuts you have in the house to mix it up a bit. Really great for the whole family, they're also especially good for second stage weaning, pregnancy cravings for your handbag or even as an energy hit for when you are in labour.

1. Preheat the oven to 180°C Fan. Line a large baking tray.

2. Put the oats, dates, pumpkin seeds and chia or flax seeds into a food processor and blend until you have a coarse texture.

3. Melt the butter in a pan, then add the butter, egg, maple syrup and bicarbonate of soda to the food processor and blend again until combined and sticky.

4. Take about 1 heaped tablespoon of the mixture, roll it into a ball in your hands, flatten and put onto the baking paper. Repeat until all the mixture is used up.

5. Bake in the oven for 10 minutes. Leave to cool and store in a Tupperware for up to 5 days.

TIP
I use molasses instead of maple syrup for extra iron.

CHEESY SEED CRACKERS

MAKES ABOUT 40 CRACKERS | **PREP** 15 MINUTES | **COOK** 20 MINUTES

3 tbsp pumpkin seeds

3 tbsp chia or flax seeds

½ tsp ground cumin

210g gluten-free plain flour (add 20g more for spelt or plain wheat flour), plus extra for dusting

130g butter (cold from the fridge)

1 egg

160g Cheddar, grated

3 tbsp sunflower seeds

I have never thought about making a cheese cracker before, but these are not only an amazing snack for kids, but also are insane with a beautiful blue cheese for an after-dinner course at a dinner party.

1. Preheat the oven to 180°C Fan and line a tray with baking paper.

2. Put the pumpkin seeds, chia (or flax) seeds, cumin and flour into a food processor and blend until the seeds have become a coarse flour texture.

3. Add in the butter in cubes and blend again until it becomes crumb like. Add the egg and cheese and blend once more until it resembles a dough.

4. At this stage you can split the dough in half; put half into a freezer bag and place in the freezer to defrost another day.

5. Dust a surface and rolling pin with flour, roll the dough into a ball and flatten and dust each side with more flour. Roll out the dough so it is about 2–3mm thick and, with a cookie cutter, cut out shapes. If you don't have a cookie cutter, you can just slice into rectangles or squares.

6. Put onto the tray and bake for 16–18 minutes. You want the crackers to be a pale colour – if they go too 'golden' they become slightly acidic tasting.

7. Take out of the oven and leave to cool. You can keep them in a Tupperware for about a week.

BEETROOT CHOCOLATE CUPCAKES

MAKES 10 CUPCAKES | **PREP** 10 MINUTES | **COOK** 15 MINUTES

120g butter

200g cooked beetroot

100g dates

4 tbsp honey (or maple syrup for under ones)

3 eggs

120g gluten-free self-raising flour (if you want to use self-raising wheat flour, the recipe works the same. Just omit the xanthan gum and use 20g more of the self-raising wheat flour)

20g cacao powder

½ tsp baking powder

¼ tsp salt

½ tsp xanthan gum

buttercream icing or whipped cream, for decorating

blueberries and choc chips, chopped up a bit, for decoration

I originally made these for Rudy at Halloween, but they seem to have come out as a regular bake in our house. They also can be turned into a cake; just add about 10 minutes onto the bake time for a 20cm round cake.

1. Preheat the oven to 180°C Fan.

2. Melt the butter in a saucepan on a low heat.

3. Put the beetroot, dates and honey into a food processor and blend until smooth. Add in the butter and blend again.

4. Add the eggs, flour, cacao powder, baking powder, salt and xanthan gum and blend again until fully combined.

5. Spoon about 2 tablespoons of the mixture into each of ten cupcake cases so the mixture is just underneath the top of the case.

6. Bake in the oven for 15 minutes. Take out and cool.

7. Decorate the cupcakes with some buttercream or whipped cream and sprinkle with the blueberries and chocolate chips.

FIRST BIRTHDAY CAKE OR CUPCAKES

MAKES 8 SLICES | **PREP** 15 MINUTES | **COOK** 30–35 MINUTES

2 bananas

1 pear or apple, cored

100g dates

3 eggs

120g butter, at room temperature

½ tsp vanilla essence

½ tbsp baking powder

½ tsp xanthan gum

160g gluten-free self-raising flour (if you want to use self-raising wheat flour, the recipe works the same. Just omit the xanthan gum and use 20g more of the self-raising wheat flour)

ADD-ONS (OPTIONAL)

4 tbsp maple syrup (for extra sweetness)

ICING OPTIONS

melted chocolate

cream cheese

whipped cream

buttercream icing

layer of berries or berry coulis

This recipe is not only great as a cake, but you can use it to make muffins or cupcakes. If you want to make a four-layer cake like the one in the photo, double the recipe, bake in two separate tins and slice each cake in half to make four. For Rudy's last birthday I used cream cheese as the icing, dyed it pink and made it into a pig! You can really use this recipe as the base for any decorations you might like. I use pear in my cakes as I find it's a little sweeter than apples.

1. Preheat the oven to 180°C Fan. Line a 20cm round cake tin with baking paper.

2. Put the bananas, pear and dates into a food processor and blend until they form a purée.

3. Add in the eggs, maple syrup (if using) and butter and blend again until combined. Add in the vanilla essence, baking powder, xanthan gum and flour and blend once more until fully combined. Spoon the mixture into the cake tin.

4. Bake in the oven for 30–35 minutes.

5. Leave to cool and then ice with whichever option you prefer.

KIDDIE FRIENDLY

Use the same recipe and bake in muffin cases for 18–20 minutes for a great snack.

TIP

If you want to make it a chocolate cake, take 20g flour out and swap it for 20g cacao powder.

INDEX

ACKNOWLEDGEMENTS

This has been the most exciting book to put together and I have loved every minute of it because of the fantastic team I have. My thanks to:

Pia Pack, my friend of 35 years, for producing the most beautiful artwork from her 'Table Talk' series for the cover of the book.

Lisa, Lawrence and Frankie for making everything look so beautiful. Your artistic vision has brought *Family Kitchen* to life and I adore working with you.

Isla and Sophie for working so hard in the kitchen on the shoot!

Kay for always making sure it all makes sense.

Laura Bond for your expertise in nutrition and for providing your knowledge on family nutrition for everyone to learn from.

Bledington Village Barn for providing us with the most exquisite location in the Cotswolds, which enabled all the team to stay in one place and for me to be close to Rudy and always be home for bath time. @bledingtonvillagebarn

Thank you to the following brands for lending me gorgeous props for the book shoot: Ekobo eco lunch boxes, Falcon enamel cookware, Staub UK cast iron ceramic cookware.

Laura Bond is a nutritional therapist (DipION) and journalist. She has a particular interest in natural approaches to healing and encourages clients to make simple changes to reduce their risk of disease and help their body eliminate toxins. Laura believes that boosting our own health and protecting the environment should go hand in hand – since the air we breathe and the ground our food is grown in has a major influence on our health. @laurabond www.laura-bond.com

Pia Pack is an artist and cartographer of social situations, documenting and painting shared meals to highlight the importance of social connectivity. @piapack www.piapack.com

Mums Know Best

www.mumsknowbest.com

First published by Mums Know Best in 2020

10 9 8 7 6 5 4 3 2 1

© Natasha Corrett 2020

Natasha Corrett asserts the moral right to be identified as the author of this work

© Photography Lisa Linder

A catalogue record of this book is available from the British Library

ISBN 9781527253193

Printed in Italy by Graphicom

Book Production by Booklabs.co.uk

FSC
www.fsc.org
MIX
Paper from responsible sources
FSC® C013123